# FOR A GOOD CAUSE?

# FOR A GOOD CAUSE?

How Charitable
Institutions Become
Powerful Economic
Bullies

John Hawks

602
HAW

A Birch Lane Press Book
Published by Carol Publishing Group

To Lisa, Ricky, Scott, Steve, and John,
the inner circle,
and to Jim Ellison,
the world's most patient editor

A Birch Lane Press Book
Published by Carol Publishing Group
Birch Lane Press is a registered trademark of Carol Communications, Inc.

Editorial, sales and distribution, and rights and permissions inquiries should
be addressed to Carol Publishing Group, 120 Enterprise Avenue, Secaucus,
N.J. 07094.

In Canada: Canadian Manda Group, One Atlantic Avenue, Suite 105,
Toronto, Ontario M6K 3E7

Carol Publishing Group books may be purchased in bulk at special discounts
for sales promotion, fund-raising, or educational purposes. Special editions can
be created to specifications. For details, contact Special Sales Department,
Carol Publishing Group, 120 Enterprise Avenue, Secaucus, N.J. 07094.

Manufactured in the United States of America
10 9 8 7 6 5 4 3 2 1

Library of Congress Cataloging-in-Publication Data
Hawks, John K.
    For a good cause? : how charitable institutions become powerful
economic bullies / John Hawks.
        p. cm.
    "A Birch Lane Press book."
    Includes index.
    ISBN 1-55972-387-4
    1. Charities—United States.   2. Nonprofit organizations—United
States.    I. Title.
HV91.H395   1996
361.7'0973—dc21                                         96-39493
                                                           CIP

# *Contents*

# Acknowledgments

WHEN I BEGAN WRITING THIS BOOK about the abuses and excesses of America's nonprofits, I made some people curious—and a few people very nervous.

Despite the enormous unchecked growth of tax-exempt groups and their unexamined influence in arenas of American life, ranging from politics to commerce, *For a Good Cause?* generated mostly questions about my ulterior motives during its genesis. I researched and wrote this book in the face of the almost unyielding refrain "What kind of ax do you have to grind, anyway?" from executives and managers at major national charities who stonewalled requests for documents in the public record to lawyers and government officials who could not believe my chutzpah in exploring this controversial topic.

In this case, the ax is actually a hatchet, a tiny collection of ideas that attempts to chop away at the weeds in the forest that obscure our view of the millions of good deeds and worthy works performed silently by nonprofit employees and volunteers across the country. It is in their ultimate defense that this book points out the cancers that weaken America's nonprofit sector.

At the risk of slighting any person by omission, I want to thank the librarians at the University of Kentucky, Murray (Ky.) State University, and the Lexington (Ky.) Public Library, who fielded every obscure reference request with skill and aplomb. Staffers with the Internal Revenue Service (IRS) in Washington, D.C., Cincinnati, and Lexington answered many questions with patience, and representatives at IRS field offices around the country copied nonprofit tax returns and replied to my letters and calls as quickly and as completely as a writer could hope to expect.

Thanks should go as well to the many leaders and rank-and-file employees and volunteers at the nonprofit entities mentioned in the book. Almost to a person, they responded to my requests and answered most of my questions, even when they disagreed vigorously with my observations and conclusions.

Jim Santini and Kenton Pattie provided generous assistance in documenting the commercial activities of nonprofit organizations in Chapter 8.

Among others, Scott Lipke, Steve Perry, Dwain McIntosh, Frank Julian, and Carol Julian took time to read the manuscript and offer comments. Every writer values his circle of personal reviewers who pat him on the back while draining their red pens dry scratching suggestions on the manuscript.

Anita Diamant and Robin Rue shepherded this book from the idea stage through the finished product. Jim Ellison saw the promise of the book immediately, gritted his teeth at times waiting for manuscript pages, and exhibited extraordinary sensitivity in shaping the book into final form.

America's nonprofits exemplify the core values of this country. I wrote *For a Good Cause?* to stimulate debate on the future of these groups and to issue a call urging them to focus again on the basic tenets of faith, hope, charity, and love that constitute their true mission.

# Introduction

AMERICA IS THE LAND OF GIVERS. Like the bald eagle and the Statue of Liberty, the image of a helping hand represents the ideals of the United States to people in all corners of the globe. "Few aspects of American society are more characteristically, more famously, American than the nation's array of voluntary organizations and the support of time and money that is given to them by its citizens," concludes *Giving in America—Toward a Stronger Voluntary Sector,* a report issued by the 1973 Commission on Private Philanthropy and Public Needs. Throughout U.S. history, individual citizens have banded together in voluntary groups—paying few or no taxes, operating under special privileges—to provide basic social services, depending on each other before turning to the government for help.

Think about the charities, trade associations, and other non-profit organizations that affect your daily routine:

- You wake up in a house purchased with the help of a real estate professional who subscribes to the code of ethics of the National Association of Realtors.
- You prepare a healthful breakfast according to guidelines issued by the American Heart Association, the American Diabetes Association, or other national health societies.
- You give your children money to buy hot lunches at school prepared according to the guidelines of the American School Food Service Association.
- On the way to the office, you drop off several jackets that family members have outgrown at the local dry cleaner, who

cleans the coats and donates them to his state association's "Give a Coat—Share the Warmth" program for needy people.

- You read an article in the morning newspaper about the annual convention of the XYZ Association being held in your city's convention center, bringing millions of dollars in economic activity to local merchants and businesses.
- Your children take part in a "design team" project at school—making race cars out of milk cartons, propelled by balloons—sponsored as a national education initiative by the Society of Automotive Engineers.
- After school, your children go to a local day-care center that adheres to standards developed by experts at the American Public Health Association. Later, the kids attend den meetings organized by the Boy Scouts of America and the Girl Scouts of the U.S.A. while you work in a quick aerobics class taught by an instructor certified by the American Council on Exercise.
- At the end of the day, you sort through the day's mail, which includes your church newsletter and a flyer from the local chapter of Mothers Against Drunk Driving (MADD) describing a program to help families affected by substance-abuse crimes.

"Every day, trade associations, professional societies, and philanthropic organizations touch your life," reads *Associations: A Family Portrait*, a brochure published by the American Society of Association Executives. "They're everywhere—at home and on the job, whether you're at work or at play."

Despite the pervasive influence of America's nonprofit groups, however, serious questions have arisen about the size, mission, and operations of the country's 1.2 million nonprofits:

QUESTION 1: *What is the proper role for nonprofits in America today?*

Whose job is it to satisfy the many fundamental social, physical, and spiritual needs of Americans that are not being met on a daily basis? Many good deeds that were once the province of federal, state, and local governments have been downsized and outsourced to private nonprofit organizations. "One of the cruel hoaxes of the current political moment," observes the director of a private foundation in New York, "is to perpetuate the myth that private giving can take the place of the government in meeting basic human needs."

Other nonprofit experts argue that charities and philanthropies must be the places to which people turn for help first, not the government itself. "Before Franklin Roosevelt's New Deal programs, we depended upon charities, churches, and families, not the government," says a senior tax analyst with a Washington, D.C., think tank. "History shows we can do it again."

Which side is right?

QUESTION 2: *Do Americans want, or need, so much nonprofit activity occurring "off the books" of the U.S. economy?*

In dollars-and-cents terms, how do the nation's good deeds stack up?

More than 1,164,000 nonprofit groups sat on the "master list" of U.S. tax-exempt organizations in 1995, compared to 99,500 nonprofits registered with the Internal Revenue Service (IRS) forty years earlier, and the IRS will process an estimated fifty thousand applications for tax-exempt status in 1996. "It's gotten way too easy to become a charity," says Rep. James Bilbray (D-Nev.). Echoes former congressman J. Pickle (D-Tex), "Once a tax-exempt organization gets on the books [at the IRS], it stays there forever, until Gabriel blows his horn."

Why do the following groups—all of which enjoy exemptions from federal, state, and local taxes, special legal privileges, or other benefits of nonprofit status—belong in the same arena as the Salvation Army and Habitat for Humanity?

National Football League
National Hockey League
PGA Tour
Professional Golfers' Association of America
Professional Bowling Association
U.S. Tennis Association

Best Western International
Blue Cross–Blue Shield health plans (many but not all)
C-SPAN
Christian Broadcasting Network (originator of the Family
    Channel)
Major hospitals, such as New York & Presbyterian Hospi-
    tals, Inc. in New York (with $2.5 billion in annual patient
    revenues and a 17 percent share of the metropolitan New
    York market)

Can Americans afford the luxury of supporting this non-profit juggernaut—offering tax exemptions and other operating benefits to almost 1.2 million organizations regardless of the relative value of their stated missions?

QUESTION 3: *How can the recent explosion of excesses, lax management, and outright swindles in America's nonprofit community be curbed?*

While leaders across the political spectrum continue to call for tighter government budgets and more accountable government programs, and business owners and workers explore every opportunity to increase productivity and cut operating costs, many organizations in America's nonprofit sector live the high life at taxpayer expense. "In recent examinations of large public charities, we are finding patterns of abuse that cause us concern," confirms IRS commissioner Margaret Richardson.

For example, some tax-exempt entities, such as Methodist Hospital in Houston, easily escape notice as charities and philanthropies. A suit filed by the Texas attorney general alleged that the hospital devotes only about $5 million annually to charitable care, even though it received in one recent year $40 million worth of tax exemptions, posted $76 million in excess revenues, and showed a cash reserve exceeding $600 million. An eighteen-month investigation of U.S. nonprofit hospitals by the *Philadelphia Inquirer* discovered that the 250 nonprofits surveyed in the report controlled more than $1 billion in commercial spin-offs, ranging from hotels and travel agencies to a duck-hunting lodge and a private airport-management company.

Many nonprofit managers have found that doing good does good for them. A recent survey, commissioned by Congress, of the pay of two thousand executives at the country's 250 largest tax-exempt organizations showed that three hundred individual managers earn salaries exceeding $200,000; of those three hundred, sixty-four receive between $300,000 and $400,000, and a few take home more than $1 million apiece. At one tax-free educational trust, four trustees are paid almost $700,000 each. By comparison, President Bill Clinton earns $200,000 per year, and U.S. Supreme Court Chief Justice William Rehnquist earns $171,500 annually.

Along with big business–level salaries come the trappings of corporate America. The Arlington, Virginia–based Freedom Forum, a small nonprofit foundation bankrolled by the Gannett newspaper chain, occupies a $15 million headquarters (including $1 million worth of artwork). Employees at the American Association of Retired Persons (AARP) (annual revenues in excess of $300 million) work in a new ten-story headquarters building in Washington, D.C., dubbed the Taj Mahal, featuring a turret, a marble lobby, and office lights controlled by state-of-the-art motion sensors. The AARP spent a reported $29 million on furniture when the building opened in 1990, including dozens of $1,800 mahogany bookcases; that same year, the AARP invested $14 million in programs aimed directly at assisting poor and indigent Americans aged fifty and older.

The overhead expenses of America's nonprofits take a large chunk from the funds generally assumed to be earmarked for charitable spending. In 1995, Girl Scouts around the United States sold more than 180 million boxes of cookies, generating $420 million in tax-free sales. Of that amount, more than $370 million is shaved off the top for various expenses, ranging from the actual cost of the cookies (80 cents per $3 box) to the operating costs of supporting more than four hundred staffers in the group's U.S. headquarters on Fifth Avenue in New York City.

Some nonprofit executives and volunteers find the sea of tax-free money too tempting to ignore. In the early 1990s, William

Aramony purchased a luxury apartment in New York City for $383,000, spent an additional $72,000 to redecorate it, took his girlfriend on vacations to London, Paris, and Egypt, and surprised her with an $80,000 sunroom added on to her home in Florida. Unfortunately, Aramony paid for these good things in life with funds siphoned under his watch as the chief staff officer of United Way of America and began serving seven years in prison in 1995 after being convicted of conspiracy, fraud, and money laundering.

Over time, some nonprofits actually cross the line into commercial activities. At the 1995 White House Conference on Small Business, more than a thousand delegates urged the federal government to adopt laws that would prohibit tax-exempt groups from engaging in commerce that competes directly with America's small businesses. These commercial activities yield big bucks for some nonprofits; for example, the American Cancer Society agreed in 1996 to endorse NicoDerm antismoking patches and Florida orange juice for an estimated $4 million in royalties, and the AARP earns an estimated $146 million in royalties and related income for its promotion of insurance policies to its 33 million members. Two members of Congress filed a bill that would make income from health-club operations taxable for nonprofit hospitals after a Wisconsin tax-exempt hospital unveiled plans for a $10 million, 72,500-square-foot health-and-fitness center. The Knights of Columbus is one of the country's fastest-growing life insurance companies; however, the group gave only $9.1 million to charitable causes in 1993 while earning $224 million in profits.

To protect these special privileges, nonprofit groups devote hundreds of millions of dollars each year to lobbying campaigns and political contributions. The American Medical Association spent more than $8.5 million in the first six months of 1996 alone in federal lobbying expenditures, and the U.S. Chamber of Commerce invested $7.5 million during the same period. Some nonprofits carry on these lobbying campaigns with one hand while depositing government funds and grants with the other;

for example, the American Bar Association received $10 million in federal grants in 1995 while at the same time campaigning against tort reform, and the National Council for Senior Citizens gave in excess of $100,000 that year in campaign contributions to selected congressional candidates and in lobbying against President Bill Clinton's health-care proposals while receiving more than 96 percent of its $86 million budget directly in the form of federal grants.

In some cases, the nonprofits themselves become exposed as elaborately planned con games designed to prey upon innocent investors and supporters under the protection of tax-exempt status. In a Philadelphia courtroom in September 1996, John G. Bennett Jr., president of the now-defunct Foundation for New Era Philanthropy, was indicted on charges of swindling philanthropists, museums, and Bible schools out of $135 million in what prosecutors described as the biggest charity fraud in U.S. history. Bennett was charged with eighty-two criminal counts, including mail fraud, wire fraud, bank fraud, and money laundering. (He pled not guilty and was freed on $100,000 bail.) According to the indictment, New Era (in bankruptcy proceedings since May 1995) persuaded donors to give money with the promise that, after a holding period usually lasting six months, they would receive twice the amount of their donation from contributions by wealthy anonymous donors. Allegedly, the group of wealthy donors never existed, making New Era in effect a nationwide Ponzi scheme in which Bennett attracted new donors to keep paying off existing ones. (As part of New Era's bankruptcy proceedings, Bennett surrendered his $620,000 house, for which he had paid cash and his 1992 Lexus automobile.) He faces indictments that could result in a $28 million fine and 907 years in prison.

Of course, many nonprofit groups continue to fulfill their tax-exempt missions with an efficiency and a zeal that public-sector agencies and private businesses can rarely match. Four out of five national charities analyzed each year by the National Charities Information Bureau meet the performance standards imposed by the watchdog group. Can America reward those nonprofits that follow the law and adhere to strict, above-board operating guidelines while at the same time rooting out dishonest nonprofit executives and con artists who abuse the system for their own personal gain?

In other words, does the idea "for a good cause" carry the same weight with the average American today?

PART I

# FROM A HELPING HAND TO BIG BUSINESS

# 1

## Charity, American Style

WHY DO AMERICANS WORRY so much about doing good things for their fellow men?

Nonprofit groups in the United States have historically exerted a much stronger influence on the country's development than have those in any other nation. Interestingly, the United States followed a pattern of "institutionalized" charity, a social model in which volunteer societies and tax-exempt organizations have largely replaced the family influences common to the heritage of Asian, Hispanic, American Indian, and African-American cultures. Moreover, nonprofit groups have grown to be more important in the daily lives of Americans than the socialistic welfare programs practiced widely today in the European countries from which many Americans' ancestors emigrated in the first two hundred years of U.S. history.

During his famous visits to eighteenth-century America, French historian Alexis de Tocqueville tried to explain this preoccupation with helping other people on a private, as opposed to a public, basis:

> Americans of all ages, all conditions, and all dispositions constantly form associations. They have not only commercial and manufacturing companies, in which all take part, but associations of a thousand other kinds, religious, moral, seri-

3

ous, futile, general or restricted, enormous or diminutive. The Americans make associations to give entertainments, to found seminaries, to build inns, to construct churches, to diffuse books, to send missionaries to the antipodes; in this manner they found hospitals, prisons, and schools. If it is proposed to inculcate some truth or to foster some feeling by the encouragement of a great example, they form a society. Wherever at the head of some great undertaking you see the government in France, or a man of rank in England, in the United States you will be sure to find an association.

In other words, what makes America most different from other countries around the world is not the free enterprise economy in which the U.S. commercial sector operates or the universal involvement of U.S. citizens in their country's political processes. Instead, says nonprofits consultant Richard Cornuelle, "Americans for nearly a quarter of a century of a millennium have found better and better ways to act directly on their common problems by forming literally millions of voluntary organizations of every imaginable shape and size."

## *In the U.S.A., Charity Begins at Home*

Before the mid-1800s, local volunteers, churches, and relatives in most cases performed their good deeds without banding together into formal organizations. "Urbanization and industrialization had already emerged as aspects of American society in the early 1800s," writes sociologist Eleanor Brilliant in her book *The United Way: Dilemmas of Organized Charity*. Until the Civil War erupted, aid to the "needy"—widows, children, the ill, and the disabled—came largely from neighbors helping neighbors, mutual aid societies, and churches, resulting in large part from colonial traditions. However, more towns began adopting public-assistance programs, paid for by local tax dollars, to help those in need (e.g., the public dole, assigned work in return for handouts, and the almshouse for the most desperately poor citizens).

During this time, the world of commerce provided the lone exceptions to the "charity begins at home" tradition. In 1724 the Philadelphia House Carpenters became the nation's first American trade association, formed along the lines of a European trade guild. Almost twenty years later, in the same city, Benjamin Franklin organized the American Philosophical Society, the oldest U.S. scientific society that has remained in continuous existence. Candle makers in New England originated, in 1762, the concept of self-regulation by associations—considered a revolutionary idea at the time, though it is a core function of trade organizations today—by forming the Association of Spermaceti Chandlers. These commercial alliances undoubtedly influenced early American political thought, captured most broadly in the protections adopted in the U.S. Constitution in 1789 that provide for the freedom of citizens to associate.

After the end of the Civil War, U.S. social and civic institutions underwent tremendous changes as the nation concentrated on patching its wounds and expanding westward into new territories. Social-welfare institutions like the Freedmen's Bureau—the federal government's first ambitious attempt to provide direct social-welfare support—grew quickly. In many instances, these organizations failed just as quickly. Founded to help newly freed slaves, for example, the Freedmen's Bureau disappeared after eight years, replaced by a network of public and private services for black Americans. At the same time, many states, following the federal government's example, began establishing their own public-aid agencies and charities.

The late 1800s also marked the birth of private coordinating groups for charities (such as the National Conference of Charities and Corrections, which sprang up in 1874) and increasing efforts by labor unions to secure better working conditions for the urban poor. Individual philanthropists like Andrew Carnegie and John D. Rockefeller emerged who expanded the national concept of charity from simply life-giving aid for the poor and needy to large-scale, high-profile donations to colleges, libraries, and research programs (gifts which, incidentally, focused for the first time considerable public attention on both the recipient charities and the donors themselves).

### *Federated Funding: Joining Forces to Raise Money*

As these new charities began competing for the same donors and volunteers, the growing needs of these groups stoked the desires of many nonprofit leaders to find a better way of coordinating local and national fund-raising efforts. Rev. S. H. Gurteen, an Episcopalian minister who had served congregations of workers and their families along the Erie Canal, traveled to England in the 1870s to study the Charity Organization Society, a community-based coalition of London-area philanthropies that had banded together to assess the needs of the city's poor and ill citizens and to divide responsibility for helping the needy among these agencies. He returned to the United States to launch the first Charity Organization Society in America in 1877, and the concept eventually expanded to include coordinated fund-raising efforts as well.

Ten years later, philanthropies in Denver launched the Charity Organization Society of Denver, considered the first federated fund-raising association in America. The group in Denver introduced the notion of raising money for many community charities through a combined citywide fund drive rather than a series of multiple solicitations, marrying the concepts of community-wide charitable support with coordinated charitable giving. Planned by an alliance of religiously affiliated city leaders, the Denver program raised $21,000 in its first campaign and lasted several years. The concept of federated charities spread from New York to Cincinnati.

In Cleveland the founders of the city's Federation for Charity and Philanthropy applied new strategies to the Denver model by hiring professional nonprofit managers to organize and operate the charities and by encouraging local business leaders to lead fund-raising drives. In 1913 the group started what nonprofit experts consider the first modern federated fund-raising program.

## Tax "Exemptions": A New Concept

While these community coordinating agencies were being formed in major cities across the country, Congress grappled with the issue of introducing the federal income tax on corporations and its potential impact on charities and philanthropies. Before 1894 all customs and other tax legislation listed specifically the entities targeted for each tax or levy. In other words, a tax "exemption" meant simply not being named in a customs or tax bill. When Congress enacted the Tariff Act of 1894, calling for a flat 2 percent federal income tax on corporate income, legislators struggled for the first time with the need to define those groups or individuals to be exempted from the new tax. Section 32 of the act lists the nation's first tax exemptions for nonprofit charitable, religious, and educational organizations, fraternal beneficiary societies, and some mutual savings banks and mutual insurance companies. The 1894 statute was set aside as unconstitutional by a court challenge, but the Sixteenth Amendment to the U.S. Constitution incorporated its basic aims, and the Revenue Act of 1913 laid the groundwork for permanently establishing the principle of tax exemptions.

Since that time, notes James McGovern, a former director in the Office of Chief Counsel of the IRS, the federal government's notions of tax exemptions for nonprofit groups "are not the result of any planned legislative scheme" but were "enacted over a period of eighty years by a variety of legislators for a variety of reasons." While the supporting reports for the 1913 act and other revenue statutes which followed do not specify the reasons for supporting nonprofit tax exemptions, many experts agree that the members of Congress thought the arguments for doing so made common sense. "One may nevertheless safely venture that the exemption for charitable organizations in the federal tax statutes is largely an extension of comparable practice throughout the whole of history," states Bruce Hopkins, one of the nation's most noted nonprofit tax attorneys. "Presumably, Congress simply believed that these organizations should not be taxed and found the proposition sufficiently obvious as to not warrant extensive explanation. . . . Clearly, then, the exemption for charitable organizations is a derivative of the concept that they perform functions which, in the organizations' absence, government would have to perform; therefore, government is willing to forgo the otherwise tax revenues in return for the public services rendered."

A 1939 report from the House Ways and Means Committee offers a rare glimpse into the policy deliberations within Congress on this issue: "The exemption from taxation of money or property devoted to charitable and other purposes is based upon the theory that the government is compensated for the loss of revenue by its relief from financial burden which would otherwise have to be met by appropriations from public funds, and by the benefits resulting from the promotion of the general welfare." In *McGlotten v. Connally*, a 1972 case in the U.S. district court in Washington, D.C., one justice observed that the federal government's charitable-contribution income-tax deduction is justified because "by doing so, the Government relieves itself of the burden of meeting public needs which in the absence of charitable activity would fall on the shoulders of the government."

## War Chests and Community Chests

World War I brought a sea change in the structure of America's tax-exempt economy. Relief efforts and war-related causes provided a national focus in an arena long dominated by local charitable efforts, and organizations such as the Red Cross and the YMCA introduced stand-alone national campaigns to raise money for their own projects. Even before the war began, after decades of growth on the state and local levels, nonprofits built along a national, vertical structure began to emerge—the Boys Club Association, the Boy Scouts of America, Goodwill Industries, and the American Cancer Society, among others.

As the war set into the consciousness of Americans, many communities embraced the idea of the "war chest," a coordinated fund-raising effort that combined the emotional appeal of the Great War with local causes. More than four hundred separate war chests sprang up in the United States, and it was claimed that every single chest reached its fund-raising goals ("oversubscribed," one source observed) by the war's end. After the war ended, in 1918, however, the war-chest movement declined quickly, largely as a result of the disappearance of the unifying appeal of the war-relief effort; by 1919, only thirty-nine community war chests remained in the United States and Canada, raising slightly more than $19 million, compared to more than $100 million the year before. To prolong the life of the war chests as communitywide charity fund-raisers and networks, many war chests transformed themselves into "community chests," preserving the wartime structure of a unified charity appeal and with new social goals consistent with a peacetime America. (The war chest in Rochester, New York, introduced the name in 1918.)

As the community-chest concept spread in the 1920s, America's business community and rank-and-file workers took on added importance in the life of these campaigns. In 1929 the Corning Glass Works won a major battle in the U.S. Court of Appeals in the District of Columbia when the court held that a contribution by the corporation to the local hospital was deductible from corporate income as a business expense because the gift satisfied the condition that "business corporations may have authority to make donations of money or property to enterprises reasonably calculated to further their general business interest." Six years later, the Community Chests and Councils of America—the national "umbrella" association of community chests—persuaded Congress to change federal tax laws to allow companies to make tax-deductible contributions of as much as 5 percent of their net income for charitable causes. In 1940, Congress began to permit banks (and, later, mutual insurance companies) to make direct contributions to community charity drives. By the mid-1930s companies accounted for 25 percent of the income of community chests; within twenty years, corporate contributions made up more than 40 percent of the funds raised in local federated fund drives. Also, nonprofits moved into the workplace as a more common fund-raising tactic, soliciting contributions directly from employees, leading later to the idea of payroll deductions sent to local charities and community chests.

These tactics helped many nonprofits survive the Great Depression, a time when economic conditions meant fewer dollars but more volunteer support from Americans anxious to help their fellow citizens. The 1930s also witnessed an expansion in the goals of many nonprofits, from simply helping the poor and needy to working on other issues, ranging from recreation to culture, as the federal government stepped into the battle with its New Deal–style agencies and social-welfare programs.

## Trade Associations: The New Bullies on the Block

As the community-chest movement evolved, nonprofit business associations received greater acceptance as well. *The New Competition*, a 1912 economics treatise by Arthur J. Eddy, generated interest for its advocacy of the "open-price system," which supported the formation of trade and commercial associations based on the theory that competition would be more effective, and waste less prevalent, if buyers and sellers had channels through which they could gain better information about inventories, prices, costs, and other market factors. On the heels of the Revenue Act of 1913, which specifically gave nonprofit business associations federal tax exemptions based on lobbying efforts by the U.S. Chamber of Commerce, the American Society of Association Executives—the trade association representing association managers—was organized in Washington, D.C., in 1920. The U.S. Chamber of Congress created a special Association Division seven years later. "Trade associations are the safeguards of small business and thus prevent the extinction of competition. . . . With wisdom and devotion, their voluntary forces can accomplish more for our country than any spread of the hand of government," declared Secretary of Commerce Herbert Hoover in 1923. The self-regulation concept pioneered by New England chandlers in the 1760s became federal policy in 1933 when the National Industrial Recovery Act included language encouraging industrial self-policing by trade associations formulating Codes of Fair Competition that operated hand in glove with such New Deal–era agencies as the National Recovery Administration.

Toward the end of the 1930s came the realization that another world war loomed on the horizon. Americans again fell under the spell of patriotism as community chests competed with state war chests and the National War Fund and almost every charity jumped on the bandwagon of the war-relief effort to raise funds. By 1944 more than $225 million was raised by 773 local community chests, thanks in large part to the wartime appeal. While President Woodrow Wilson failed in his attempt to introduce a national coordinating board to govern charitable appeals during World War I, President Franklin Roosevelt proved more successful (a case in point: the United Service Organizations [USO], formed from seven independent national agencies to operate programs for U.S. civilians and soldiers overseas). When the federal government began mandatory withholding of federal taxes from workers' paychecks in July 1943, that practice further paved the way for future charitable payroll deductions that would later ensure the success of United Way of America and other national charities.

## The United Way Model

As World War II came to an end, the country faced demographic and social changes similar in scope and force to conditions after the Civil War. Wartime economic demands had changed the makeup of urban populations, and wartime industrial technologies held great promise for the mass production of consumer goods unequaled in American history. In the U.S. nonprofit sector, wartime fund-raising appeals had to give way to peacetime solicitations, and the plethora of war chests and war funds that had arisen in the early 1940s had to cope with the loss of their key mission. To mobilize the leaders of U.S. charities in a new direction, automobile mogul Henry Ford II called a meeting in July 1947 to plan and launch the United Health and Welfare Fund for the State of Michigan. The United Fund, as it came to be known, attacked two core concerns of nonprofit groups following the end of the war: the burgeoning numbers of independent charities and fund-raising campaigns in many cities and the need to convince corporate America to take on a bigger role in charity fund-raising. The United Fund combined the concepts of workplace solicitations, payroll deductions, and direct corporate support with the idea of limited access to employees; in other words, charities that did not take part in the United Fund's one-time-a-year workplace drive could not solicit employees at other times of the year. This tactic did not sit well with national health agencies, such as the American Cancer Society, determined to conduct their own independent fund-raising initiatives.

To cope with the changing nature of U.S. nonprofits, the national organization of community chests changed its name in 1956 from Community Chests and Councils of America to the United Community Funds and Councils of America (UCFCA). As the group continued to grapple with internecine struggles, such as disagreements with national health charities, the 1960s brought tremendous social upheavals, from the integration of public schools and colleges to the Vietnam War. Presidents John Kennedy and Lyndon Johnson championed the advent of Great Society entitlement programs designed to lift poor Americans out of poverty. In many ways, America's nonprofits were slow to react; for example, the UCFCA waited until 1963 and 1964 to adopt an affirmative-action policy for its employees. After a major internal examination of its policies and priorities, the UCFCA moved in 1970 to change its name to United Way and to reestablish its position as the unofficial leader of America's nonprofit community.

Since the 1970s, U.S. nonprofits have continued to search for their proper role in the country's political, social, and cultural structure. Indeed, the very idea of a "tax-exempt organization" is undergoing constant redefinition and expansion. (The concept of a "nonprofit organization" finds its root generally in state law, while "tax-exempt organizations" are sourced in federal tax law.) "Simply put, the voluntary sector represents the vast array of institutions, organizations, and acts of giving, caring, and serving which increase the quality of life in America," points out John Glaser, the former chief operating officer of United Way International. "It is called 'voluntary' because its support and activities are derived from the efforts of millions of citizens who donate their time and money to solve others' problems or enhance another's quality of life in ways that are not provided by [other economic] sectors."

# 2

# *The Nonprofits Explosion*

IN AMERICA, DOING GOOD has become big business.

In 1945 the Internal Revenue Service listed 99,500 nonprofit groups on its master list of tax-exempt organizations. By September 1995 that number had mushroomed to 1,164,789 groups—up from 992,461 nonprofits in 1989 and an increase of more than 1,200 percent in less than fifty years. Religious organizations constitute two-thirds of the nonprofit world, but growth in the sector since 1970 has come largely in the secular categories. In fact, more than 56 percent of the human services, education, health, and arts and culture nonprofit organizations in existence today came into being after 1970. (While one-third of America's religious nonprofit groups date their founding before 1900, only 5 percent of secular nonprofits can make that claim.)

Nonprofit work in the United States is a growth industry. After World War II, the IRS processed roughly seven thousand applications for tax-exempt status annually. "In one year, however—1965—the number more than doubled, to over fourteen thousand, probably as a consequence of the Great Society programs of the federal government," said Burton Weisbrod, a professor of economics at the University of Wisconsin who has studied the historical development of nonprofits in the United States. As the number of tax-exempt applications continued to rise, the IRS continued to approve as many as 80 percent of the requests. "Until I looked, I thought being declared a nonprofit was pretty hard," said Ted Chapler, executive director of the Iowa Finance Authority, a public corporation charged with helping nonprofits arrange tax-exempt financing for their projects. "Then I found something like 95 or 99 percent who apply get approved. It's like getting your driver's license." In the year that ended on September 30, 1994—the last period for which data are available—the IRS approved a record 46,887 applications from petitioners seeking tax-exempt status and rejected only 520. "The total was up 7 percent from 1993 and 21 percent from 1991," confirmed an IRS spokesperson. Most of the applications for new nonprofits came from the religious and charitable sectors, with 40,276 approved applications in 1994, an increase of 9 percent from the previous year.

Nonprofits control more than $1 trillion in assets—enough value, if liquidated, to issue every adult and child in the United States a check for more than $4,000. They earn nearly $700 billion annually, or about 10 percent of the U.S. gross domestic product; compared to other major sectors of the economy, nonprofits make six times more money than America's farms, five times more than public utilities, and twice the earnings of the construction industry. They employ 7 million people—one of every eighteen working Americans, or more employees than the federal government and the fifty state governments combined. After World War II, nonprofits became the single fastest-growing sector of the U.S. economy; in fact, they have grown four times faster than the U.S. economy as a whole since 1970.

One in two adult Americans volunteer their time for nonprofit causes, totaling more than 15 billion hours each year. Calculating the work year for a full-time employee at two thousand hours, these volunteers equaled the unpaid labor of an additional 7.5 million workers, or 6.1 percent of the employed labor force in the United States. Seven of ten adults belong to at least one trade, professional, charitable, or advocacy association, estimates the American Society of Association Executives. (One in four belongs to four or more such groups.)

While it is relatively easy to grasp the immense size and scope of Fortune 500 multinational corporations and major federal agencies, it is startling to picture the operations of the country's largest and most powerful nonprofit organizations. For example, the American Association of Retired Persons (AARP) now counts one of every two Americans over age fifty in its membership rolls. For eight dollars annually, AARP members receive a variety of benefits, ranging from discounts on travel, prescription drugs, and insurance products to monthly copies of *Modern Maturity*, the largest-circulation magazine in the United States. With 33 million members, the AARP ranks second only to the Roman Catholic church as the country's largest nonprofit institution. The AARP boasts more members than Canada has citizens. Its Washington, D.C., mail room has its own zip code.

What accounts for this incredible growth?

Societal trends have fed into the development of nonprofits in two critical ways. First, government contracts and grants for social services performed by nonprofits have dried up in the last twenty-five years, and until recently, so had private contributions.

Nationally, nonprofits draw about 30 percent of their annual revenues from federal, state, and local governments, according to the Independent Sector, an alliance of charities and foundations based in Washington, D.C. That amount roughly doubles the funds received from individual charitable contributions, with the remainder stemming from endowment income, fees charged for services, and unrelated business income.

While the National Endowment for the Humanities and the National Endowment for the Arts have received the brunt of publicity surrounding their dependence on government funds, the groups which depend most on tax dollars are those that provide health care, job training, educational assistance, and other services to poor families and children. The funds for these programs fall under the "discretionary nondefense" sections of the federal budget—sections for which Congress plans to reduce expenditures by $87 billion, or 26 percent, by 2002, according to the Congressional Budget Office. Under several budget-reduction schedules, this section of the U.S. budget would be the only broad-based budget category with less money in 2002 than today.

A study commissioned by Independent Sector claims that congressional balanced-budget plans would reduce direct federal support for nonprofits by $263 billion from 1996 to 2002. Even with the most optimistic forecasts about growth in individual charitable contributions, the study concludes, nonprofits could be facing a $235 billion shortfall in coming years. "Under some scenarios, it would be just about impossible for private giving to make up for the federal cuts," said Alan Abramson, the study's coauthor. "It would require levels of giving far beyond what has ever occurred."

In the private sector, total giving by businesses, foundations, and individuals rose to about $143.85 billion in 1995, up 11 percent ($15 billion) from 1994, after remaining flat or declining in the early 1990s, according to *Giving USA 1996*, a report issued by the research arm of the American Association of Fund-Raising Counsel (AAFRC). Individual donations constitute 81 percent of total giving; they have risen slightly but remain below 1980s levels. Corporate giving rose 7.5 percent to $7.4 billion (not including sponsorships or cause-related marketing), and foundation gifts rose 8.06 percent from 1994 totals. Breaking down the results by nonprofit types, religious groups garnered the lion's share of contributions (44.1 percent of all donations, up 5.39 percent from the previous year). Public benefit philanthropies raised 17.35 percent more in contributions in 1995, followed by environmental and wildlife groups (12.53 percent), health-care nonprofits (9.23 percent), educational institutions (8 percent), and arts, cultural, and humanities organizations (2.85 percent); giving to international-affairs groups slipped by 6.59 percent; human-services giving, by 0.15 percent.

Rather than a greater sensitivity to the needs of nonprofit groups, *Giving USA 1996* attributes much of the rise to onetime factors and anomalies such as the booming stock market at the peak of the giving season, an increase in personal income at the fastest rate since the 1990–91 recession, and Capitol Hill debate over proposed changes in tax policies (such as a flat tax) that would make future charitable giving less advantageous than in 1995. AAFRC officials also cite a fourth potential factor: an increase in the quantity and quality of fund-raising activities. "There is no doubt that nonprofits and fund-raising professionals are thinking more creatively and more strategically," said AAFRC chairman Nancy Rabin. "The survey results show that when people have increased capacity to support the nonprofit sector, their impulse is to do so, particularly when the organizations have made a clear case and painted a compelling picture of how their programs will serve and enhance communities. However, we have to keep fighting for those dollars, because last year's favorable conditions will not last for long."

Indeed, some experts say that American giving patterns have already begun moving the other way. Lester M. Salamon, director of the Johns Hopkins Institute for Policy Studies, claims that even if state and local governments hold their support at current levels, in the face of federal cuts in nonprofit aid, private gifts will have to grow at twenty times the current rate. To replace both direct-funding cuts for nonprofits and overall reductions in federal social services, private giving would have to increase by 86 percent in 1997 and by 247 percent in 2002. Salamon's study reports that giving patterns for Americans have moved the other way; measuring contributions in constant dollars, growth in personal donations has fallen to less than 1 percent a year. Discounting factors such as stock market gains, the percentage of household income given as nonprofit donations dropped from 2 percent in 1989 to 1.7 percent in 1993.

Even America's churches have been hit hard by declines in benevolence. Less than a penny of each dollar earned by the average churchgoer is given to church charity (spending unrelated to church operations), and benevolence contributions have fallen for eight consecutive years, according to a 1996 survey of twenty-nine Protestant denominations released by empty tomb, a research organization in Champaign, Illinois. Members of the twenty-nine groups gave 0.43 percent of their income to church charity in 1993, the last year for which figures are available. Total church contributions—benevolence and operations—were 2.52 percent of income in 1993, down from 3.14 percent in 1968. "People who are looking to the churches really ought to be aware of these trends because they are very strong," said Sylvia Ronsvalle, executive vice president of the research group. "They do not suggest, as it stands now, that there is an informed body of people who have been willing on a voluntary basis to meet these kinds of needs."

Whereas in the past nonprofits courted wealthy supporters as a principal source of large gifts, these benefactors by no means account for the bulk of what Americans donate to charity. In her 1996 book *Why the Wealthy Give: The Culture of Elite Philanthropy*, Harvard sociologist Francie Ostrower points out that lower-income Americans give as much money, measured as a percentage of household income, as upper-income households. Moreover, the charities that wealthy Americans support today generally deal with the arts and culture, not with the concerns of poor families and children. Like many people, Ostrower contends, the rich expect government to assume such responsibilities.

Furthermore, recent legislative moves, such as the privatization of government-sponsored social services and the reform of welfare and public-assistance programs, have pushed more activity from taxpayer-supported agencies to private-sector nonprofits. Even charities that do not receive direct government financial aid will be affected, as Congress and state governments set time limits on welfare programs and cut the growth of such programs as Medicare and food stamps. Catholic Charities USA, the nation's largest private human-services network, helped 11.1 million people in 1994, up 5 percent from the previous year.

Larry Kressley, executive director of the Public Welfare Foundation in New York, which funds housing and social-services projects around the country, doubts that nonprofits will be able to boost services substantially to absorb increasing demands for aid as a result of government social services cuts. "I really do think one of the cruel hoaxes of the current political moment is to perpetuate this myth that private giving can take the place of the government in meeting basic human needs. The numbers simply don't stack up," he said.

The combination of declining contributions and increasing requests for aid have led some nonprofit leaders to call for more favorable government incentives to encourage charitable giving. "America needs a renaissance of private giving," concludes a 1996 report from the National Commission on Economic Growth and Tax Reform, chaired by Jack Kemp. Included in the recommendations of the report is a call for raising federal individual tax deductions for charitable donations—an idea that wound its way through Congress as an element of the Charitable Contributions Legislation (H.R. 1493) and the Giving Incentive and Volunteer Empowerment Act (H.R. 1575). Both bills died in 1996.

While all levels of government have continued to reduce their roles and responsibilities and to ask charities in turn to provide more services, some nonprofit officials have identified the need for stronger tax incentives as a uniquely efficient way to encourage voluntary contributions for public purposes. "Charitable giving would have to increase nearly 250 percent—fifty times greater than it has in recent years—to make up for proposed cuts in federal funding alone," says Sara Melendez, president of Independent Sector, an alliance of major U.S. nonprofit groups. "While taxpayers contribute to charities because they believe it's the right thing to do, the amount the taxpayer contributes is very much influenced by the charitable deduction." According to Independent Sector calculations, charitable contributions in the United States would fall an average of 32 percent if the federal tax deduction for donations were eliminated altogether.

Some nonprofit sector observers believe that such measures may not turn the tide. "Giving may increase in some respects, but we will not be able to bridge the gap that may be created by these cuts [in government support]," said Helmer Eckstrom, president of the American Association of Fund-Raising Counsel. "The math doesn't work."

On the other side of the argument, conservatives say that nonprofits are engaging in hyperbole to avoid catching up with the times. "When you lower taxes, charitable contributions rise," noted Jeff Beach, a senior tax analyst with the Heritage Foundation, a conservative think tank in Washington, D.C. "Americans are very charitable people. When they have the money, they give it up." According to Beach, nonprofits have to do more in the coming years to attract the support of baby boomers, who will receive record amounts of accumulated wealth through housing and stock appreciation and through bequests from their parents, and to streamline their operations and reduce overhead in the same way as have private corporations. In Beach's view, the days of relying on government support are gone. "Before Franklin Roosevelt's New Deal, we depended upon charities, churches, and families, not the government," he said. "History shows we can do it."

Kimberly Dennis, executive director of the Philanthropy Roundtable, contends, "As more and more support for nonprofits is channeled through government, the independent sector's allegiances have shifted to Capitol Hill and the federal bureaucracy. A mentality has developed that sees institutional, and hence societal, well-being as a function of government generosity. It views for-profit ventures as second-rate, morally inferior, and perhaps even evil. The leaders of tax-funded nonprofits apparently would rather see people eat in soup kitchens than in diners, live in a 'habitat for humanity' than in a trailer park." In Dennis's view, direct government support of nonprofits comes with strings attached in that the aid changes nonprofits' incentives by rewarding them with funds when caseloads go up and diluting their core tax-exempt missions and messages with bloated bureaucracies. Few national charities have been able to avoid this trap. "Even the Salvation Army has stopped requiring church attendance as a condition of its assistance in areas where it accepts government funds," which now account for about 15 percent of the Salvation Army's budget, Dennis notes. "The charity that stays genuinely independent from government is still the exception.

"In short, while charities are supposed to offer an alternative to government-run social welfare, most have become so dependent upon and aligned with government that they no longer represent a way out of the welfare state. If we place our faith in private nonprofits as they are currently organized, we are in for a big disappointment. Before we can rely on charities to help us dismantle government, they must wean themselves off the dole."

In some cases, nonprofit organizations must also erect barriers to protect the erosion of their tax-exempt missions as they step forward to lend a helping hand. The welfare reform bill signed by President Clinton contains a "charitable choice clause" that allows states to contract with religious organizations to provide social services. "Charitable Choice represents a historic shift in the care for the needy from the federal bureaucracy to private charity," observes James Geoly, a Chicago attorney who advises nonprofit organizations. "It is a shift that's already been taking place at the state level. Driven by the inefficiency, unresponsiveness, and corruption of the public welfare system, states have long contracted with private and religious groups to provide programs like job training, foster care, child-rearing classes, adult education, day care, and drug rehabilitation."

For example, the state of California could turn to the Fresh Start Program, a twelve- to eighteen-month program serving addicts on Los Angeles's Skid Row by offering personal counseling, work training, physical education, and Bible study. Officials in Denver can strike a deal with New Life Rehabilitation, a mission serving about a hundred men and women by operating a manufacturing business so that these recovering addicts can learn skills and earn money assembling musical equipment.

The new law gives these "faith-based charities" the right to retain control over the "definition, development, practice and expression of [their] religious belief[s]." Good news for all sides? "The devil, if you will, is in the details," reports Rev. Stephen E. Burger, executive director of the International Union of Gospel Missions, an association of 245 religious rescue missions. A "limitations" clause in the welfare reform law states that "no funds provided directly to institutions or organizations to provide services . . . shall be expended for sectarian worship, instruction or proselytization." "What if I, as a preacher of the gospel, say, 'God loves you!' to comfort a woman who's been living on the streets with her children, and she feels that's against her religion?" Burger asks. "Will daily or weekly Bible studies be allowed as part of our drug-rehabilitation programs, which, by the way, have a higher success rate than those run by the government? Until these tough questions have been answered, faith-based charities will not line up to help the government overhaul the welfare state for fear of being dragged into court."

James Geoly downplays such fears, noting that the "charitable choice" clause in the 1996 welfare-reform law intends to prevent these harms by allowing religious groups to administer government-supported programs without having to create separate entities, cover up religious symbols, or change their hiring practices. "At any rate," he says, "charitable choice is an entirely voluntary program. No religious group will be forced to run government programs."

Based on the latest surveys, some sectors of the nonprofit world have bucked these depressing trends. The Association for Healthcare Philanthropy (AHP)—the Falls Church, Virginia–based national alliance of nonprofit hospitals and health-care institutions—reported in July 1996 that contributions to its members rose 29 percent in 1995, to $4.92 billion. While the proportion of cash gifts to total giving decreased from 63.6 percent to 53 percent, interest and endowment income made up the difference. Pledges (up 13 percent) and planned gifts (up 23 percent) also helped boost the overall total. Individuals gave almost 54 percent of the cash gifts, while businesses gave 19 percent of the total dollars raised. Foundations provided 15.4 percent, and charities and civic groups provided another 12 percent. "As the nation's health-care-delivery system changed around us, one direct result of these changes is that, for the first time, multihospital systems raised more charitable dollars than community hospitals," reports AHP spokesperson Kathy Brady. Multihospital systems represented 15 percent of the survey respondents but accounted for $1.36 billion of the total giving. Many AHP members relied on foundations for their fund-raising programs (69.5 percent), bringing in 77.5 percent of all gifts, while the remainder used stand-alone fund-raising departments to do the job.

Accompanying these trends is a phenomenon relatively new to the nonprofit world: cutthroat competition. With too many groups chasing too few dollars, competition among tax-exempt organizations with similar missions or constituencies has heated up. For example, Americans concerned about the environment can choose among a number of major national nonprofits with different strategic missions: the Sierra Club, which focuses on influencing public policy debates; the in-your-face advocates at Greenpeace USA; the public-education projects supported by the Audubon Society and the Wilderness Society; or the public land trusts of the Nature Conservancy.

As thousands of new nonprofit organizations enter the economy each year, the immediate and long-term consequences of these births—in terms of foregone tax revenues, increased tax subsidies, and competition against for-profit companies and social-services providers—remain largely unknown and unexamined. Burton Weisbrod wrote in *The Nonprofit Economy*:

> Although unrestricted entry into the private market economy has a great deal to commend it on grounds of competition, the same cannot be said for the nonprofit economy, given the public subsidies it receives and given that this special treatment attests to the belief that there are important differences between the nonprofit economy and the private enterprise economy. Under existing law, however, the IRS, as the principal regulatory body for nonprofits, has no authority to deny entry on grounds of "excessive" competition; neither, for that matter, is it authorized to encourage new entrants by relaxing its rules if, for example, increased competition were deemed desirable. The IRS is not even authorized to inquire into the effects of the massive rate of entry of nonprofit organizations, such as the effect on the rate of exit of existing nonprofits.

Nonprofits feel the pinch of this competition on the front lines of their fund-raising efforts. Despite raising $394 million in

1995, an increase of 3.5 percent from the previous year, the American Cancer Society (ACS) did not cheer the results. "The growth is not exactly what we had been hoping for," concluded ACS spokesman Steven Dickinson. "The charitable market is growing, but there are so many good charities competing for every dollar that distinguishing yourself is getting tougher."

As a result of these competitive trends, nonprofits today have become much more aggressive and business oriented. Traditionally, nonprofit groups have relied heavily on donations and dues to subsidize their operations. However, these income sources make up only 23 percent of the average tax-exempt organization's revenues today. Instead, nonprofits have made a significant shift toward charging for their products and services. Seventy-six percent of the money now comes from sales, for-profit subsidiaries, and other new sources of income, according to a study conducted by the U.S. Small Business Administration (SBA). "In effect, the nonprofits are growing in economic significance, and the way they are financing that growth is basically through nontraditional revenues from sales and services," concluded an SBA report to a congressional committee in 1988.

In fact, these financial pressures have focused attention on the favorable competitive advantages which can be exploited when operating a business venture under the aegis of the tax-exempt status. Many sports fans in America may not realize, for example, that the nation's most prominent and profitable sports leagues—responsible for hundreds of millions of dollars annually in corporate sponsorships, ticket sales, logoed merchandising, and broadcast revenues—enjoy nonprofit status.

The National Football League (NFL)—the organization governing professional football teams and players in the United States—became a nonprofit group in 1966 when Congress included the NFL in the same section of the Internal Revenue Code that exempts local chambers of commerce and boards of trade from federal taxes. NFL commissioner Paul Tagliabue earns a reported $1.5 million salary annually, and the league rents prime office space in Manhattan for $1.5 million; however, the NFL spent less than 1 percent of its $42 million budget in

1995 on activities which could be deemed educational and charitable in nature.

Based in Montreal, the National Hockey League (NHL) also operates in the United States in the same tax-exempt category as the NFL. The league president earned more than $500,000 in salary and benefits, and the league's most recent federal nonprofit tax reports list $165,418 in European scouting expenses.

In 1994, the Federal Trade Commission (FTC) launched an investigation of PGA Tour Inc., the highly profitable nonprofit group which comprises the Senior PGA Tour, the Nike Tour, the PGA Tour Productions television production subsidiary, and a national network of Tournament Players Clubs. PGA Tour controls assets exceeding $200 million, 1995 revenues of $279 million, and a pension fund estimated in 1994 at approximately $20 million. A PGA Tour spokesman confirmed that the FTC has been "in a fact-gathering position" since 1990, examining the rules under which PGA Tour members—touring professional golfers—are allowed to take part in "unofficial" or nonsanctioned golf events.

In fact, the list of other nonprofit professional leagues reads like a who's who of American sports: the Professional Golfers' Association of America, the Professional Bowling Association, the U.S. Tennis Association, and the players' associations in football and major league baseball.

Many sports nonprofits benefit greatly from another perk: tax-exempt financing vehicles. A record 5.1 million individual tax returns reported tax-exempt interest for the 1994 tax year, up 8.4 percent from 1993, according to IRS statistics examined by the Public Securities Association, a New York–based trade group. Two-thirds of the filers showed taxable incomes under $75,000, proving that more middle-class investors have turned to tax-exempt bonds and funds that were once considered the province of wealthy, in-the-know investors. The promise of tax-exempt investment income—and the prospect of luring the Oilers professional-football franchise—persuaded voters in Nashville, Tennessee, to approve a $60 million tax-exempt stadium bond sale in the summer of 1996. The Nashville bond sale is a drop in the bucket compared to other tax-exempt projects in the works around the country: a $200-million Baltimore Ravens (formerly known as the Cleveland Browns) football stadium; a $210-million Miami Heat basketball arena and a separate $212-million Florida Panthers hockey arena; a $300-million Arizona Diamondbacks expansion-franchise baseball stadium, and the proposed Cincinnati Reds and Bengals baseball and football complex rumored to cost a whopping $540 million. While sports team owners and fans argue that these investments bring measurable returns for local economies, the nonpartisan Congressional Research Service (CRS) estimated that Baltimore's football stadium subsidies will cost $127,000 for each new job created by the project, or twenty-one times the cost of creating a job through Maryland's existing economic development fund ($6,250). "Almost all stadium spending is spending that would have been made on other activities within the United States," the CRS report concludes. In some cases, cities that spend their own budgeted funds on stadium construction projects find themselves forced to resort to federal-aid requests to satisfy other community needs. Sen. Daniel Patrick Moynihan (D-N.Y.) introduced legislation in 1996 to remove federal tax exemptions on bonds used to build sports facilities; though the bill slowed the Nashville bond sale for a few weeks, it died eventually, deadlocked in committee.

Many famous consumer services and brand names belong to businesses that operate under nonprofit rules. Best Western International, one of the world's most recognized hotel chains, is classified as a nonprofit association of hotel owners—allowing Best Western to conduct marketing campaigns and expand its locations without paying taxes on corporate revenues.

Few Americans who use the Blue Cross–Blue Shield network of health-insurance plans realize that these insurers were exempt until recently from paying federal taxes because they claimed nonprofit status as providers of low-cost health insurance. In 1986, Congress decided that the eighty-plus Blue Cross–Blue Shield organizations around the country were substantially the

same as their commercial competitors, and their tax-exempt status was stripped. Despite this decision, however, a number of
states and cities still give the plans tax breaks as nonprofit
groups, making them strange hybrids in the sense that they pay
taxes at the federal level yet operate as nonprofits in certain
parts of the country. An even stranger legal arrangement will
allow Empire Blue Cross and Blue Shield of New York, one of
the nation's largest nonprofit health-care insurers, to seek permission from New York State regulators to convert to a for-
profit company and establish a charitable foundation that would
own 100 percent of the new company's stock. The Empire move
has drawn criticism from advocates of health-care services for
the poor who believe that the "Blues" have forgotten their original calling. "Any time a nonprofit feels compelled to abandon
its charitable mission of serving the public interest, it is sad, because it speaks to the larger trend in our society of commercial-
izing the delivery of health care," noted J. David Seay, vice
president of the United Hospital Fund of New York.

Even highly commercialized industries, such as cable television, have their share of anomalous nonprofit entities that operate for all intents and purposes in the same manner as their
for-profit counterparts. C-SPAN offers two channels of programming, providing televised coverage of Congress and major
public-policy forums and debates as well as a range of shows
dealing with political commentary and current affairs. In 1992,
the last year for which public tax records are available, C-SPAN
received more than $19 million in revenues, almost all of which
came from subscriber fees paid by for-profit cable companies.
That same year, C-SPAN showed more than $3 million in prof-
its, and its president received a salary exceeding $200,000.

One of the most egregious examples of nonprofit chicanery
is the Christian Broadcasting Network (CBN), the tax-exempt
entity founded by Rev. Pat Robertson to launch the Family
Channel in 1968. From $1.1 million in revenues during its first
year, CBN has grown as a nonprofit to an astounding $211 mil-
lion in revenues for 1995—and 57 percent of those funds come
from commercial advertising which Robertson began selling in

1981 (despite an initial vow not to sell such ads). CBN did pay unrelated business income tax on its commercial revenues, but by the late 1980s the enormous cash flow from commercial activities forced Robertson and his son Tim to set up a for-profit company, International Family Entertainment (IFE), to purchase the Family Channel from CBN in 1989. Using $250 million in convertible notes from IFE, Robertson arranged in effect for CBN to loan money to the for-profit IFE, which IFE agreed to pay back to CBN with interest and for which CBN handed over the Family Channel as an asset valued at a quarter of a billion dollars. "The deal is a classic case of 'borrowing from Peter to pay Pat,' guaranteed to generate profit for Robertson's company and himself while keeping the tax men at bay," concluded Elizabeth Macdonald, a financial writer for *Worth* magazine who investigated the deal. In return for an initial investment of $150,000, the Robertsons now control IFE stock valued in excess of $123 million. Currently, the IRS is reviewing IFE's 1990 tax return, and Rep. Pete Stark (D-Calif.) has introduced legislation imposing penalty excise taxes on the excess benefits that accrue to nonprofit insiders like Robertson as a result of such deals. (For the second quarter of 1996, IFE reported that its net income more than tripled, outpacing analysts' projections, due to gains from asset sales in the United Kingdom and strong advertising and subscriber fees for the Family Channel, and that its revenue for the first six months of 1996 grew 20 percent, to $150 million. The cable network now reaches 64.9 million households, up from 60.9 million in 1995.)

Students who take college entrance examinations may not realize that these tests are administered by nonprofit entities, such as the Educational Testing Service (ETS) and the American College Testing Program, which compete against for-profit testing services but pay no federal taxes on their earnings. This advantage has helped make the ETS the largest testing company in the world, responsible for the Scholastic Assessment Test (SAT), the Graduate Record Examinations (GRE), Graduate Management Admission Test (GMAT), and other major exams. One ex-ETS employee has calculated that the ETS controls a tax-exempt endowment larger than those of all but a few hundred select colleges in the United States.

When Quincy Jones produced the star-studded Oscars show in the spring of 1996—an awards broadcast seen by more than 1 billion people around the world—he paid for the show with an $8 million budget provided by the Motion Picture Academy of Arts and Sciences, a nonprofit trade association based in Beverly Hills, California.

While Quincy Jones is known for his production talents, several Catholic organizations have gone Hollywood in search of profits from making films. Gregory Productions, an Alabama-based Catholic relief organization, combined funds from endowments to bankroll the production and release of the 1996 surprise hit *The Spitfire Grill,* which garnered a $10 million tax-free deal with Turner New Line Cinema for national distribution. Rev. Ellwood Kieser, founder of Paulist Productions, debuted the Catholic order's second feature film in September 1996, *Entertaining Angels: The Dorothy Day Story,* based on the life of a pioneering human-rights advocate in New York City. The Day film cost the order $1 million from its savings and $3.5 million in additional funds, but the film opened in both New York and Los Angeles and is expected to make money. According to Kieser, some volunteers at the order feared that the production costs should have been dedicated instead to aiding the poor, but he believes that the film will inspire good in other ways. "Jesus told stories to make a point, and I tell stories through movies," he says.

Many major hospitals in the United States used tax subsidies and tax-exempt rules to triple their segment of the health-care industry throughout the 1980s, according to figures provided by the American Hospital Association. Hospitals are now the single largest segment of America's nonprofit economy, with nearly one-quarter of nonprofit assets. New York City residents have seen the power of nonprofit hospitals firsthand, for a rash of mergers and near mergers has erupted from the cost-cutting consolidations of some of the city's best-known health-care institutions.

In June 1996, Mount Sinai and New York University medical centers agreed to merge both their hospitals and their medical schools. One month later, in an effort to achieve an estimated $60 million in operational savings, New York Hospital–Cornell Medical Center and Columbia-Presbyterian Medical Center agreed to merge, creating one of the largest nonprofit hospital corporations in the United States. The new entity—New York & Presbyterian Hospitals Inc.—boasts patient revenues of $2.5 billion, seven thousand hospital beds, twenty-eight hundred physicians (plus another eight thousand doctors in affiliated hospital networks), more than twenty different health-care facilities (ranging from actual hospitals to nursing homes and ambulatory-care centers), and a domineering 17 percent share of the lucrative New York City market. "This is the big bang—the other mergers in this city and around the country have been pops," an exultant Dr. William T. Speck, president of the new nonprofit, told the *Wall Street Journal.* "It's like [merging] Coke and Pepsi."

A 1995 survey by the Kaiser Family Foundation discovered that Americans think generally that for-profit health-care organizations give better, more efficient care than their nonprofit competitors; however, 46 percent responded that a hospital's profit status makes no difference in where they would go for care. The foundation argued that the mixed results reflect a general public ambivalence: While Americans want health care to become more efficient and responsive, they are not completely comfortable with the idea of health decisions being made strictly on a businesslike basis. One misperception highlighted in the study: Fifty-four percent of Americans believe that the trend toward for-profit health facilities is a "bad thing" for health care generally due to the belief that for-profit hospitals are more expensive. However, even though they enjoy substantial tax-exempt benefits, as a general rule nonprofit hospitals do not charge lower rates than their for-profit competitors.

"For-profit entities are known, for many reasons, to engage in charity, and nonprofits to withhold it . . . yet this meeting of a public need by a provision of services cannot be the sole distinguishing characteristic that leads to an automatic property tax exemption," wrote one U.S. district court judge in *Utah City v. Intermountain Health Care*, a 1985 case pitting a municipality against a nonprofit hospital. "It may very well be, as a matter of public policy, that *all* [emphasis his] hospitals, for-profit and nonprofit, should be granted a tax exemption because of the great public need they serve. . . . Neither can we find on this record that the burdens of government are substantially lessened as a result of the [nonprofit's] provision of services. . . . Indeed it might be argued that for-profit hospitals relieve a greater portion of the public 'burden' because they provide medical care without public subsidy."

In fact, the IRS changed its definition of charity care in 1969 as a result of lobbying by hospital interests, so that (contrary to popular belief) nonprofit hospitals may decline to care for indigent patients seeking elective medical services without losing their tax-exempt status. "I continue to believe that if we make our case and do our job well, we can appeal to our customers just as effectively as the for-profits can and beat them at their own game," said Dr. Forrest Calico, president of Appalachian Regional Healthcare Inc., a nonprofit alliance of hospitals in eastern Kentucky, describing the need for nonprofits to compete more effectively against for-profit hospital chains.

Sometimes nonprofit classifications make no discernible sense at all. The MITRE Corp. in Bedford, Massachusetts, provides engineering consulting services for government agencies, with a focus on defense systems. The nonprofit company earned $8 million on revenues of $572 million in 1991, largely through projects such as the development of early-warning aircraft-defense technology, but MITRE operates as a tax-exempt competitor, paying none of the federal taxes assessed on other major U.S. defense contractors. Nonprofits like MITRE ignore classical economic definitions of charities and philanthropies. "If nonprofit organizations perform a useful role, they must provide outputs that cannot be provided profitably by private enterprise," said nonprofits economist Burton Weisbrod.

In many cases, the lax rules governing nonprofit practices constitute an open invitation to criminals and flimflam artists to prey upon the public under the guise of doing good. Form 1023—the IRS application for tax exemption—contains a series of straightforward questions asking, for example, the names and addresses of the group's incorporators and a description of the intended charitable activities for which the nonprofit is being organized. Understaffed and handcuffed by the lack of punitive legal options, the IRS approves the great majority of applications without conducting a thorough check of the veracity of the answers or the appropriateness of the nonprofit's intended mission. "We simply accept at face value the statements provided on these forms," said Marcus Owens, director of the IRS's Exempt Organizations Technical Division, charged with approving Form 1023 requests. As a result, the IRS rejected only 520 applications for tax-exempt status in 1994 (the last year for which IRS records are available) while approving 46,887. Given those figures, applicants braved a one-in-sixty chance of *not* being accepted, compared to a one-in-twenty-seven rate in 1980.

Edwin E. Whitis II filed a Form 1023 request with the IRS office in Austin, Texas, on December 31, 1987. The IRS approved the application to establish America's Battered Children, a tax-exempt social-services agency for abused children operated by Whitis, his wife, Deanna, and Rev. Harvey Couts. (Later, federal investigators discovered that Reverend Couts had died in 1983, five years before the application for tax-exempt status was filed.) Whitis's Form 1023 described ambitious plans to operate a five-hundred-bed health-care clinic for seriously injured children on a ranch owned by Whitis and his wife, with funds raised through television and direct-mail appeals and neighborhood car washes and bingo games.

If Whitis had not been indicted and sentenced in 1988 to five and a half years in federal prison for bilking investors out of more than $3 million in "advance fees" for fraudulent loans, he and his wife would have perhaps enjoyed many years of tax-free largesse. After Whitis's indictment was announced, an IRS auditor discovered that the charity's assets included $433,282 in cash accounts and 375 gold bars valued at $175,000. In addition, the charity had purchased, for $223,541, the ranch for which Whitis

had paid $174,500 eighteen months earlier. Expenditures ap-
proved by Whitis and his wife included $6,043 for draperies,
$11,374 for an atrium, $3,395 in landscaping, $6,866 on car-
peting, and nearly $33,000 on carpentry. Based on these find-
ings, the IRS revoked the tax-exempt status of America's
Battered Children on March 7, 1991, retroactive to 1987. From
federal prison in Louisiana, Whitis lost the case on appeal.

"Nobody ever asked me about my past," Whitis told reporters from the *Philadelphia Inquirer* in 1993. "You don't have
to submit a resumé or anything, and the application doesn't take
that into account. They don't even ask if you have a criminal
past. If they had, I would have told them. I wouldn't have tried
to hide it." If Form 1023 had included a question about previous criminal convictions, Whitis might have needed extra blank
lines, given his eight arrests in the 1970s for charges ranging
from forgery to heroin possession and his two prison terms for
check kiting and forgery. At the time of the revocation of
Whitis's tax-exempt status, the IRS's Marcus Owens stated that
the application for nonprofit status did not need to ask about
criminal histories because, in his experience, few criminals actually apply.

Abuses of nonprofit status can be difficult to define and
prove. The articles of incorporation filed for the average nonprofit organization generally run to vagueness in describing the
group's tax-exempt mission. Federal and state laws and regulations applying to the operating practices of nonprofits can be
hazy in their construction and scattershot in their application.

Also, the "halo effect"—the unassailable aura of doing good
that many nonprofits tout in their aid appeals and annual reports—takes the sting from many would-be objections to questionable uses of a group's nonprofit privileges and benefits. "A
business has discharged its task when the customer buys the
product, pays for it, and is satisfied with it. Government has discharged its function when its policies are effective," observed
management consultant Peter Drucker in his seminal text *Managing the Nonprofit Organization: Principles and Practices.*
"The 'non-profit' institution neither supplies goods or services

nor controls. Its 'product' is neither a pair of shoes nor an effective regulation. Its product is a *changed human being* [Drucker's emphasis]. The nonprofit institutions are human-change agents. Their 'product' is a cured patient, a child that learns, a young man or woman grown into a self-respecting adult; a changed human life altogether."

Without the special competitive advantages of nonprofit status, however, these nonprofits would have to pay as much as 34 percent of their operating income in federal corporate income taxes as well as up to 28 percent in capital-gains taxes on investment income and applicable state and local taxes on property and sales. Instead, a 1990 study by reporters at the *Philadelphia Inquirer* analyzing 630 large nonprofits found that these groups returned an average profit margin of 9 percent—more than double the average of Fortune 500 companies.

Clearly, America's nonprofits have grown too big to ignore.

# 3

# *What Do a Thousand Points of Light Really Cost?*

WHEN PRESIDENT GEORGE BUSH SALUTED the concept of nonprofit work with his "Thousand Points of Light" program in the late 1980s, he echoed a long-standing sentiment of U.S. public policy, which is often expressed in politics but seldom practiced in practical terms: Government—and, by extension, nonprofit organizations that enjoy tax-exempt benefits—should be empowered to engage in only those activities which individual citizens cannot perform for themselves.

Through the years, federal statutes and court rulings have largely followed this principle. "Philanthropy," wrote one state supreme court justice in a 1969 case involving Dartmouth College, "is the very possibility of doing something different that government cannot do, of creating an institution free to make choices government cannot . . . which stimulates much private giving and interest."

That philanthropic "possibility" has much to recommend it. By their independent, nongovernmental nature, nonprofits can tackle some nagging societal concerns that federal, state, and local taxpayer-supported agencies cannot or should not confront. "Forty years ago, most Americans already no longer lived in small towns, but they had still grown up in one," explained

36

noted management consultant Peter Drucker. "They had grown up in a local community. It was a compulsory community and could be quite stifling. Still, it was a community. Today the great majority of Americans live in big cities and their suburbs. They have moved away from their moorings, but they still need a community. And it is working as unpaid staff for a nonprofit institution that gives people a sense of community, gives purpose, gives direction—whether it is as a helper in the local Girl Scout troop, as a volunteer in the hospital, or as the leader of a Bible circle in the local church. Again and again when I talk to volunteers in nonprofits, I ask, 'Why are you willing to give all this time when you are already working hard in your paid job?' And again and again I get the same answer, 'Because here I know what I am doing. Here I contribute. Here I am a member of a community.' "

With private leadership (and, in most cases, private dollars), they can apply their funds more efficiently than the government. Also, their successes in addressing these problems further the cause of pluralism in what has become an increasingly fragmented U.S. society. According to Drucker, nonprofits today are central to American society and can be described as its most distinguishing feature—"central to the quality of life in America, central to citizenship, and indeed carr[ying] the values of American society and of the American tradition."

However, these nonprofit good deeds do not come cheaply.

When an individual nonprofit organization qualifies for the federal tax exemption, that ruling allows the group to piggyback other waivers and exemptions onto it: state corporate income taxes, local property taxes, sales taxes at all levels. Furthermore, the nonprofit can take advantage of loans and financing deals from publicly authorized authorities that have the power to issue bonds that carry lower interest rates for the nonprofit than conventional loans and that do not incur taxes for the bond buyers on the earned interest.

When more than 1.2 million nonprofit groups operate independently of the nation's tax rolls—avoiding various federal, state, and local levies on their operating incomes, sales, and

property—the foregone tax revenues quickly become a staggering figure. Many government officials and economists have no
idea of the scope and cost of these exemptions. "Through the
years we've never really been asked to conduct any estimate of
the impact of these nonprofit arrangements," conceded a
spokesman for the Congressional Budget Office. "They go all the
way back to 1913, when the federal income tax was introduced,
and no one has thought to include an estimate since then."

IRS analysts now estimate that the federal government alone
loses $44.5 billion each year by extending tax exemptions and
subsidized rates to nonprofit groups (the largest share: an estimated $22 billion from income-tax deductions for charitable
contributions). That amount equals the taxes paid in 1995 by
the 25 million Americans earning between $12,000 and $25,000
annually, or more than five times the current budget of the IRS
itself. "There's no way you can take 10 percent of the tax base
[represented by nonprofits] and put it aside and not have the
rest of the folks who are still paying taxes not pay more," observed Paul Streckfus, a former IRS examiner who specialized in
tax-exempt organizations.

When the federal government began writing tax exemptions
into law in the 1920s, they were granted to organizations that relieved the government of providing a service—schools, hospitals,
and community service agencies, among others. These charitable
groups relied primarily on private donations to fund their services.

Today, however, this concept of local groups relieving government of burdensome social responsibilities has become
sharply distorted. "The idea that tax-exempt organizations always wear white hats in the community, going around doing
things that benefit everyone and helping the poor . . . as opposed to that other part of society that gropes for money all day
long, is not something that is rooted in fact," said Marcus
Owens at the IRS. Over time, nonprofits began charging fees for
their services. Federal programs ranging from Medicare to Social Security began paying for these services. Responding to special interests, Congress expanded the scope of its exemptions,
resulting in twenty-five categories of nonprofits today, ranging

from trade associations to cemeteries and credit unions. These factors have combined to lead to a nonprofit juggernaut that effectively shields 10 percent of the nation's economic sector from the tax system that affects the remaining 90 percent.

Nonprofits enjoy exemption from a number of federal taxes, levies, and user fees beyond the corporate income tax. For example, Congress passed a law in 1982 that requires larger for-profit corporations that are granted patents to pay a fee equal to 100 percent of the costs incurred by the U.S. Patent & Trademark Office in awarding the patent; nonprofit organizations (as well as some small businesses and independent investors) are charged only 50 percent of the costs. Moreover, IRS rules exempt certain nonprofits from specific import and customs duties. "While this may not benefit every nonprofit corporation," said attorney Ted Nicholas, "one whose program involves the import of artwork from overseas, for instance, would be able to escape the sometimes hefty duties imposed by U.S. Customs."

Most nonprofits extend the value of their federal tax exemption by applying for similar exemptions at the state and local levels. In fact, most states and municipalities consider the awarding of the federal exemption the ipso facto requirement for their own exemptions. At the state and local levels, the exclusion of billions of dollars worth of sales and property from tax laws—especially the funding mechanism for school districts and municipal services—puts a much greater strain on existing taxpayers. In Minneapolis, for example, 23 percent of the city's real estate is tax-exempt. That figure rises to 39 percent in Pittsburgh and 40 percent in Syracuse, New York. The District of Columbia loses an astounding $98 million in tax revenues each year from tax-exempt real estate—a figure that does not include government buildings.

The property-tax exemption and similar waivers cause concern because local governments must provide police, fire, and other public services to nonprofits, which pay no property taxes in return to support those services. In some cases, nonprofits have made voluntary payments in lieu of taxes, but such arrangements are not common and almost never compulsory.

"The primary reason for the increase in governmental attention [to the impact of tax exemptions] is that the number of tax-exempt organizations has grown so much in the past decade or two that the phenomenon is considered in some quarters to be a serious threat to the tax-base stability of many political jurisdictions," advises attorney Ted Nicholas in *The Complete Guide to Nonprofit Corporations*, one of the leading how-to texts for launching a tax-exempt organization. (Cover blurbs on the book jacket include "Completely and legally avoid payment of federal income tax!" and "Slash postage costs.") "Churches, hospitals, nursing homes, chambers of commerce, charities, social service agencies and the myriad other nonprofit organizations in most communities may have tax-free real estate holdings," says Nicholas. "In some cities and towns, a substantial portion of the entire lot of privately held real estate is owned by tax-exempt organizations. This means there isn't any revenue flowing into local tax coffers from this sector. . . . [A]s corporate and individual taxes rise, those who must pay them often fault the tax-exempt sector as a prime reason for the increases. Even the tax-exempt status of churches, protected from the very beginning of the tax code, has been questioned in recent years, particularly in reference to church investments in secular properties."

In Hawaii, state legislators have begun investigating the structure of the Bishop Estate, a vast nonprofit organization which owns more than 367,000 acres of land in the state, including two major resort hotels on beachfront property, as well as 300,000 acres of Michigan timberland and a part interest in the Robert Trent Jones–designed golf course near Washington, D.C., where President Clinton regularly plays. Under federal and state laws, the estate is tax-free because the land holdings were willed by Princess Bernice Bishop in 1883 to create schools for Hawaiian children. In 1994 the Bishop-controlled schools accepted a total of three thousand children; however, the estate paid no taxes on net revenues of $303 million, and its five trustees were paid an annual compensation of $915,238.

The Nature Conservancy, the country's "granddaddy" of public land trusts, founded in 1951, controls more than 7.9 million acres of ecologically significant land now worth almost $1 billion. When the nonprofit group purchases or takes over a piece of land, the property is removed from local tax rolls. "That has a serious effect on local economies," says Greg Ruehle, associate director of the National Cattleman's Association. "There has to be a balance between environmental goals and the economic interests of landowners."

Taxpayers fighting the loss of these tax revenues face an uphill battle. In Colorado supporters of a constitutional amendment to force nonprofits to pay taxes on their property gathered the fifty-two thousand signatures needed to put the measure on the November 1996 ballot. If approved, the amendment would have made Colorado the first state to tax nonprofit properties.

Proponents of the Colorado measure say that the chief goal is fairness. "Churches and charities pay their utility bills. Fire and police protection are utilities also, and they ought to pay their share of those as well," said John Patrick Murphy, a Colorado Springs lawyer and one of the bill's chief sponsors.

Under the amendment, real property—land and buildings—would be taxed, while personal property, ranging from office equipment to furniture, would remain exempt. Colorado collected $2.5 billion in property taxes in 1995. State treasurer Bill Owens noted that the extra revenue—estimated at $70 million by backers of the amendment—would help taxpayers in the short term but would hamper private charitable efforts. "Churches and nonprofits provide many services much better than government can," Owens said. "This [measure] would be extremely negative and is very shortsighted."

Rev. Gil Horn, pastor of the 1,350-member Montview Boulevard Presbyterian Church in Denver, calculated that his congregation would lose $15,000 of its $660,000 budget to property taxes under the new rules. "That certainly won't shut us down," he said, "but it will limit the amount we give to other charities."

Responding to such charges, Murphy noted that the additional state revenues could lead to lower tax rates or rebates for other property owners. "The state doesn't get that money, and the Vatican doesn't need it," he said. "We're taking money out of the pulpit and putting it back in the pews. Individuals would be free to donate to any charity."

At a 1985 symposium on nonprofit management at Yale University, economist Henry Hansmann discussed the findings of his study of the relative importance of nonprofit subsidies in various states. While the value of the federal exemptions remains largely constant for nonprofits based in any state, the differences in state and local tax structures across the country gave Hansmann a defensible basis for determining whether there is a systematic relationship between the size of a state's nonprofit subsidy (largely in the form of foregone tax revenues) and the influence of nonprofits in that state compared to for-profit companies. Hansmann found that the higher the level of a state's taxation of private business, the greater the competitive value to a nonprofit of exemption from those taxes. States that assessed higher rates of property taxes, sales taxes, and corporate income taxes in effect gave nonprofits based within their borders a greater subsidy than states with lower tax rates. Consequently, nonprofits in the higher-rate states enjoyed a greater competitive advantage and in many cases held a higher share of the market in a given industry compared to their for-profit competitors. "In the competition between nonprofit and proprietary firms, tax exemption of nonprofits makes a difference—particularly the exemption from sales and corporate income taxes," Hansmann reported. "Exemption from property taxation gives nonprofits a particular incentive to locate in city centers, where property tax rates are usually high."

Perhaps the greatest example of exemption largesse comes in the construction boom of athletic stadiums and ballparks around the United States. By the year 2000, at least forty-five new stadiums and arenas will have been built at a cost exceeding $9 billion—more than the IRS will spend in its 1996 budget. Of forty-nine major league football arenas and stadiums in the United States, forty-four were built with public money. More than $4 of every $5 spent in the 1990s on arena and stadium developments came from public sources, at a time when politicians have won and lost campaigns on the basis of their stance on new taxes. "It's an epidemic," says Charles C. Euchner, professor of urban politics at Holy Cross College. "Cities have two choices: forget about major league sports or feed the monster."

The "monster" of stadium construction feeds largely on tax exemptions. A 1996 Congressional Research Service (CRS) study discovered that federal tax exemptions alone provide as much as one-third of the public subsidy for many stadium projects, at a cost of more than $1 billion over the next ten years. After diverting funds to stadium construction, these cities then soak up additional millions in federal aid sought to meet other pressing local needs.

Many large public-works projects, such as arenas and ballparks, are financed with tax-exempt bonds. These securities carry lower interest rates than taxable bonds of equivalent risk because the federal government agrees to forgo the taxes it normally would receive on those investments. That practice costs taxpayers indirectly, not in taxes they pay but in taxes the government does not receive. While the bulk of construction funds comes from state and local sources (including tax exemptions at those levels of government), Sen. Byron Dorgan (D-N.D.), an outspoken critic of these projects, estimates that North Dakota taxpayers pay an extra $6 million annually as a result of arena and stadium projects, even though their state has no big-league teams. "Do we have enough money to finance stadiums for owners worth $500 million and players who make $1 million a year at the same time we are cutting Head Start programs?" Dorgan asks. "That's a logical public-policy question."

Dorgan requested a CRS study that concluded that a $225 million stadium built today and fully financed by tax-exempt bonds would receive a subsidy as high as $75 million over thirty years. "Stadiums are the only healthy public-housing program we have left in this country," he notes. Though Senator Moynihan has introduced legislation that would remove the tax exemption from bonds issued for sports facilities, Sens. Mike DeWine (R-Ohio) and John Glenn (D-Ohio) lined up a bipartisan coalition to defeat the measure.

Proponents of tax-exempt financing for sports facilities argue that their regions need the economic boost that new arenas and stadiums can bring. "I know there will be a huge return on investment for the people of this area if we proceed with plans for downtown stadiums for the Detroit Lions and the Detroit Tigers," claims Detroit mayor Dennis Archer. Under the current construction plan, private investors (including the teams' owners) would supply $265 million, or 52 percent of the estimated $505 million cost. Along with $100 million from a county tax on hotel rooms and rental cars and a $55 million grant from a state economic-development fund, the city will provide $85 million largely through the sale of tax-exempt bonds. Archer cites an analysis by a city-affiliated development agency that predicts $66 million in positive economic impact during the first year of operations alone. "Strong city centers make for strong metropolitan areas, with tax bases to provide better services," he says. "Removing one of the key tools for urban renewal [tax exemptions on bonds for sports complexes] would leave cities stranded on an uneven playing field."

In many cases, however, stadium subsidies do not pay off locally. The CRS found that the move of the Cleveland Browns professional football team (now called the Baltimore Ravens) to Baltimore in 1996 will cost Maryland taxpayers $331,000 per job, more than fifty times the cost of other state economic-development efforts. The city of Cleveland refused the demands of the team's owner for a new stadium because it has already lost $60 million on facilities built for its professional baseball (Indians) and basketball (Cavaliers) teams, at a time when the state has taken over the city school system, saddled with $150 million in debt. In fact, no stadium development in the past thirty years has increased living standards in its community, according to economist Robert Baade at Lake Forest (Ill.) College.

The ultimate example of a taxpayer-subsidized "white elephant" sports complex is Miami Arena, built in 1988 at a cost of $52 million, $46 million of which was publicly funded. Though the arena is barely eight years old, it is considered obsolete by the Miami Heat (National Basketball Association) and the Florida Panthers (National Hockey League) because it was not built with enough luxury skyboxes and other amenities that the teams insist are needed to generate competitive revenues. The teams pitted Dade County (where Miami Arena is located) against neighboring Broward County in a bidding war that resulted in approved plans for a new $212 million arena in Broward County for the Panthers and a new $210 million sports complex in downtown Miami for the Heat. When the new arenas open in 1998, Miami Arena will remain empty, with about $38 million still to be repaid on the thirty-year tax-exempt bonds issued to fund its construction, according to Jerry Bernfeld, executive director of the Miami Sports and Exhibition Authority.

Once in place, nonprofit tax exemptions at all levels of government are rarely revoked. In fact, Treasury and IRS examiners at a 1991 congressional hearing were stumped when asked how many of the nation's 3,200 nonprofit hospitals had lost their exemptions in the last twenty years. "It's a handful of revocations, as I understand it," replied Deputy Assistant Secretary of the Treasury Michael J. Graetz. "I think it's more than one, but certainly less than a dozen." According to the hearing transcript, Graetz updated his guess later in the day: "I think the answer . . . is five, but I was not certain of it," he said. At the end of the hearing, John Burke—an assistant IRS commissioner—provided an estimate of one.

Beyond foregone tax revenues, the federal government loses more than $3 billion a year in the form of reduced tax rates or subsidies for specific programs, such as nonprofit postal rates. In any enterprise, postage is a standard, and sometimes sizable, budget item. Under the current system of rates proposed by the U.S. Postal Service and approved by the Postal Rate Commission, nonprofit organizations can mail materials related to their tax-exempt mission at rates substantially below those charged to their for-profit counterparts. To qualify for these rates, nonprofits must submit an application to the U.S. Postal Service for a special permit. With this permit, nonprofit mailing rates can run as low as 11.1 cents per letter, or by taking full advantage of bar coding and presorting discounts, as low as 5.4 cents per letter. The same piece of mail could cost a for-profit business 19.8 cents or the average consumer the full 32 cents for first-class postage.

The latest mail-classification-reform package—the proposed rate changes and procedural improvements which govern "regular" and nonprofit mail—set to take place in late 1996, would include "moderating increases" for nonprofits, including the possible lowering of nonprofit rates for flats (nonletters, such as advertising circulars) and automated mail, according to Lee Cassidy, executive director of the National Federation of Nonprofits.

Subsidized postal rates take on critical importance for many nonprofits that rely on the mail to communicate with supporters and to raise funds. The more mail the nonprofit generates in the course of its daily operations, the greater the benefit from discounted postal rates. "Nonprofit corporations that rely on membership income can use the mail even more extensively to service their members, so potential savings from a special mailing permit are considerable," said attorney Ted Nicholas.

Burton Weisbrod argues that postal subsidies for nonprofits should be replaced by less restrictive subsidies. "When government encourages nonprofits, it should be neutral with regard to the inputs nonprofits employ; there is little if any justification for providing more aid to organizations that use the mails to raise funds or otherwise to carry out their activities than to nonprofits that use telephones, newspapers, radio, or television," he said. "Moreover, such special-purpose subsidies pose continuing administrative and legal challenges, as, for example, how to determine whether a postal subsidy for fund-raising by mail applies to 'informational' material that accompanies the request for funds. Public subsidies should encourage the desired activities without distorting the means of carrying them out."

Other legal operating advantages enjoyed or sought by nonprofits carry costs not in terms of actual dollars spent by taxpayers but opportunity costs and legal loopholes that give them in many cases an unfair advantage against for-profit corporations. Certain types of nonprofits, based on their 501 (c)(3) tax exemption, can become eligible to receive grants from both public and private sources on a tax-free basis. Individual donors to these groups can claim personal federal-income-tax deductions of up to 50 percent of adjusted gross income for donations made to 501 (c)(3) groups (classified as traditional charities and phil-anthropies, as opposed to trade associations and other types of "commercial" nonprofits). When a person dies, the estate can claim a full federal-estate-tax exemption for bequests made to 501 (c)(3) nonprofits.

Although many states have eliminated or limited this privilege, some states still allow nonprofit charities to be immune to tort liability. The immunity is limited to damages resulting from the negligence of a nonprofit's agents or employees (protecting the organization itself, not the actual agents or employees). For example, a bus driver for a nonprofit group who causes a traffic accident and is ruled at fault may be fully and personally liable for negligence, but the nonprofit would be immune from any responsibility for the accident. In those states which permit such exclusions, nonprofits enjoy substantial savings by avoiding liability-insurance premiums paid by for-profit companies.

The National Labor Relations Act and statutes in a number of states exempt nonprofits from the rules of union collective bargaining, meaning that a tax-exempt group cannot be forced to engage in collective bargaining on wages and benefits with its employees even if they should already be represented by a labor union. In addition, some states allow nonprofits to forgo taxes, like state unemployment compensation fund levies, that other employers must pay. "Considering that these contributions by employers usually amount to anywhere from 1.6 percent to 9.1 percent of payroll costs, the possible savings in the operating budget for the nonprofit corporation can be significant," said Daniel Porter, associate tax counsel for the Council of State Governments.

The halo effect, which confers on nonprofits the aura of doing good deeds, carries over into benefits for nonprofits that are actually subsidized directly by businesses. For example, some large department stores and discount warehouses extend lower membership rates to nonprofit employees. In part to satisfy federal broadcasting regulations, many radio and television stations (as well as newspapers and magazines) donate free space and time for public-service announcements touting the messages of nonprofit advocacy groups.

PART II

# THE SEVEN DEADLY SINS OF NONPROFITS

# 4

# *"What Do You Think We Are— A Charity?"*

DO YOU EXPECT TO FIND marble foyers, valet parking, and gourmet meals at your local hospital?

Try Methodist Hospital in Houston, which earned $500 million in tax-free revenues last year. The Texas attorney general filed suit against Methodist, alleging that the hospital did not deserve its nonprofit status because it excluded nonemergency uninsured patients unless they could pay a deposit equal to the entire cost of their care. The suit charged that Methodist devoted only about $5 million annually to charity care, even though it received $40 million in annual tax exemptions, posted $76 million in excess revenues (the nonprofit equivalent of profits), and showed a cash reserve exceeding $600 million.

Though the judge later dismissed the lawsuit, television news reports about the hospital's well-appointed suites and amenities for high-paying "guests" led to the passage of a landmark Texas statute in 1993 requiring tax-exempt hospitals to devote a set percentage of their revenues to charity care. (The Texas requirements contrast greatly with federal tax guidelines, which do not require tax-exempt hospitals to offer certain levels of indigent care in return for their nonprofit status.)

Despite compelling photographs in their annual reports and public-service announcements, some nonprofit groups take full advantage of their tax-exempt benefits without fulfilling their charitable responsibilities under the letter, or at least the spirit, of the law.

In no other sector of the nonprofit economy does this issue surface more frequently than in the case of major national foundations—nonprofit organizations which manage endowments and funds held in trust for the purpose of providing scholarships, research grants, and other gifts deemed to serve the public interest. The IRS defines a foundation as "a private, nonprofit organization with a narrow base of financial support whose goal is to maintain or assist social, educational, religious, or other activities deemed to serve the public good." In 1995, U.S. nonprofit foundations disbursed approximately $10 billion in grants and awards, according to the Foundation Center. Since 1975, foundation assets have grown from about $30 billion to $179 billion, due largely to boosts in the stock market and favorable federal tax rulings.

Foundations pay no federal income tax on these assets or the investment income generated by their holdings. If they were taxed at the same rates which apply to the income of for-profit corporations, they would be liable for approximately $4.5 billion each year in federal taxes. Most foundations pay simply a 1 percent excise tax on their investment income, compared to 34 percent for corporations.

More than thirty-three thousand nonprofit foundations exist in the United States today, but the ten largest foundations account for 20 percent of the assets and 12 percent of the grants. The directors of these foundations control an enormous amount of wealth which remains off the tax rolls at the federal, state, and local levels, and they answer largely to themselves in terms of how their funds are invested and spent. In hearings before the House Banking Committee in 1972, congressional leaders noted that 1 percent of America's foundations control 63 percent of the assets owned by all nonprofit groups; today that percentage has jumped to 68 percent. While private foundation grants obviously support worthwhile causes in many instances, the question remains whether the long-term impact of removing a significant portion of private dollars from the nation's taxable economy is worth the benefits.

Congress did enact several changes to federal tax codes in the 1970s to curb excessive wealth gathering by nonprofit foundations. The most important legal change requires foundations to give away a minimum of 5 percent of their assets each year in the form of grants and awards. However, many foundations take full advantage of the fine print in this statute which allows many general and administrative expenses to be included in the 5 percent total. "It has been much easier to make money than to spend it wisely," said the late W. K. Kellogg, who established his own foundation in 1930. Today many nonprofits seem to be following his advice, concentrating more on making money and enjoying the fruits of their labors than on improving the quality of the world around them.

Take the nation's largest private nonprofit foundation, the Ford Foundation. Its twelve-story glass-and-steel headquarters in New York City—complete with an enclosed one-third-acre garden under an immense skylight—could be mistaken for the corporate headquarters of a multinational corporation. Fifteen staffers coordinate the foundation's $6.7 billion investment portfolio. Despite two inches of paperwork in its 1994 tax filing that describe $278 million in grants—an amount half again as large as the second-ranked W. K. Kellogg Foundation—the Ford Foundation still gave only about 3.75 percent of its total assets in grants for the 1994 tax year. In fact, the group reported receiving no private contributions or gifts, but it earned $72 million in interest on savings and $284 million on dividends from its stock investments (while giving away $278 million in grants).

The record is the same for many other juggernaut foundations. The Robert Wood Johnson Foundation—funded by an endowment from the family which founded the Johnson & Johnson consumer-products empire—showed $175 million in contributions and $267 million in interest, dividends, and capital gains in its 1994 tax return, while it handed out $93.5 million in grants.

The difference between income and grants becomes more pronounced when comparing the records of the nation's largest foundations, which control the great bulk of nonprofit wealth, and the smallest foundations, which depend much more heavily on charitable contributions and donations. According to data from the IRS and the Foundation Center, 19 percent of the revenue of large foundations comes on average from contributions, whereas the smaller groups receive as much as two-thirds of their income from private donors. Foundations with $100 million or more in assets pay out 4–5 percent of their assets on average, while foundations with $100,000 or less in assets pay out about 11 percent. In fact, the larger foundations usually give away as grants about one-half of their investment income, while the smaller nonprofits distribute twice as much as their investments earn.

Even before the federal income tax was approved by Congress in 1913, many government officials were concerned about the prospect that large nonprofit foundations could use legal loopholes to set up repositories for corporate wealth. In 1912 a congressional commission recommended that foundations be required to give away every cent of their income each year. In 1954 a congressional advisory committee suggested that foundations be required to spend themselves out of existence after no more than twenty-five years, but the idea never became law. In the Tax Reform Act of 1969, Congress did not include a recommendation that foundations should be phased out after no more than forty tax-free years, but new federal regulations did require nonprofit foundations to give away 6 percent of their assets or their net income, whichever was greater. That amount was cut in 1976 to 5 percent. In addition, federal legislators approved a 4 percent excise tax on foundations' investment income to support more oversight by the IRS; in 1978 the tax was cut to 2 percent, and in 1985 foundations could pay 1 percent if their grants reached the 5 percent threshold successfully. Despite the weakening of these regulatory provisions, some nonprofit leaders still groused about what they described as "hostility" against foundations on the part of the IRS.

"Congress does not like private philanthropic foundations, and, in all likelihood, never will," Terrance Keenan, an official of the Robert Wood Johnson Foundation, wrote in a 1992 pamphlet outlining the future of America's foundations through the 1990s. "[Congress] is very uncomfortable with the foundation as a center of power and wealth which has no such accountability. The congressional hostility toward foundations has been manifest since the passage of federal income tax legislation."

Compared to the task of fulfilling the spirit of their nonprofit missions, many foundations and other nonprofits seem to get more caught up in the spirit of spending money to make money. IRS records indicate that foundations spend typically between 15 and 40 cents for every dollar given in grants, with an average of 20 cents for every dollar. A 1972 study by the House Banking Committee pegged the amount at closer to 50 cents on administrative costs for every dollar given away. "The cost of producing and distributing charitable benefits by private foundations is staggering by any standard," the study concluded. "When funds that are intended for charity are selfishly and wastefully diverted to the administration and management of these foundations, it is charity that is being cheated."

Few nonprofit executives have proved the power of personal connections in doing good works more than Allen H. Neuharth, former chief executive officer of Gannett, founder of *USA Today*, and former chairman of the Freedom Forum in Arlington, Virginia. The reception room in Neuharth's offices—headquartered on the top floors of a high-tech glass tower facing the Potomac River—features dozens of photographs depicting Neuharth posed with world leaders. Neuharth relied on these contacts to support the programs of his foundation (formerly known as the Gannett Foundation) in funding journalism programs around the world.

An examination of the forum's tax returns from 1989 to 1993, however, yields interesting questions about the group's ability to accomplish its charitable mission at a reasonable cost. In fiscal year 1993, for example, the group spent more than $1.70 in general and administrative expenses for every dollar dedicated to nonprofit journalism projects—more than eight times the average for all nonprofit foundations. With assets pegged at $698.5 million that year, the group spent $34.4 million in administrative costs and awarded grants totaling $20.2 million. These overhead costs grew from 36 cents for every grant dollar in 1989 to the present level of $1.71.

Where did the additional funds go? During the five fiscal years examined, spending on salaries more than doubled; Neuharth earned $131,000 in 1992 as head of the foundation, and president Charles Overby earned $278,040. Leasing and occupancy costs for the foundation's new offices quadrupled. Spending on travel and meetings quadrupled, with board of directors meetings held in Hawaii, Mexico, and Russia.

The New York attorney general's office investigated the forum briefly in 1992, but no findings of the inquiry were ever released. (A spokesman for the forum refused to discuss the tax filings in question.)

When Rev. Pat Robertson founded the Christian Broadcasting Network (CBN) in 1988, he described its nonprofit mission as follows: "[Preparing] the United States of America . . . and other selected nations of the world for the coming of Jesus Christ and the establishment of the Kingdom of God on Earth. CBN's ultimate goal is to achieve a time in history when the 'knowledge of the Lord will cover the Earth as the waters cover the sea.' " After more than a decade of nurturing under its nonprofit wings the growth of the Family Channel—a popular family-oriented cable network whose revenues soon dwarfed those of the nonprofit's religious broadcasts—CBN spun off the network in a shady deal that netted the Robertson family a tidy profit of approximately $90 million. Today Reverend Robertson earns more than $400,000 in salary and bonuses from the holding company which controls the network (as well as the FIT-TV cable network and the MTM Entertainment syndication packager), and his son Tim earns $475,000 as the company's chief executive officer. In a 1992 interview Robertson described these salaries as "embarrassingly low by media-industry standards." Robertson lives in a $1-million red-brick house with stables (allegedly paid for with royalties on his books) on the 500-acre, $68-million campus that houses the two companies and Regent University, his private college for fifteen hundred students training to become "regents" (those who rule during the absence of a king, or Jesus Christ in this case). The house is protected by a high-tech security system operated by the tax-exempt CBN. Robertson also enjoys free access to the CBN country estate in Hot Springs, Virginia, and the nonprofit's twenty-four-seat BAC-111 jet, once owned by country singer Kenny Rogers.

Through a collection of trusts and direct shares, the Robertsons own 16 to 25 percent of the holding company, which is reportedly being courted by CBS, NBC, and the Sony Corporation of America for a possible programming deal or an outright purchase. The Family Channel posted its best three-month results ever in the first quarter of 1996, averaging a 1.4 prime-time rating, with 934,000 households watching, making it the fastest-growing major cable-network primetime household-audience delivery (an increase of 52 percent); more viewers from key demographic groups watched the Family Channel than ever before. "Entertainment should bring a viewer a sense of excitement and wonder," declared Tony Thomopoulos, the executive who directs programming development for International Family Entertainment, in an advertising insert in *Advertising Age* for cable network ad sales. "For the Family Channel to be successful, we must not only bring these elements to the viewer, but they must carry positive values for every member of the family."

Rev. Barry Lynn, a former cohost of a radio show supported by Robertson who now serves as executive director of Americans United for Separation of Church and State, stated: "I just am flabbergasted that he can say with a straight face that he needs more and more financial contributions at a time when he is personally sitting on top of the enormous wealth he currently possesses. The average person who gives money to *The 700 Club* [the daily talk show hosted on CBN by Robertson himself] does not have a clue to the existence of the undergirding financial empire that [Robertson] possesses. They would be shocked if they knew."

The National Collegiate Athletic Association (NCAA) describes its chief mission as a nonprofit organization as governing and policing collegiate sports. In 1994 the NCAA earned more than $120 million, mostly from television broadcast rights, merchandising royalties, and corporate-sponsor revenues. Its Overland Park, Kansas, headquarters includes a separate state-of-the-art visitors center, a marketing subsidiary, a real-estate holding company, and a foundation. The bulk of the NCAA's budget is devoted to promoting college sports—market research, video production, legislative relations, and general marketing expenses. At the same time, the NCAA Enforcement Department accounts for less than 2 percent of the annual budget. The NCAA currently employs fifteen investigators to cover more than a thousand member institutions, or one investigator for each seventy-two schools.

Until 1969, many hospitals in the United States "earned" their nonprofit status by giving away a substantial amount of care to poor and indigent patients. In fact, federal tax regulations required tax-exempt hospitals to provide free medical care to the extent of their financial resources—what was known as the "financial ability" standard. Under intense pressure from hospital lobbyists, however, the IRS dropped the financial-ability standard and adopted the "community service" standard, which held that hospitals could qualify as nonprofits if they promoted health services in their communities.

The IRS ruling reads: "Like the relief of poverty and the advancement of education and religion, [hospital care] is one of the purposes in the general law of charity that is deemed beneficial to the community as a whole, even though the class of beneficiaries eligible to receive a direct benefit from its activities does not include all members of the community, such as indigent members of the community."

Despite evidence that the new community-service standard gutted federal regulations which had forced tax-exempt hospitals to hew more closely to their stated nonprofit missions, federal officials have defended the change. "A community-benefit standard reflects the long-standing proposition that the promotion of health is a charitable purpose and recognizes the potential for a variety of means of fulfilling that purpose," Assistant Treasury Secretary Michael J. Graetz told the House Ways and Means Committee in 1991.

Using this new standard as a spur for development, non-profit hospitals now form the single largest segment of America's nonprofit economy, accounting for nearly 25 percent of assets in the sector. Since 1950, their assets have grown tenfold, from $19 billion to $195 billion, after adjusting for inflation. As the hospital sector has expanded, many individual hospitals have become overbuilt and overstaffed; in some U.S. cities, as many as one-third of all hospital beds lie empty every night. Meanwhile, the average cost of a hospital stay has skyrocketed from $615 in 1970 to $5,500 in 1995—an increase of more than 790 percent, or more than three times the rate of inflation. During that same period, nonprofit hospital revenues jumped from $14 billion to $160 billion, or four times the rate of inflation.

IRS officials estimate that the value of federal and state tax exemptions for U.S. nonprofit hospitals totals $8 billion. Do they provide sufficient care for poor and indigent patients to "earn" their tax-exempt status? The American Hospital Association (AHA) gauged the free treatments provided by nonprofit hospitals at approximately $9 billion in 1989, the last year that the trade group calculated the figure. "The problem is one in which we are seeing the indigent and the uninsured patients that are showing up at our hospitals at a greater and greater number, with nowhere to shift that cost," Jack W. Owen, acting AHA president, told Congress in 1991. However, a 1990 General Accounting Office study of nonprofit hospitals in five states discovered that 57 percent provided less charity care than the tax benefits they enjoyed. In 1986 hospitals spent an average of 6.5 percent of their annual budgets on charity, according to AHA studies; by 1994 that figure had dropped to 5.7 percent. Methodist Hospital System in Houston, with its marble foyers and valet parking for patients, spent less than 1 percent of its gross patient revenues on indigent care.

Existing notions that government subsidies are needed to underwrite better care for poor patients do not bear the scrutiny of further study. "Evidence that nonprofit hospitals serve the public better than proprietary hospitals do, for example . . . is by no means overwhelming," nonprofits economist Burton Weisbrod concluded. "The days of the nonprofit hospital are over," writes Henry Hansmann, an attorney and economist at Yale University who specializes in tax law for hospitals. "They are vestigial institutions whose nonprofit form no longer has meaning. As a matter of tax policy, we may not want to do away with nonprofit hospitals, but that doesn't mean we still want to subsidize them." In his testimony before a congressional committee in 1988, Hansmann concluded: "The critical question is whether the nonprofits in question provide the kind and quality of service that is unavailable from for-profit firms in the same industry. If they do not, then the case for tax exemption is quite nebulous. At most, it will simply produce a larger volume of services . . . and if this is what is desired, then we must ask why we do not extend the tax exemption to the for-profit firms as well."

Hansmann's test can be applied to commercially oriented nonprofits, such as the Hazelden Foundation in Center City, Minnesota. Known around the world as a drug and alcohol rehabilitation facility, Hazelden receives 95 percent of its annual revenues from patient fees, publishing, and investments. In 1994, 45 percent of its $45 million operating revenue came from treatment fees; the remainder came largely from its stake in book publishing. While Hazelden officials insist that the books are simply an extension of the center's therapeutic mission and thus deserve exemption from taxes, critics question the fact that Hazelden paid almost no federal taxes on more than $30 million in book and magazine sales in 1994; in one instance, Hazelden paid one author more than $1 million in royalties.

In the broadest sense, some cases of self-serving nonprofit excess do not even attempt to hide under the banner of selfless charity. Atwater Entertainment Associates, an investment group vying for the rights to operate a riverboat casino in Detroit, created the Atwater Foundation to help its case. The charity plans to give up to $12 million in local grants, but only if the company wins a municipal contract giving it exclusive rights for riverboat gaming. Harrah's, the gaming concern which runs fifteen casinos nationwide, donates money to many different groups, including one which helps compulsive gamblers. "There's a tremendous amount of enlightened self-interest in the gaming field," observed Bill Eadington, an economist at the University of Nevada at Reno who specializes in gaming.

Nonprofits in many other fields have learned the fine art of public relations in describing their "charitable" works and the resulting revenues. Judge George Levin called the Hamot Medical Center in Erie County, Pennsylvania, on the carpet in 1990 in a ruling on a tax case involving $57 million earned by Hamot in the 1980s. "Hamot contends these funds are not profit but are revenue over expenses which are reinvested in operations," Levin wrote in his opinion. "The evidence showed otherwise. Called profit or revenue over expenses, $57 million remained after expenses from 1981 to 1989. Hamot's revenue over expenses is profit, whether Hamot chooses to call it such or not. . . . 'What is in a name? That which we call a rose would by any other name smell as sweet.' Profit is profit, no matter where it is spent or what it is called. This level of profit is sweet by any name."

In many cases, nonprofits have learned how to reinvest these surpluses into profitable sidelines. An eighteen-month investigation of U.S. nonprofit hospitals by reporters at the *Philadelphia Inquirer* yielded startling results. Hospitals in the study had moved more than $3 billion into tax-exempt foundations and holding companies to make the hospitals appear less wealthy; the hospital foundations in Pennsylvania invested just 5 percent of their funds in hospital services, while 39 percent went for overhead and salaries and 56 percent went into investments. More than $40 billion in excess earnings helped to build new hospital buildings, offices, and parking garages. From a study of 250 hospital forms, the newspaper discovered more than $1 billion invested in commercial spin-offs, including book publishers, hotels, laundries, pharmacies, travel agencies, a duck-hunting lodge, and (in the case of the Mayo Clinic) a private airport management company. Based on a rash of state court rulings curtailing the for-profit activities of these hospitals, the IRS altered its auditing practices for nonprofit hospitals to focus more attention on commercial subsidiaries. "There's no question, hospitals are a good example of how some large nonprofits have changed, becoming businesslike, even investing in for-profit ventures," admitted Marcus Owens. "They present one of the most challenging areas for us." Daniel Fox, president of the nonprofit Milbank Memorial Fund, agreed: "Congress has been asleep on this issue. It allowed the IRS to set both tax and health policy and then provided no oversight. For the last twenty years, hospitals have essentially had a free ride."

That free ride has translated into substantial investment portfolios for some nonprofit hospitals. The Mayo Foundation in Rochester, Minnesota, owns more than $550 million in stocks, bonds, and securities as well as real estate worth $800 million. Besides its private airport, Mayo funded new clinics in Jacksonville, Florida, and Scottsdale, Arizona, to welcome patients who have retired to warmer climates. The Methodist Hospital System in Houston at one time held investments worth $600 million and commercial property worth $408 million, including the "Chez Eddy" gourmet restaurant and a duck-hunting lodge. In the late 1980s, Methodist's holdings generated $100 million in revenue, but the hospital reinvested only 3 percent of that amount in hospital services, while prices rose an average of 7 percent a year.

What has not changed is the brazen attitude with which many nonprofit managers and consultants continue to encourage apparent abuses of the spirit of nonprofit tax exemptions. "When your machines are turned off, what else could they be doing? When a space is empty, how could it be filled?" urges Dr. Richard Steckel, an "enterprise coach" for nonprofits, in his book *Filthy Rich & Other Nonprofit Fantasies*. "It's hard to believe that a hospital cafeteria could be known for good food, but that's the case at the Great Falls Hospital in Montana. The cafeteria also had down times between meal services when they [sic] could prepare extra food. So hospital administrators decided to capitalize on their asset. They opened a catering service, first catering just staff parties, and now expanding to community functions."

Despite the incredibly elastic interpretations applied by some nonprofits to federal tax laws, the IRS rarely revokes exemptions; in fact, a spokesman confirmed that the agency cannot produce even a partial list of nonprofits that have lost their exemptions. "We don't keep them on file that way."

# 5

# *Over-the-Top Overhead*

AT MANY U.S. NONPROFITS, "downsizing" is an unknown term. While they admit on the one hand that donations and other income streams are growing more scarce and the demands for their charitable services are increasing steadily, nonprofit groups face greater temptations to invest heavily in Fortune 500–level salaries and benefits, opulent headquarters and capital assets, and other perks to a degree that seems at variance with their tax-exempt missions—avoiding, all the while, an estimated $30 billion in federal taxes every year. These excesses stretch the principle of "no private inurement," defined by IRS assistant commissioner James McGovern to mean that nonprofit groups "must benefit the public and not the individuals who run them."

When it comes to valuing the good deeds performed by chief executive officers, directors, and other major employees of nonprofit groups, the traditional standard that psychic rewards matter more than payroll has been largely abandoned. A recent congressional survey of the pay of two thousand executives at America's 250 largest nonprofits showed that three hundred executives earned salaries exceeding $200,000. Of those three hundred managers, sixty-four received between $300,000 and $400,000; a few took home more than $1 million apiece. At one tax-free educational. trust, four trustees are paid almost $700,000 each.

A 1996 survey of 184 nonprofits by the *Chronicle of Philanthropy* confirmed the fact that some tax-exempt groups are also very charitable with their top managers. Among the respondents, 154 groups paid at least one executive more than $100,000, and 83 of them posted at least one salary at $200,000 or more. One hundred twenty groups increased the pay of their chief executive officer from 1995 to 1996, while thirty-four reduced compensation and the rest reported no change.

Some of the highest-paid executives included Harold M. Williams, president of the J. Paul Getty Trust, at $610,001; William G. Bowen, president of the Andrew W. Mellon Foundation, at $455,389; and Harvey W. Schiller, executive director of the U.S. Olympic Committee, at $444,331. By comparison, President Bill Clinton earns $200,000 per year, and William Rehnquist, chief justice of the U.S. Supreme Court, earns $171,500 annually.

"I think [nonprofits] are giving more in money in order to retain the talent that they have," said Daniel Langan, spokesman for the National Charities Information Bureau, a national watchdog organization policing U.S. charities. "It's up to the board of directors how much they have to pay to employ somebody who is going to improve their programs, their revenues, their overall operation. What they also have to keep in mind, however, is that it is public record."

A study of nonprofit tax filings by the *Philadelphia Inquirer* found that at a time when 37 million Americans cannot afford health insurance, more than one thousand executives and doctors at nonprofit hospitals and insurance companies were paid salaries ranging from $200,000 to $1.2 million. "A lot of people are being priced out of health-care coverage," said Ron Pollack, executive director of Families USA, a Washington-based health-advocacy organization. "What people get paid—whether it's physicians or administrators of hospitals or CEOs of insurance companies—is a factor. Somebody has to foot the bill for these salaries, and that somebody is you and me."

Nonprofits offer several arguments to justify the high salaries paid to their top executives. In today's ultracompetitive, increasingly complex business environment, nonprofit managers contend with more stressful workloads and responsibilities than in the past. To find qualified top-level managers, nonprofits must compete with private companies in terms of salaries, benefits, and perks. Many nonprofit executives are drawn today from the ranks of private industry, where salaries tend to run higher than traditional nonprofit positions. Finally, nonprofit managers (particularly those who run nationwide charities and philanthropies) operate in the same social and financial echelons as Fortune 500 executives, and therefore, the argument goes, deserve the same consideration when it comes to compensation.

"Many tax-exempt organizations are very large and complex," observed Marcus Owens. "Whether the compensation package paid to the chief executive is reasonable would depend, I think, on looking at a number of factors. What are the responsibilities? What are the decisions? Does it involve large amounts of money?" Robert Ochsner, director of compensation for Hay Associates, an employee-benefits firm in Philadelphia, agrees. "It used to be that the not-for-profit sector was its own world. You signed on after you got out of college, like if you joined the government, and you stayed there. There also was the realization that you never expected the same money you might earn in the for-profit world. Now we see people are crossing over. It's more common for people to go out of the not-for-profit to the for-profit sector, but it also works the other way around. Therefore, the markets are moving toward each other and the pay is catching up."

Beyond the point of catching up, however, how much is too much? Consider the salaries of these nonprofit chief executives, compared to the popular impressions of the charities and tax-exempt groups that they run:

- Paul Tagliabue, commissioner, National Football League (NFL)—$2 million plus
- Walter Cabot, president, Harvard Management Company—$1,486,446
- Clifton Wharton Jr., chairman and chief executive officer, Teachers Insurance & Annuity Association and the College Retirement Equity Fund (TIAA-CREF)—$1,283,650

- John Rowe, president, Mount Sinai Hospital/Medical Center/School of Medicine—$1,116,996
- William J. Flynn, chairman and chief executive officer, Mutual of America Life Insurance Company—$1,058,702
- Paul Marks, president and chief executive officer of Memorial Sloan-Kettering Hospital/Cancer Center/Institute for Cancer Research, New York—$983,579, as well as a reported $1 million "signing bonus" when he became president in 1988
- Donald Fehr, president, Major League Players Association—$950,000 plus
- Jack Valenti, president, Motion Picture Association of America—$800,000 plus
- William Whaley, division president, Children's Television Workshop—$671,000 plus
- David Hamburg, chief executive officer, Carnegie Corp. of New York—$597,877
- Franklin Thomas, chief executive officer, Ford Foundation—$548,371
- James Todd, executive vice president, American Medical Association—$528,496
- Joseph Volpe, president, Metropolitan Opera Association—$444,000
- Edwin Feulner Jr., president, Heritage Foundation—$439,538
- Walter H. Annenberg, president, Annenberg Foundation—$425,000
- Gilbert Grosvenor, president, National Geographic Society—$419,691
- Peter Goldmark, president, Rockefeller Foundation—$408,383
- Gene Budig, president, American League—$400,000
- Dennis O'Leary, chairman, Joint Commission on Accreditation of Healthcare Organizations—$388,191
- Jim Awtrey, chief executive officer, Professional Golfers' Association of America—$386,788
- Nancy Cole, president, Educational Testing Service—$323,296

- Horace Deets, president, American Association of Retired Persons (AARP)—$286,940
- Peter Tomasulo, chairman, American Red Cross—$270,080
- Elizabeth Dole, president, American Red Cross—$201,299
- Keith Geiger, president, National Education Association—$240,340
- Al Shanker, president, American Federation of Teachers—$209,045

These healthy salaries for nationwide nonprofit positions have helped raise the tide for executives at other types of nonprofit groups. Foundation chief executive officers earned a median salary of $81,600 in 1995, according to the Council on Foundations. The council's annual salary report found that most foundations granted or planned to grant a salary increase in the previous year. In their 1994 book *Unhealthy Charities: Hazardous to Your Health and Wealth*, James T. Bennett and Thomas J. DiLorenzo estimated that the American Heart Association, the American Lung Association, and the American Cancer Society spend more money on salaries than any other single expense category (in the case of the lung association, as much as 43 percent of annual revenues).

The news is not as rosy for the average nonprofit staffer, who will receive a budgeted salary increase in 1996 of 4.5 percent, the same as 1995 figures, according to the 1996 Cordom Salary Survey of Nonprofits. "The changes [in salary increases] over the past five years have been largely incremental. There's nothing startling in these percentages," reports Damon Cordom, the principal of Cordom Associates, the firm that conducts the semiannual survey. Eighty-eight percent of the responding nonprofits said they plan to increase their payroll budgets between 3 percent and 5.9 percent. Most of the nonprofits confirmed that they use performance as the sole means of granting salary increases, while a third use a combination of cost-of-living and merit factors to award pay raises.

The sea change in compensation philosophy for nonprofit managers has spread to other levels of governance in the tax-exempt community. In the past, people who served on nonprofit boards of directors were called *trustees*, a term that reflected their basic role: guarding the integrity of a charity and ensuring the protection of the group's assets and nonprofit mission. Today many nonprofits adhere to a corporate structure, calling their advisory groups *boards of directors* and paying board members to attend meetings.

The John S. and James L. Knight Foundation, a tax-exempt foundation created by the Knight brothers, who launched Knight newspapers (now the Knight-Ridder media conglomerate), has paid its trustees fees ranging from $1,500 to more than $20,000 (the average: $11,250). The Freedom Forum, once run by *USA Today* founder Allen Neuharth, offers its part-time directors between $8,500 and $99,500 (average: $60,000). Mutual of America Life Insurance Company paid its directors more than $275,000 in 1994, or an average of $4,200 per director per meeting. The American College of Physicians and Surgeons spent more than $1 million in 1994 on directors' fees and expenses; "many of our trustees devote a substantial amount of time, and these fees are a way of compensating them for their lost practice time," a spokesman explained.

By comparison, the average compensation for outside directors of America's 150 largest industrial corporations was about $42,000, according to a 1994 survey by Hewitt Associates.

Corporate-style perks extended to nonprofit executives also include performance bonuses, low-interest loans, housing allowances, the use of cars, and more generous vacation and retirement deals. For example, besides her $323,296 salary, Educational Testing Service president Nancy Cole lives rent-free in a posh home owned by the nonprofit college entrance exam organization in Princeton, New Jersey. In 1992, NFL commissioner Paul Tagliabue negotiated a low-interest loan of $950,000.

A 1996 survey by the Hay Group in Philadelphia showed that 15 percent of the nonprofits polled offer some type of "variable compensation plan" for their managers, to compete more effectively in the job market and to reward performance, and 30 percent were considering such a plan. A similar study by William

M. Mercer, Inc., in New York found that more than half of the larger foundations and trade groups involved in the study supplemented managers' salaries or offered a form of deferred compensation. "Even if directors approve such a plan, however, they don't always want to talk about it," said Ellen Prior, director of Hay's not-for-profit group. "It's a sensitive area." "Compensation based on performance is a good idea for nonprofits," said Mark Rosenman of the Union Institute, a Washington-based think tank, "but rewards should not be keyed to dollars but to job promotions or awards, and they should not be limited to top executives." In fact, the use of bonuses has been singled out in several lawsuits challenging the tax-exempt status of a nonprofit organization. In a Pennsylvania case involving a hospital president who earned a $37,980 bonus on a salary of $206,991 in 1991, the judge chastised the nonprofit, saying, "Incentives based on profit are directly contradictory to a lack of profit motive. Each executive who participates in these benefits knows that he or she will receive more money if the institution generates more profits. . . . How is such a payment possible without a private profit motive?"

Bonuses for nonprofit executives come in all shapes and sizes. When Dr. Buris Boshell, the part-time executive director of the Diabetes Trust Fund in Birmingham, Alabama, took early retirement from his post at a clinic run by the University of Alabama at Birmingham in 1989, the trust fund's board of trustees voted him a onetime bonus of $300,000 in addition to his $100,000 salary. The group's 1989 tax return explains that the board "voted the executive director a special onetime bonus in the amount of $300,000 for his past services to the trust fund. This equates to a salary of about $20,000 per year for the first fifteen years of the trust fund, when the executive director served without compensation."

"My board went to the university and explained that [early retirement] certainly would create financial distress for me," Boshell explained in an interview. "They asked for a golden parachute for me, and to make a long story short, the university said 'no.' The board then decided that I should get $300,000 for the many, many years I had put in to the clinic." After receiving the bonus, he continued to run another diabetes clinic in Birmingham and remains in his part-time, $100,000-per-year position as executive director of the trust fund.

Transcripts from a 1992 board of regents meeting at the University of California revealed that some board members were concerned about the appearance of a $797,000 lump-sum retirement package approved for outgoing president David Gardner (in addition to his annual pension of $130,000). Gardner had served as the university's president for ten years. "If the legislature gets hold of this . . . when we're increasing fees . . . it's very difficult to reconcile," regent Frank Clark stated during the meeting.

After provisions in the Omnibus Budget Reconciliation Act of 1993 capped compensation at $150,000 for calculating pension benefits under qualified retirement plans, many nonprofits followed the example of major corporations in restoring benefits to their top managers via legal loopholes in the act. A 1996 Towers Perrin survey discovered that 56 percent of the association chief executives polled had restructured their compensation packages to recover benefits that might have been lost due to the reduction in pensionable earnings limits (mean base salary found in the study: $170,200). In July 1996 the U.S. Senate approved H.R. 3448, the small-business-tax bill that reinstates 401(k) retirement plans for nonprofits. Now sitting in a House-Senate conference committee, the Small Business Job Protection Act of 1996 also restores the Section 127 tax exclusion for employer-provided educational-assistance programs. The move to allow nonprofits to offer 401(k) plans to employees was part of President Clinton's proposed fiscal 1997 budget; therefore, the bill is expected to become law as soon as the full Congress approves the conference committee draft.

In its 1994 tax return, the National Collegiate Athletic Association (NCAA) lists more than $1 million in outstanding loans made to NCAA officers and directors. In 1990, then–executive director Richard Schultz owed $247,016 on a mortgage loan in addition to drawing a $328,438 salary. (Ironically, the NCAA regularly enforces rules governing loans made to college athletes;

in 1992, for example, the NCAA suspended Demetrius DuBose, an all-American linebacker at Notre Dame, for two games for accepting a $600 loan from two boosters.)

Even when they put themselves out of business, nonprofit executives can find ways to line their pockets. When Blue Cross & Blue Shield of Ohio—one of the nation's largest nonprofit Blue Cross health insurance plans—agreed in July 1996 to merge with the for-profit hospital giant Columbia/HCA, Jack Burry, the chairman of Blue Cross & Blue Shield of Ohio, agreed to a $3 million payment under a "noncompete" agreement and a $7 million payment for managing the merger. Chief counsel Jerome Rogers earned $3.5 million in the deal. The insurer's outside lawyer also earned $3.5 million. Despite grumblings that the nonprofit's leaders rigged what Ohio attorney general Betty Montgomery termed "platinum parachutes" for themselves while selling the insurance plan ($2 billion a year in premiums) for a measly $300 million and a move by the national Blue Cross organization to prohibit Columbia/HCA from using its trademarks, the merger is scheduled to be completed if the Ohio legislature approves the deal. "There appears to be no money going to anybody but the folks who structured the deal," said Columbus lawyer Thomas Dutton.

Of course, not every nonprofit chief executive lives the high life. In the *Chronicle of Philanthropy* salary study, several top managers, including Robert C. Macauley, chief executive of the AmeriCares Foundation, and Ferdinand Mahfood, president of Food for the Poor, skewed the pay averages by reporting no salary or benefits for their work. Habitat for Humanity founder Millard Fuller receives $46,450 each year to manage a global nonprofit organization with 1995 revenues of $49.9 million. While David Mercer, head of the YMCA of the USA, earned $269,207 annually, YWCA of the USA head Prema Mathai-Davis earned just $74,769. Kenneth Hodder, national commander of the Salvation Army, is paid $57,421 per year, including benefits, for managing an organization with a $354 million annual budget and offices around the United States. "I believe that the special mission of nonprofits separates us from profit-making companies," he said. "I really can't speak to why other organizations pay what they do. But I can tell you that people who come to work at the Salvation Army don't come into this work because they are looking for money. If that was our overwhelming passion in life, we would go elsewhere."

Beyond the questions of salary and benefits lies the next best thing for nonprofit executives: the trappings of corporate America, embodied in opulent headquarters buildings and other perks of power. Before Allen Neuharth took over as chairman of the Arlington, Virginia–based Freedom Forum, the small nonprofit operated in rented offices in New York and made grants to support journalism projects in the cities where Gannett published newspapers. In 1989, however, Neuharth moved the forum to Virginia and approved $34 million in additional expenses, such as $15 million for a new headquarters (a figure that included $1 million for artwork).

The nine business divisions of the American Association of Retired Persons sustain an annual cash flow exceeding $10 billion, with revenues of more than $300 million annually. Its new ten-story Washington headquarters on K Street—leased for approximately $16 million a year—has been dubbed the Taj Mahal by neighbors. Described by the architectural critic of the *Washington Post* as "a knockdown surprise," the building boasts a turret, a state-of-the-art radio and TV broadcast studio, a marble lobby, and office lights operated by motion sensors. The building is filled with stained-glass windows, dozens of mahogany bookcases (reported cost: $1,800 each), and other furnishings that cost the seniors organization $29 million when the building opened in 1990. That same year, the AARP spent $14 million on programs aimed directly at assisting poor and indigent Americans aged fifty and older.

The building costs actually come in second to the $43 million spent each year on salaries for more than eleven hundred headquarters employees and $10 million spent for outside consultants (including one contract for experts to train AARP employees in how to pack their belongings into boxes for the 1990 move). Such over-the-top overhead poses a tantalizing challenge for other nonprofits in the AARP's niche. "If I could, I'd walk into AARP and immediately shift the money around," said Kurt Vondran, a lobbyist with the National Council on Senior Citizens.

An estimate prepared by the *New York Post* in a 1995 series on nonprofit abuses found that the National Football League is excused from commercial rent taxes and business income taxes paid by for-profit companies in New York City on its posh Park Avenue headquarters; at the standard 6 percent rate, the league apparently saved about $150,000 in taxes on the $2.4 million in rent it paid in 1993.

Other perks on par with the highest levels of corporate America have included a leased Jaguar for an executive of the J. Paul Getty Trust ($36,000), a skybox at Three Rivers Stadium in Pittsburgh for executives of Blue Cross of Western Pennsylvania ($377,101 over five years), and tent rentals and catering for an event in Palm Beach, Florida, for trustees of the National Museum of Polo & Hall of Fame in Lexington, Kentucky ($9,000).

While for-profit public corporations have shareholders, Wall Street analysts, and federal securities regulators to monitor their administrative spending, there are no natural watchdogs for America's nonprofit groups. Although the IRS says it has begun to pay closer attention to the executive salaries and benefits that must be listed for a nonprofit organization's top five officers in the group's annual Form 990 tax return, the agency has not conducted a comprehensive study of executive compensation or of general and administrative expenses among tax-exempt groups. In fact, Marcus Owens, the top IRS official in charge of nonprofit tax-code enforcement, freely admits that the issue of nonprofit salaries and administrative expenses is "a very gray area." Since the last hearing on executive compensation more than a quarter century ago, Congress has provided little encouragement or oversight on the issue of overhead for nonprofit groups.

In many cases, the board of directors of a nonprofit organization is compromised in its oversight powers because the board members are accustomed to higher levels of executive pay in corporate America and, in some instances, count the nonprofit itself as an important business client. "Trustees too often are on the board simply as fund-raisers, or worse yet, as vendors of legal, financial, construction, real estate, medical, and other services," Nancy Kane, a professor at the Harvard School of Public Health, testified before Congress in 1991.

Federal law states that compensation and benefits—no matter how they are determined or in what form they are paid—must be reasonable in order for a nonprofit to retain its tax-exempt status. Excessive compensation may violate the legal doctrine of private inurement, which holds that pay must be calculated based on comparable data from related sources and must not exceed benchmarks for similar types of jobs. Though they are not always enforced, IRS regulations stipulate that the compensation agreement must be negotiated "at arm's length," specify the amount of control that the executive exerts over the nonprofit organization, and set a "ceiling of reasonable maximum limit" beyond which the executive cannot be paid, among other factors.

A smoldering dispute between the publishing arm of the Evangelical Lutheran Church in America (ELCA) and its former chief executive officer turns on these questions. On July 30, 1996, both parties filed charges and countercharges in a Minneapolis court based on three questions surrounding Gary J. N. Aamodt's tenure as president and chief executive officer of Augsburg Fortress, Publishers: (1) What expenditures did Aamodt authorize as benefits for himself? (2) Did he unfairly structure these benefits as financially favorable to himself, to the detriment of his nonprofit employer? and (3) What payments did he authorize for himself to take care of the tax liabilities resulting from these benefits?

Aamodt, who resigned under pressure in April 1995, accused the Augsburg board of directors of breach of contract, fraud, and defamation of character over the terms of his employment in 1992 and his dismissal. Augsburg then filed a countersuit in Hennepin County District Court charging that Aamodt improperly spent more than $500,000 in Augsburg funds to buy an annuity and life insurance and to pay for personal tax liabilities resulting from the insurance purchases and from a leased Mercedes-Benz.

Aamodt was hired in 1992 at a $150,000 annual salary plus a benefits package that included retirement benefits, life insurance, a car, two club memberships, social security, health insurance, and disability insurance. The Augsburg board did not have specific figures on the cost of these benefits when Aamodt came on board, acknowledged H. George Anderson, then chair of the Augsburg Fortress board and now presiding ELCA bishop. After the man who became chairman of the board the next year pressed Aamodt for a detailed breakdown of the benefits cost, the board discovered that Aamodt had allegedly received $826,665 in total compensation for 1993; of that amount, the board maintains that it did not approve $548,576 of the payments. At the April 1995 board meeting in Toronto, the Augsburg executive committee decided to accept a report from legal counsel recommending that Aamodt resign immediately or be fired. According to Aamodt's lawsuit, the chairman, the board's attorney, and two members of the ELCA bishop's staff went to his hotel room and gave him thirty minutes to decide his fate. The publishing house posted security guards at Aamodt's office in Minneapolis who escorted the deposed chief executive officer from the building when he tried to enter his office upon returning from Toronto. The locks on the office were also changed.

According to Augsburg's countersuit, Aamodt used the nonprofit's funds to pay for a Lutheran Brotherhood annuity in his name for $234,027, a $300,000 life insurance policy for $129,634, $311,034 in personal taxes resulting from the insurance purchases, and $3,515 in personal taxes for the leased car. In doing so, the suit claims, Aamodt is guilty of "deceitfully receiving excessive unauthorized income," avoiding disclosure of the excess income, and jeopardizing Augsburg's nonprofit status. ELCA presiding bishop Anderson says he supports the Augsburg board fully, adding that through "their efforts to discover and remedy problems existing at Augsburg Fortress, they exercised their appropriate role as directors. Their decisiveness has restored confidence in our publishing enterprise."

For his part, Aamodt claims that Augsburg's accountants knew about the expenditures and in several instances recommended the actions he ultimately took. "This is all about promises made and promises not kept and about a bungling board that had an employment arrangement with me that it did not carry out," he says. "It's about an investigation that I knew nothing about prior to an hour before the executive committee meeting [at the April 1995 board meeting in Toronto]." Aamodt says he is seeking a jury trial as soon as possible to clear his name.

John Glaser, a former executive of United Way of America for twenty-three years, has suggested capping top salaries of chief professional officers of nonprofits who raise funds from the public at $200,000—the salary of the president of the United States—and keeping closer ratios between the pay of the chief staff officer and the lowest-paid worker. "An argument that a nonprofit must be able to compete with business to attract qualified people is fallacious for anyone but businesspeople," he said. "The reasons people go into nonprofit work are entirely different from those which motivate people to go into the commercial sector. . . . One argument voiced by people is that nonprofit executives can make a fortune in business. That's beside the point. We chose the nonprofit field, and we must therefore be bound by its constraints imposed by the public."

Glaser cites the comparison of executive salaries in the United States and Japan as an example of equitable pay scales. "Many of America's corporate executives make eighty-five times what the average blue-collar worker makes. In Japan, the ratio is closer to ten to one."

"Nothing points to the need for a major overhaul in the U.S. tax code for nonprofit groups more than these excesses," concludes Sally Covington of the National Committee for Responsive Philanthropy. "The tax-exempt code hasn't been updated for decades and decades and decades. In my view, tax-exempt privileges must be reviewed. If organizations have nothing to do with charitable purposes, then they simply shouldn't be tax-exempt."

# 6

# *Robbing Peter to Pay the Fund-Raisers*

IN 1993, BETH DENTON BEGAN asking questions about the Thin Mints. As one of the adult volunteers serving as a troop leader in Troop 370 of Girl Scouts of the U.S.A. in West Haven, Connecticut, Denton cheered on five young girls who sold 407 boxes of Girl Scout cookies during the organization's annual cookie drive. Girl Scouts have traditionally peddled the cookies door-to-door to foster volunteerism among the nation's 2.8 million members and to raise funds for Girl Scout programs. While safety concerns have made door-to-door selling a thing of the past in many regions—leaving parents in the unenviable role of peddling the cookies to coworkers and neighbors—the cookie sale continues to define the success of the Girl Scout movement and remains a requirement for any Brownie or Girl Scout to participate in special activities, such as camp and field trips, throughout the year.

However, Denton wondered where the money went. She complained to the local Girl Scouts council that her girls forwarded almost $900 to the council's headquarters, yet kept only about $100 for the troop itself. Checking with other troop leaders, she discovered that the average troop keeps less than 15 percent of the purchase price of the cookies for its own programs.

(Though the price of a box of Girl Scout cookies varies slightly from region to region, the national breakdown of the average sales price of $3 per box is 40 cents for the troop, 80 cents for the bakery, and $1.80 to one of 330 local Girl Scouts councils and, in turn, the group's national hierarchy of professional staffers and national volunteers.)

Girl Scouts around the United States sold more than 180 million boxes of cookies in 1995, generating more than $420 million in tax-free sales. Of that $420 million, more than $370 million is shaved off the top for various types of operating expenses. The cookie sale is the pinnacle of the organization's national fund-raising efforts—measures that support more than four hundred staffers at the headquarters of the Girl Scouts of the U.S.A. on Fifth Avenue in New York, $127 million in total assets, and a $35 million surplus in 1995. (The remaining funds for Girl Scout activities come from various participation fees and sales of uniforms and merit badges.)

Denton continued her quest to find out more about the ultimate use of the Girl Scout funds. Eventually, her inquiries resulted in an investigation of the local council by the Connecticut attorney general's office. However, Denton was ultimately drummed out of the movement for causing the stir.

Questions about the ultimate beneficiaries of the traditional Girl Scout cookie sale point to a larger issue that affects many nonprofits today: the struggle to raise additional funds to support existing programs and the rising costs of securing those funds. To be sure, many nonprofits have honed their fund-raising skills to a new art, becoming very effective and efficient in generating ongoing financial support for their causes. "People are having a tougher time getting funds for nonprofit causes, and they are looking at many different ways, like product fund-raisers, to get the job done," reports Russell Lemieux, executive director of the Association of Fund-Raisers and Direct Sellers, a national trade group representing companies that produce merchandise for resale by charitable groups. The association's membership has mushroomed from 70 companies in 1990 to 720 in 1996.

Of the 366 major nonprofit organizations monitored by the New York–based National Charities Information Bureau, more than two-thirds meet all of the watchdog group's financial standards. However, the drive to raise new dollars can lead even the most established charities to overextend themselves. The American Cancer Society (ACS) learned a painful lesson in 1992 when it hosted an elaborate charity ball in Washington, D.C. The event raised more than $400,000, but after the society paid the evening's bills—ranging from the all-you-can-eat lobster bar to the dancers on stilts and the catering staff on roller skates—the net proceeds totaled a mere $194,771. Refocusing its efforts the next year, the society earned more than twice that amount at its ball. Nationally, the ACS spends 76 percent of every dollar on actual programming services—a ratio matched roughly by most large U.S. philanthropies.

Of course, some major national charities with household names and causes spend far less on their causes. The Shriners Hospitals for Crippled Children spends a little over 50 percent of its annual revenues on health-care services each year; the remainder goes to overhead and fund-raising expenses. In fact, some local Shrine temples have been accused of organizing circuses and other charity events ostensibly to generate funds for the hospitals when the money was actually being spent on temple operations. National Shrine policies now require local temples to state clearly on their fund-raising materials whether the money raised will go to the temples or the hospitals.

The telemarketing firm which raised $30.2 million for Mothers Against Drunk Driving in 1994 kept more than $15 million of the donations as its fee. An egregious example of out-of-control fund-raising costs at the state level is the Maryland-based Walker Cancer Research Institute, which raised almost $3 million in one recent year but spent less than a penny of every dollar taken in on cancer research. Fifty-four percent of the take went directly to pay fund-raising expenses and administrative overhead, while 44 percent paid for "public education" campaigns, such as antismoking programs.

While the ACS struggles to dedicate 76 percent of its annual revenues to cancer research and education programs aimed at helping patients and their families, the soundalike Cancer Fund of America (CFA) spends 86 percent of its annual budget on direct-mail and telemarketing campaigns and other fund-raising expenses, leaving a scant 13 cents on the dollar for cancer-related programs. "Cancer Fund of America is the organization we get more questions about than any other charity in the U.S.," notes a spokesman for the National Charities Information Bureau, estimating the number of calls annually at several hundred. "People call us all the time and say, 'Isn't that the group that has been sued by so many states?'" By piggybacking on the phrase "cancer fund"—claimed by the ACS as one of its more common nicknames—critics charge that the CFA has intentionally misled thousands of people into believing that they are actually supporting the larger, more well-established ACS. A lawsuit filed against the group by Pennsylvania regulators in 1994 claimed that the CFA had adopted the ACS "signature" method of raising funds—door-to-door solicitation drives led by neighborhood residents—in an attempt to confuse donors about the true recipient of their dollars.

Several trends in nonprofit management have encouraged the move toward exorbitant fund-raising campaigns. First, donors—particularly people who feel a strong personal connection to a nonprofit group or cause—have become harder to target and identify in solicitation appeals. A 1996 study of nonprofit donors by the Direct Marketing Association found that half of each generation group (baby busters, baby boomers, builders [ages 50–68], and seniors) agreed that it is important to have a meaningful relationship with a nonprofit group. However, those respondents actually reporting that they currently have such a bond with a nonprofit cause varied. Only 37 percent of baby busters confirmed that they feel that close to a nonprofit cause, compared to 45 percent of baby boomers, 52 percent of builders, and 42 percent of seniors.

In addition, those donors who give consistently have become much more picky about their investments in the nonprofit world.

Fund-raisers targeting aging baby boomers estimate that as much as $10 trillion in inheritances will pass from one generation to the next in coming years. How much of those funds will end up in charitable coffers is another matter. "Some baby boomers will 'get religion' and give to charity, but it won't be a universal notion," predicts Lester Salamon.

Unlike the Rockefellers and Carnegies, however, the recipients of this transferred wealth will make different choices about their bequests. "The new wealth is paper wealth," Salamon notes. "Old money was based on physical capital that did not fluctuate as much as today's fortunes." Therefore, baby boomers will be preoccupied with maintaining family legacies before they turn their attention to charities. "Endowed advocacy"—giving a sum of money for a very specific purpose, cause, or program—will be more common than large, undesignated gifts. Tapping into these currents of future philanthropy will require more skilled fund-raisers and targeted solicitation techniques, both of which carry hefty price tags. (Even the most traditional fund-raisers have begun experiencing greater levels of resistance among consumers, donors, and volunteers. "I sometimes wondered, What do we get out of this?" asked Kim Burton, a veteran of the annual Girl Scout cookie sales in Lexington, Kentucky. Burton sold boxes of cookies for her daughter Heather by posting and circulating order forms to attract coworkers at her office. "Basically, it's the parents who end up doing the sales. What do the girls learn from that?")

Another factor affecting the cost of fund-raising programs among nonprofits is the set of lax accounting rules that allow tax-exempt groups to hide fund-raising expenses in many different parts of a nonprofit's budget. In 1987 the American Institute of Certified Public Accountants adopted a ruling, at the request of several major nonprofits, allowing charities to allocate a percentage of the cost of a fund-raising project (such as a solicitation letter or a telemarketing campaign) to program expenses if the project contains "educational" content (called the "allocation of joint costs" ruling). Thus, a nonprofit group can downplay the amount of money invested in fund-raising efforts each year by attributing some of the fund-raising and administrative costs to program-expense line items within the budget. The result: The nonprofit group can claim a much more aggressive and appealing ratio of dollars raised to dollars spent on services. As long as the marketing brochure mentions the need to eat fruits and vegetables several times a day, then the message of good eating habits actually saves the nonprofit's image as a responsible organization because the group's accountant can hide the costs of the brochure in the "public education" category. Watchdog agencies, such as the National Charities Information Bureau, weed out such dubious billings when they prepare their own financial statements for the charities they monitor. However, the accounting institute's standard has become the generally accepted accounting principle for nonprofit financial reporting, with no prospects on the horizon of reversing course. Using the rule, the CFA claimed $8.5 million in expenses in 1992, or 41 percent of all funds taken to date. However, CFA leaders admit that almost $3 million in expenses had been coded to "public education" when they were in reality fund-raising costs.

The old adage "You have to spend money to make money" summarizes the third factor stimulating the increases in fund-raising expenses. The average Christmas season, for example, brings hundreds of national direct-mail fund-raising campaigns tailored to known and prospective donors. "There's a free-for-all at the end of the year," observes Jerome Pickholz, chief executive officer of Ogilvy & Mather Direct, the New York–based direct-marketing unit of WPP Group's Ogilvy & Mather. "There's no question there's competition for the mailbox, competition for the mind, and competition for the wallet. But the last thing you want to do is step away from the fray. If you're not out there, you get nothing."

Many cost elements in fund-raising are extremely competitive compared to for-profit business expenses. For example, postal rates on third-class mail for nonprofits can be as low as half the rates on commercial mail. However, many nonprofits find that the real financial "nut" comes in donor prospecting— finding new names to become new givers. Donor-acquisition programs may use rented or loaned donor lists as the foundation of the campaign; associated costs can include creating, renting, or buying lists of donors and structuring them to fit the needs and messages of the nonprofit group. "Donor prospecting can be so costly that sometimes in the first year of a group's campaign you may actually spend much more than you take in due to printing, list rentals, computer services, and other costs," says Kenneth Albrecht, president of the National Charities Information Bureau.

Another factor increasing fund-raising costs is compliance with federal, state, and local laws governing nonprofit solicitations. For example, fund-raising programs conducted for tax-exempt groups by for-profit consultants may be covered under new Federal Trade Commission (FTC) telemarketing regulations. "In situations where a for-profit company makes interstate calls to solicit donations for a nonprofit organization but offers no goods or services as an inducement to make a donation, the activity is not covered," reads a guide published jointly by the Direct Marketing Association and the FTC. "However, if goods or services (such as a book, a subscription, or a membership) are offered to induce donations and the goods or services are of more than a nominal value, the activity is covered, and the required oral disclosures [e.g., stating the group's refund policies] must be made." "Get all the facts before you get on the phone," recommends Jill M. Cornish, publisher of *Association Trends* magazine. "Also, when you are choosing an outside telemarketing provider, be certain they understand your concerns and address them specifically in the contract. The company should be fully familiar with the nonprofit's objectives and the laws which govern nonprofit fundraising."

"We know it doesn't look good on the first year. We're going to stand up and take our lumps," said Bill Grein, the retired U.S. Marine Corps major who serves as head of operations for the U.S. Marine Corps Reserve Toys for Tots Foundation in Quantico, Virginia. Grein was referring to the discovery on Christmas, 1992, that the nonprofit did not have enough money to make planned purchases of toys. In July of that year the foundation hired a professional fund-raising firm to operate a national mail campaign; however, the fund-raising costs ate up the $9.3 million raised during the first half of the year. Formed in 1989 to provide a year-round source of funds for the foundation, the Toys for Tots program expects to earn more than $1 million from the seeds sown in the initial direct-mail campaign which ended in an embarrassing deficit.

More than sixteen hundred full-time, nonprofit, fund-raising consultants now belong to the National Society of Fund-Raising Executives, a trade association based in Alexandria, Virginia. The group has seen its membership grow by 30 percent in the last five years, according to Patricia Lewis, the organization's president. Hiring an expert moneymaker does not come cheap, however. David Davenport, a private fund-raising consultant in Norfolk, Virginia, who specializes in church-related projects, charges between $8,000 and $10,000 for a campaign that involves part-time work and might charge up to $40,000 for a multimillion-dollar on-site campaign. "National firms might charge up to $40,000 for midsize campaigns and up to $200,000 for a multimillion-dollar campaign," he said.

Do such expensive techniques work? "I don't think the diocese has ever achieved a fund-raising success like this," said Brian Hunt, comptroller for the Episcopal diocese in Lexington, Kentucky, which needed to raise $1.2 million in 1995 to renovate the Cathedral Domain camp and conference center in a neighboring county. The diocese hired Holliman and Associates, a Pennsylvania company that specializes in coordinating fund-raisers for about three hundred Episcopal churches around the country. "With Holliman's help, we hit our pledge goal within a year," Hunt remembered. "My gut instinct says we wouldn't do as well" without the consultants.

# 7

## *Donations Gone Astray*

WILLIAM ARAMONY ENJOYED the good things in life. Because he frequently traveled to New York City on business, he decided to purchase a luxury apartment on the city's Upper East Side for $383,000; one year later, he invested an additional $72,000 to redecorate it to suit his taste. The sixty-seven-year-old executive shared his largesse with his twenty-five-year-old girlfriend, treating her to vacations in London, Paris, and Las Vegas, and to mark the anniversary of their first date, the pair traveled to Egypt for a weeklong cruise on the Nile River. He surprised her by investing $80,000 to build a sunroom onto her home in Florida.

The good life fell apart later that year, however, when the news leaked that Aramony—president of United Way of America for more than twenty-two years and the man credited with making the organization into the country's most visible "umbrella" association for community service groups—had used United Way funds to pay for these extravagances. After a stormy trial in Alexandria, Virginia, in which Aramony claimed that brain atrophy had impaired his ability to distinguish between right and wrong, he was convicted on twenty-five counts of conspiracy, fraud, and money laundering.

The Aramony case provided one of the most current and extreme examples of the lax financial controls in place at many

U.S. nonprofit organizations. Accounting rules for nonprofits have fallen behind comparable standards for for-profit corporations, and nonprofits sometimes fail to observe the rules, based on a lack of proper financial training or on simple negligence, and the boards of directors and other officials charged with ensuring the financial integrity of the nonprofits that they serve have a history of failing to exercise proper oversight to ensure that the money collected by nonprofits goes to the good causes for which it is intended.

From its beginning in Denver in 1887, United Way has tapped literally millions of Americans as donors and helped countless thousands with a variety of social services. A 1994 public-service announcement touted the good works of United Way affiliates throughout the country: "Last year, United Way agencies helped 27,500 people with drug or alcohol problems. Gave comfort to 9,952 abused children. Provided 151,870 nights of shelter for the homeless. And served over 417,000 hot meals to the hungry. As you can see, thousands need us. That's why we need you." In 1995, United Way raised more than $3.5 billion, which went to forty-seven thousand agencies, ranging from soup kitchens to after-school programs.

Building on early-twentieth-century trends toward community coordination of social services, United Way evolved into a national network of local and regional councils composed of autonomous nonprofit groups that come together to coordinate their charitable activities and improve community standards of nonprofit operations. "Local United Ways are still committed to the three major functions of the earlier organizations from which they emerged: coordination and planning for community needs; fund raising; and the distribution, or allocation, of funds raised," observes Eleanor Brilliant, associate professor of social work at Rutgers University in her book *The United Way: Dilemmas of Organized Charity.* "However, the way that these core functions are carried out has become considerably more complicated over the years, and it now involves United Ways in another whole set of service activities, including marketing, research, technical assistance to agencies, government relations, and public relations—all related to an increasingly competitive philanthropic environment and necessitating a more complex organizational structure."

Aramony took the helm of United Way in 1970 and began immediately to address these concerns. Under his aggressive development of corporate donors, the United Way grew through the 1980s to include twelve hundred dues-paying member organizations in the United States and fifteen international affiliates, from Canada to South Africa. These members pay about 1 percent of their funds to the national organization, which provides training, technical assistance, and national advertising to the locals. In the average year United Way of America provides partial funding for as many as 10 percent of the IRS master list of charitable organizations.

The federated approach to fund-raising championed by United Way—particularly workplace solicitations in which employees of a company view presentations showing the good work of the local United Way affiliate and are encouraged to make an immediate donation or an ongoing payroll deduction—made the nonprofit one of the most recognized charities in the United States. Today more than 50 percent of United Way contributions come from employees in major corporations and small businesses, compared to 25 percent from direct gifts from large companies. "No other fund-raising organization has yet been able to obtain the same kind of access to the workplace, and the old 'community'—or residential—(house-to-house) campaign has almost disappeared," Brilliant notes.

In February 1992 a column by investigative reporter Jack Anderson entitled "Charity Begins at Home for United Way" outlined several allegations of wasteful spending and misappropriated donations at the charity. That report started a frenzy of reporting that uncovered concerns about Aramony's $463,000 in annual salary and benefits, the hiring of Aramony's friends and relatives in key United Way posts, and the creation of spin-off corporations through which Aramony allegedly funded vacations for his girlfriend and a luxury New York apartment. On February 28, Aramony resigned as president of the charity, but ensuing investigations resulted in a seventy-one-count federal indictment in 1994 targeting Aramony; Stephen Paulachak, president of one of the United Way spin-off companies; and Thomas Merlo, United Way's chief financial officer from 1990 to 1992. The primary charge was that Aramony and his aides diverted $2.74 million from the trade group to Partnership Umbrella, Inc., the spin-off company created to help charities obtain discounts on goods and services but which in turn provided Aramony with what amounted to personal spending money for gifts and extravagances.

Despite a spirited defense at the March 1995 trial, in which Aramony's attorneys contended that brain atrophy resulting from a fall in the 1980s had impaired his ability to "process information and compute figures," Aramony was convicted on twenty-five counts and began serving a seven-year prison sentence.

Elaine Chao, a former director of the Peace Corps, was brought in to succeed Aramony, and she began immediately to address the damage done to United Way's image by the scandal. She cut the group's budget expected from donations by local affiliates, and after one year United Way's staff and budget were one-third smaller than the year before Aramony's departure. "We have installed new financial controls, a new governance structure, a new code of ethics, and new measures of accountability," she told reporters in 1993.

The United Way scandal points to lax accounting procedures as one critical reason that nonprofits may allow their funds to be used for purposes other than their charitable mission. Asked to explain how Aramony was able to cover his profligate spending habits, Rina Duncan—Aramony's former secretary, who had a three-year affair with him—said she used "creative coding" on his expense reports. Funds invested in United Way's spin-off corporations were not monitored effectively by United Way accountants, and the spin-off firms' tax returns were often incomplete.

In many cases of nonprofit financial fraud, the accounting principles that are violated may be very elementary. The American Contract Bridge League lost more than $1 million when its executive director pled guilty in April 1995 to embezzling the funds. Her method: She exercised sole authority to sign checks for the group for any amount of money, whereas established accounting procedures for businesses similar in size normally recommend two signers for checks exceeding a certain amount. The embezzlement was discovered only when the league's bank sent an overdraft notice by mistake to one of the group's volunteer officers rather than the executive director.

Jerry Wilhoit, a certified association executive who headed the Richmond, Virginia–based Phenix Corp., an association management firm, embezzled more than $960,000 in funds from three different clients: the American Society of Post-Anesthesia Nurses, the Association of Pediatric Oncology Nurses, and the American Urological Association Allied. He used a similar check-writing scheme to steal the funds from association accounts without raising suspicions from his partner in the firm or association executives. The judge ordered Wilhoit's assets sold to repay a portion of the debt, but Wilhoit "is close to the date where he's required to be released," according to his attorney.

When it came time to pay a large hotel bill after the National Association of Royalty Owners (NARO) convention in Oklahoma City in 1995, founder and president Jim Stafford discovered that approximately $50,000 of the $90,000 in receipts from that meeting had disappeared, leaving the nonprofit in financial distress. A subsequent investigation uncovered that Millard Andrew Fowler, who had served as the NARO's outside accountant for fifteen years, had misappropriated $133,801 over an eight-year period. Using his total check-writing authority in making payments to contractors and suppliers, Fowler told association executives that he was building the group's reserves by buying certificates of deposit. Instead, Fowler siphoned money from association accounts for his personal use and never bought the certificates. During the investigation, authorities discovered that Fowler was never a bonded certified public accountant, as he had claimed. In February 1996, Fowler was found guilty of twenty-one counts of embezzlement. However, he received a light sentence—twenty-three years in prison, with twenty-two years suspended—and was ordered to pay $3,300 in restitution.

The NARO—a five-thousand-member association representing owners of oil and gas royalty and mineral rights—has revamped its accounting procedures, bringing most of the tasks in-house and requiring at least two signatures on every check. "We are whittling down our debt from the theft, and despite this tremendous setback, the NARO remains alive and plans to continue to be one of the nation's most active energy-related associations," Stafford said. (Fowler allegedly embezzled $69,000 from another private organization in Oklahoma, but the group decided not to press charges, according to Stafford.)

In June 1996, Justice Donald Alexander sentenced former Maine Grocers Association executive director John Joyce in Kennebeck County (Me.) Superior Court to three years in jail and four years of probation for embezzling $705,000 from various association accounts, including the group's health-insurance trust fund. Joyce must also give up 10 percent of his annual gross income to repay the association. Convicted on May 31, Joyce was fired in the fall of 1995, after nine years as chief executive officer of the state grocers group.

Claiming that a mental disorder combined with stress led her to embezzle an amount estimated between $1.5 million and $2.2 million, Ellen Cooke—the fifty-two-year-old former treasurer of the Episcopal Church—said she will appeal her September 1996 sentence of five years in prison meted out by U.S. district court judge Maryanne Trump Barry in Newark, New Jersey. In her ruling, Barry said that Cooke had "systematically looted" the denomination's treasury. Cooke surrendered cash accounts and a farm to repay the church for her admitted theft but said she does not think she deserves to go to prison for her actions.

Greed is not the only motivation for nonprofit frauds. Frank Williams, the charismatic executive director of the American Parkinson's Disease Association (APDA), revealed in an interview with *Fortune* magazine that he had stolen about $80,000 a year for ten years from the charity. Williams crisscrossed the country raising millions of dollars for research on the progressive brain disease, building the Staten Island–based nonprofit into a major health charity, with ninety chapters and five hundred support groups nationwide and bringing boxing legend Muhammad Ali onto its board. At the same time, Williams began using a bank account which had been set up in North-field, Minnesota, to hold funds from a walkathon temporarily as a front for receiving association donations and diverting the money to his personal use. His reason? He told reporter David Stipp that he resented the family that dominates the charity's board, including APDA president Salvatore Esposito Jr. and his brother-in-law, who serves as the group's scientific director. "I wore myself into the ground, but nobody ever compensated me. I was making $109,000 a year when I left after thirteen years. I raised funds in every possible way. I did PR, marketing, direct mail, special events. Anyone else in my position [at comparable charities] was making about $200,000. They didn't even give me life insurance." For the record, Esposito counters that Williams's salary was $112,856 ("a great salary") when he left and that the charity did provide Williams with life insurance. Some APDA chapters chose to transfer their allegiance to the rival National Parkinson Foundation, based in Miami. Williams is now the tar-get of a federal investigation. "I left a trail a mile wide," he said. "I knew I would get caught. It was like a monkey off my back, and I was relieved. I couldn't function any more knowing what I'd been doing."

Especially for the nonprofits that find themselves hardest hit with ethical lapses, it can be difficult to find the road back to re-spectability. After three and one-half years as William Aramony's successor as the head of United Way of America, Elaine Chao de-cided in June 1996 that her work was done. Those United Way affiliates that had left the fold following Aramony's misdeeds had returned, 1995 contributions exceeded 1991's record $3.1 bil-lion, and Chao had set the personal example of accepting $195,000 in salary (compared to Aramony's $463,000) and re-fusing subsequent raises. However, Chao raised a firestorm when she quit, as word leaked out that seven members of the national United Way board of directors had made plans to give her a total of $292,500, privately and anonymously, as a "goodbye" pay-ment. (The $292,500 amount equaled the money Chao would have been paid if she had been fired by the board during her five-year contract, and the United Way of America executive committee approved the deal apparently without knowing the names of the seven board members posting the money.) By preparing to accept the payment, Chao appeared to be violating the ethics code she had pioneered upon her arrival at United Way. "No employee should accept any gratuity or favor for doing his or her job. [United Way of America] employees do not solicit or accept gratuities, gifts, or favors." After initially describing the money as a payment "to recognize me for the tremendous work I accomplished" rather than a gift or favor, Chao reversed course and said in a prepared statement that she would forgo the payment—intended, she said, as an expression of gratitude—"to spare United Way any criticism however unjustified." Chao denied in media interviews that the payment was connected in any way to her position as the wife of Sen. Mitch McConnell, the prominent Republican senator from Kentucky.

"This whole thing looked crummy," groused editorial writer Michael Gartner in a *USA Today* column following Chao's announcement. "The seven [board members] shouldn't have offered the money. Chao shouldn't have agreed to take it. The executive committee shouldn't have approved it. And the rest of the board—citing the ethics code—should have stopped it. . . . This looked bad for the givers—their names would have come out; they always do—and for Chao. It looked bad for the United Way. And it could have looked bad for McConnell. . . . That's why Chao's eleventh-hour decision . . . is the right one."

# 8

# *Crossing Into Profitable Territory*

THE FOUNDERS OF A NEW HEALTH CLUB in Washington, D.C., took great pains to outfit the club with the latest in physical-fitness equipment and facilities. Throughout the seven floors in the club's choice midtown building, they built such amenities as an Olympic-size swimming pool, a full-service spa, a "virtual reality" golf course, and other state-of-the-art amenities designed to lure new members away from competing clubs in the nation's capital.

Travelers in the know who visit New York City stop at one of the city's most distinctive gift shops to purchase upscale souvenirs. At the main store on Fifth Avenue and Eighty-second Street (as well as its satellite stores in other cities), the shop offers coffee mugs, notepads, clothing, umbrellas, and art reproductions showcasing the work of the art world's most well known citizens, from Vincent van Gogh to Claude Monet. The shop even created a catalog several years ago, allowing shoppers across the country to purchase items and leading to the eventual development of a mail-order operation boasting seven-figure revenues.

Charges of sexual harassment leveled in 1993 against the company president by a former employee led the *Belleville* [Ill.] *News-Democrat*, a weekly newspaper serving southwestern Illinois, to investigate the tax records of Catholic Shrine Pilgrimage, Inc., a large tour company based in Belleville that sold package vacations to destinations in the United States, Mexico, Ireland, Greece, Italy, France, Israel, Portugal, Canada, Poland, Germany, and the United Kingdom. From 1986, when the company's tax return showed $935,592 in revenues, Catholic Shrine Pilgrimage earned $3,034,555 in 1991 (the last year for which the newspaper reviewed tax records); that same year, the company spent $2,666,024 in expenses and reported total assets of $1,448,340.

Under different circumstances, these three companies would receive accolades from supporters of free enterprise for their impressive growth and marketing savvy. However, they differ from other businesses in their fields because they operate with one critical competitive advantage: They enjoy tax-exempt status as nonprofit corporations. Because they have filed successfully under the provisions of Internal Revenue Code 501 (c) to be considered tax-exempt in their missions, these "pseudobusinesses" vie for market share and revenues against for-profit companies in what many business owners term unfair competition.

"Nonprofit groups have cultivated these competitive strengths for many, many years, and they have launched a deliberate assault on tax-paying, for-profit businesses," charges Kenton Pattie, executive director of the Business Coalition for Fair Competition (BCFC), an Alexandria, Virginia–based alliance of more than twenty small-business trade associations. Affected industries combating unfair competition through the efforts of BCFC include the gamut of America's small-business community: food-service outlets, testing laboratories, bookstores, computer dealers, travel agencies, tour companies, recreation centers, plant nurseries, day-care centers, hearing-aid technicians, veterinarians, blood banks, consulting engineers, medical-equipment suppliers, pencil manufacturers, specialty advertisers, hotels, printers, construction companies, laundries, janitorial services, waste haulers, and electrical, plumbing, heating, and air-conditioning contractors. At the 1995 White House Conference on Small Business, more than a thousand delegates adopted a resolution calling for President Clinton and leaders in Congress to "enact legislation that would prohibit government agencies and tax-exempt and antitrust-exempt organizations from engaging in commercial activities in direct competition with small businesses." Compared to other resolutions addressing concerns, such as health-care coverage and tax reform, the measure garnered enough votes to rank fourteenth among more than four hundred issues discussed at the Washington, D.C., conference.

In theory, what constitutes unfair competition? "We define unfair competition in very precise terms," says Jim Santini, a former four-term member of Congress who now serves as the Washington lobbyist for the National Tour Association, a four-thousand-member trade association based in Lexington, Kentucky. "Unfair competition results when a tax-exempt entity, such as a nonprofit agency, sells goods and services using its unique, taxpayer-supported privileges. The nonprofit competes directly with private businesses instead of working through these companies to sell its goods and services." Many of the nation's 1.2 million nonprofits have become much more aggressive in seeking outside sources of income to replace decreases in federal grants and private donations. "Many fundamental conditions have changed dramatically for associations, probably altering forever the environment in which associations exist and operate," says Tracy Casteuble, associate director for research and information at the American Society of Association Executives (ASAE). According to Casteuble, a 1996 ASAE survey found that more than a quarter of U.S. trade organizations bundle different products and services and market them aggressively to members, "a practice that is likely to increase as the ability to track information and the knowledge of increasingly sophisticated marketing research methods grows."

Seventy-six percent of the average nonprofit's revenues come from the sale of products and services, the income of for-profit subsidiaries, and funding sources other than donations, dues, and grants, according to a Small Business Administration study cited by the BCFC. "Nondues revenue is where the growth is," concurred J. Scott McBride, president of Marketing General Inc., which conducted a 1996 survey of nonprofit marketing practices for the Greater Washington Society of Association Executives. Based on a sampling of two thousand nonprofit managers, the study found that 54 percent of associations report that nondues revenue is growing faster than dues income (the most popular nondues-revenue programs: convention registration fees, publication sales, and exhibits). "If nondues revenue is where the growth is, we have to become more involved in product development," said McBride. "It means committing more financial revenues to make that happen."

Nonprofits engaged in unfair competition take advantage of a wide range of competitive edges. If their commercial activities can be judged to further their legally stated tax-exempt missions, nonprofits enjoy exemption from federal, state, and local income taxes. At the same time, almost every state extends that exemption to sales taxes that might have been levied on a nonprofit's commercial revenues, and most cities forgo property taxes for the same reason. "[A]ny net damage to nonprofits will result in a diminution in the benefits associations provide to American society," warned ASAE president William Taylor in testimony submitted to the House Ways and Means Committee to oppose comprehensive tax-reform legislation that might have curbed some tax exemptions for nonprofit groups.

Nonprofits that qualify under Internal Revenue Code 501 (c)(3) as charitable foundations enjoy reduced postal rates to attract members, solicit funds, or promote their activities; in many cases, these rates amount to a discount of as much as 50 percent on the rates paid by for-profit businesses. Nonprofits can use federal and state tax exemptions to arrange tax-exempt bonds or similar financing instruments to finance their programs. Certain rules regarding social-security deductions, unemployment-insurance payments, workers' compensation, and other programs that apply to small businesses do not necessarily apply to nonprofit employers. Finally, nonprofits enjoy the advantage of the halo effect, in that the public generally confers a higher status on a product or service bearing the imprimatur of a tax-exempt organization, even though similar or better products and services are available from for-profit companies at a comparable price. The public's conviction that a nonprofit organization and its for-profit affiliates operate on behalf of the public welfare and therefore are not tainted by the profit motive gives nonprofits a valuable marketing advantage. This halo effect, the least quantifiable benefit attributed to unfair competitors, may be considered their most important competitive edge.

Bill Shore, founder of Share Our Strength, a Washington-based antihunger nonprofit group with fund-raising programs throughout the United States, believes that more nonprofits should use these advantages in entrepreneurial ventures. "Traditionally, America's nonprofits are rich in compassion and idealism, but they are entrepreneurially bankrupt," he wrote in a March 26, 1996, editorial in *USA Today*. "They're stuck settling for leftover wealth—the excess funds people and companies donate after their primary needs are met. Depending on leftovers to fight poverty or promote economic development is about as effective as trying to move a truck by asking passersby to push—what you need is a powerful engine."

According to Shore, that "engine" is independently created revenue sources. Shore started Share Our Strength by partnering with American Express to create the "Charge Against Hunger" corporate marketing campaign that has generated more than $5 million during each of the past three years for antihunger programs. "Once nonprofit leaders begin to think like business executives, they'll be able to forge relationships that benefit both the public and private sectors. Then they can take this approach a step further. In fact, a new breed of entrepreneurs is doing just that—completely reinventing the nonprofit sector by creating new wealth," he observed. Shore calls these new hybrids "community wealth enterprises," using Share Our Strength and actor Paul Newman's food company, Newman's Own, as examples. "Of course, nonprofit organizations should raise every private and public dollar they can," he concluded. "But they should not limit themselves to philanthropic dollars. Nonprofits that rely solely on government funds, charitable solicitations, and foundation grants are redividing the ever-shrinking philanthropic pie rather than taking steps to create a bigger one. If nonprofits are going to fill even some of the holes left to them by federal spending cuts and escalating social problems, they must become nonprofits for profit."

Many consultants and managers in the nonprofit world echo Shore's sentiments that the commercial activities of tax-exempt groups should be welcomed and encouraged and that fears of unfair competition are exaggerated at best. "Tax-exempt organizations and taxable organizations are fundamentally distinct," says Steven D. Simpson, a Raleigh, North Carolina, attorney who specializes in nonprofit legal issues. "A tax-exempt organization must be organized and operated exclusively for one or more exempt purposes. It must serve a public rather than a private interest. A nonprofit organization may serve the public interest through many kinds of activities, such as education, fostering self-help, or promoting cultural activities. A taxpaying entity that also conducts one or more of these activities may also serve the public good, but its primary purpose is to make money. Private investors will not tolerate a for-profit entity that does not make money. In contrast, no private individual has any profits or ownership interest in a nonprofit organization. A for-profit organization distributes its excess revenue over expenses to its owners as profits; a nonprofit organization is specifically prohibited from doing this. Finally, a for-profit entity will only provide goods or services that eventually make a profit. On the other hand, tax-exempt organizations may provide services that are not economically viable, since they can receive charitable contributions or can operate the business on volunteer time."

Based on these points, Simpson argues, the idea of "unfair competition" is basically a direct attack on the actual concept of tax-exempt status. "Rather than face the issue head-on, the business community has chosen to make self-righteous, not to mention self-serving, statements about a problem that simply does not exist," he says. "The business community complains about any competition rather than unfair competition. I submit that current law is certainly adequate to provide a level playing field between exempt and nonexempt organizations. In the health-care and publishing fields, current law puts exempt organizations at a decided disadvantage."

Tell that to John Kimelman, a writer for *Financial World* magazine, who decided in 1994 to find out what steps would be required to turn his publication—operated as a for-profit business venture fueled by subscriptions and advertising sales—into a public charity under the conditions set forth in section 501 (c)(3) of the U.S. Internal Revenue Code. In Kimelman's scenario, Financial World Partners (the magazine's owners at the time) would have to reincorporate as a nonprofit entity in the state of New York. As part of the reincorporation, the magazine would approve a new "educational and scientific" mission statement, forgo any stockholder's ownership interests, and restructure its finances so that "excess revenues" (read "profits") would be retained by the new charity. Thomas Hyatt, a lawyer with Powers, Pyles, Sutter, & Verville in Washington, D.C., wrote the new mission statement: "This organization is established solely for charitable, educational and scientific purposes, including the dissemination of information on a wide array of financial and investment topics in order to enhance the education of the public and promote better understanding of the U.S. economic system."

Next, the magazine would have to secure the approval of the IRS. As an IRS-approved charity, the magazine would not have to pay federal and state income taxes and local property taxes and would likely qualify for reduced nonprofit postal rates. It could accept tax-deductible gifts from individuals and private foundations, including foundations tied to corporations that would otherwise be magazine advertisers. *Financial World* could continue to charge subscription fees as long as the profits are retained by the charity. Advertising would still be allowed as long as traditional product advertising did not get out of hand. "The IRS code clearly permits tax-exempt organizations to have paid commercial advertising," said Marcus Owens. "So [*Financial World*] could join the ever-growing Charity Army," Kimelman concludes. "But on reflection, we're not going to pass the hat just yet."

The name's the thing in many instances of unfair competition as nonprofit groups seek to extend their halo effects into the commercial arena. In the age of $40 million Olympics sponsorships, some of the nation's largest nonprofits have learned to cash in on the value of their own names and reputations by licensing them to consumer-goods companies. The American Red Cross has approved bottled water, designer watches, and swimwear, with its logo displayed prominently on each item. Tetley Tea Co. is selling a Veterans of Foreign Wars (VFW) brand of coffee at supermarkets in selected East Coast markets, with the goal of moving more than a million cans in the first year of distribution. "It may be the beginning of a long line of products," a VFW spokesman told *USA Today* when the brand was launched. (The VFW receives about 30 cents from the sale of each can.) The World Wildlife Fund has approved the sale of a logoed line of outdoor clothing.

In October 1994, Johnson & Johnson's McNeil Consumer Products Co. unit unveiled a new line of pain relievers bearing the logo and name of the nonprofit Arthritis Foundation. The Arthritis Foundation Pain Relievers—acetaminophen (in daytime and nighttime formulas), ibuprofen, and coated aspirin—contain the same chemical composition as other competing brands. The deal calls for Johnson & Johnson to exploit the cachet of being endorsed, in effect, by the nation's leading organization for people with arthritis, while the foundation itself receives a guaranteed rights fee of at least $1 million annually, to be used in funding research programs aimed at finding a cure for arthritis. The Arthritis Foundation (1993 revenues: $72.3 million) raises money for research projects, refers people with arthritis to physicians specializing in the disease, and operates health-education programs around the country. Most of the foundation's money comes from individual donations and membership fees, but drug companies have given as much as $5 million a year to foundation causes. The foundation has endorsed pharmaceutical products in other instances, such as McNeil's Tylenol FastCap easy-to-open packaging, but the branding deal is the largest agreement entered into by the nonprofit group.

While the Arthritis Foundation's board of directors approved the project by a thirty-eight-to-one vote, critics point out that some supporters of worthy causes may be dismayed to see their nonprofit organization's name used to hawk products and services. "The real societal question is whether there is any difference between for-profit and nonprofit organizations in this country anymore," observed George Annas, director of the law, medicine, and ethics program at Boston University. "Persuading arthritis sufferers to purchase a certain brand of aspirin hardly serves the organization's tax-exempt purpose," said tax analyst Lee A. Sheppard.

"It is simply critical that in these alliances the terms should be properly disclosed to consumers and supporters, particularly the amount of the sale which directly benefits the philanthropy or nonprofit group," observes Bennett Weiner, director of the Philanthropic Advisory Service of the Council of Better Business Bureaus in Arlington, Virginia. (In the case of the Arthritis Foundation Pain Relievers, each package features a generic disclosure.) Other observers pointed out that the Johnson & Johnson–brand pain relievers cost on average 20 percent more than the equivalent generic products. ("What's actually for sale here? Mostly the Arthritis Foundation," fumed *Consumer Reports* magazine.)

Other nationally known nonprofits have struggled with the ethics and the operating challenges of endorsements and licenses. The American Dental Association (ADA) has been researching potential means of securing reimbursements for the cost of its popular "ADA" certification program for consumer dental-care products, such as toothpaste and toothbrushes. An ADA spokesperson confirmed that the association spends more than $1 million annually to examine products and award the seals of approval. "We want people to know that we take this [certification] process seriously and that no company can simply walk up and buy the ADA seal," he stated. After discarding a seal-of-approval program in the face of objections to the group's charging a recommendation fee to cover its program costs, the American Heart Association (AHA) tried another tack in the fall of 1994, distributing brochures in grocery stores to advise shoppers how to read the new federally mandated labeling on food products. In addition to deciphering the labels, however, the "Heart Fest" pamphlets given out by AHA volunteers (the group currently lists more than 3.7 million members on its roster) contained coupons for products ranging from Healthy Choice Pasta

Sauce to a home cholesterol-testing kit; in fact, two-thirds of the available space in the pamphlet consisted of coupons.

The AHA defended the Heart Fest program, saying that the promotion enabled the nonprofit to deliver its "good health" message to millions of consumers nationwide. On the other hand, consumer advocates and medical ethicists have accused the AHA of selling out in the name of raising money. "The one thing groups like the AHA bring to the country's medical discussions is that they are generally considered to be above the marketing fray," says Donald Kennedy, former commissioner of the U.S. Food and Drug Administration and former president of Stanford University. "Once a nonprofit has lost its reputation for objectivity, one of its key weapons is gone forever."

The nonprofit-endorsement bonanza is not limited to consumer products. In a move generally considered a veiled signal to millions of older Americans to consider managed-health-care plans, the American Association of Retired Persons (AARP) agreed to begin lending its name for a fee to selected health maintenance organizations (HMOs) around the United States beginning in the fall of 1996. Already a major player in the insurance industry—endorsing insurers that offer AARP-approved auto, homeowners, and Medicare supplement policies to the nonprofit's 33 million members in return for an estimated $146 million in royalties and related income in 1994 alone—the AARP declared its intention to select only those HMOs that could meet its standards on financial stability, commitment to quality, price, and popularity with current AARP members. Retaining a consulting firm, Health Benefits America, the AARP began screening hundreds of managed-care plans in the summer of 1996, seeking formal bids before selecting one or more providers in each of sixteen regional markets spanning the United States. Under the terms of the proposed agreement between the AARP and the selected HMOs, the nonprofit would assign its name and logo to the HMO for use in marketing health-care services; in return, the AARP retains the right to keep the HMO under continuous review and, if necessary, revoke the licensing agreement if the HMO's services fail to measure up to standards. Each HMO would gain access to the AARP's membership database (giving the company instant contact with millions of potential customers), promotions in AARP mailings and *Modern Maturity* (the AARP's monthly magazine), and advice on marketing services to consumers who are at least fifty years old. Among the major managed-care companies interested in submitting bids are Cigna, Kaiser Permanente, Humana, Prudential Life Insurance, U.S. Health Care, and the national Blue Cross and Blue Shield Association. (Tax experts predict that the AARP's move to endorse HMOs could invite renewed examinations by the IRS of the AARP's commercial activities; in the spring of 1993, the AARP paid the IRS an estimated $135 million to settle a dispute over its endorsements of insurance policies and other products.)

While the federal government and many national companies have embraced HMOs as an effective means of controlling health-care costs, and Medicare HMOs have become one of the fastest-growing types of managed-care programs, the AARP runs the risk of endorsing businesses for its elderly members that, as part of the cost-containment process, routinely limit or refuse medical services not judged essential according to each HMO's policies. A rash of such moves could upset AARP members, who traditionally have considered the organization their "water carrier," charged with defending health-care programs for the elderly. "Endorsing these deals could raise questions about whether the AARP can continue to maintain its credibility as a neutral broker in the ongoing debate over health care in this country, especially for seniors," said Bruce Vladeck, chief administrator of the federal Medicare program. "Getting into that business is high-risk stuff," agreed Marilyn Moon, a researcher in the economics of Medicare at the Urban Institute in Washington. "If some of these companies turn out to be bad actors, it will have a definite impact."

In August 1996 the American Cancer Society raised the bar on endorsement deals, selling its name on an exclusive basis to NicoDerm antismoking patches and Florida orange juice for at least $4 million in royalties. The deals were announced in conjunction with the national introduction of NicoDerm CQ, the second nicotine patch to be made available as an over-the-counter drug. SmithKline Beecham PLC, the big British-based drug manufacturer, will pay the society at least $1 million per year in royalties for three years. In exchange, the society's logo will appear on NicoDerm boxes and advertising materials, along with a reference to the two as partners in promoting efforts to stop smoking. The related deal with the Florida citrus marketers association will net the society at least $1 million for one year. "After very serious consideration and review, we determined that companies that are producing products that support the missions or programs of the American Cancer Society would be acceptable business partners for us," said society spokesperson Elizabeth Bridgers.

"We're going to end up with the health equivalent of the Olympics," griped Paul Root Wolpe of the Center for Bioethics at the University of Pennsylvania. "I deeply understand the temptation [to make money]. However, if they want to endorse products, they should do it in the spirit of an educational agency, not as a paid shill." Wolpe predicts that medical nonprofits will soon endorse every kind of consumer product, "from tires and chewing gum to sneakers."

In other niches of the nonprofit economy, endorsement deals are strictly a matter of capitalizing on the value of some of the world's most recognized names in the field of culture and altruism. In 1995, United Media—the publishing conglomerate that merchandises Snoopy and other Classic Comics characters on behalf of its syndicated artists—signed an agreement with the National Geographic Society to create a global licensing program to extend the "National Geographic" brand. A unit of Cincinnati-based publisher E. W. Scripps Co., United Media became the exclusive worldwide licensing agent for most major categories of products and promotions. "We've been working to expand the name of National Geographic by focusing on the group's educational projects," a United Media spokesperson said. The company plans to unveil age-specific branding agreements for products aimed at both adults and children. In 1994 the Sierra Club won a major bout in the U.S. Tax Court when the IRS threatened to levy a 40 percent tax on the $400,000 earned by the nonprofit from purchases made by supporters on a cobranded affinity credit card. "Groups like the Sierra Club rely upon these new types of fund-raising techniques," said Holly Schadler, a Washington tax lawyer representing the nonprofit. "They're now the bread and butter for raising money."

While endorsements and licensing agreements generally require minuscule investments of effort and money on the part of the sponsoring nonprofits, many groups have expanded their moneymaking programs to enter the commercial arena directly. Instead of establishing partnerships with for-profit companies, the nonprofit sets up a commercial subsidiary or simply posts a shingle and begins operating a business using its existing offices, assets, and staffers. "It's kind of a moneymaking thing," Rev. Richard Reynolds told the *Wall Street Journal* in 1995, when the newspaper investigated the tour programs offered by the South Bethlehem United Methodist Church in South Bethlehem, New York. The pastor's twenty-trip schedule for the year included a motorcoach tour to the Amish countryside and longer excursions to Hawaii and Scandinavia. "Any profit, the church gets," Reynolds explains.

For-profit travel agents and tour operators argue in turn that nonprofits like the South Bethlehem United Methodist Church use their tax-exempt operating privileges to steal business from the taxpaying businesses that subsidize nonprofits in the first place. "When it comes to nonprofit travel sales, we're not talking about the once-in-a-lifetime pilgrimage to the National Cathedral or a regional shrine," claims Jim Santini, the Washington representative for the National Tour Association. "We're seeing deluxe cruises to Greece, with a one-hour excursion to a cathedral along the way, and national and international tours going every week and every month. And because nonprofits don't pay taxes on these trips, they can undercut tour companies' prices by as much as thirty percent or more." Group Leaders of America, a marketing alliance of nonprofit travel packagers, counts more than three thousand churches among its thirty-two thousand members, carrying an estimated 1.2 million passengers on trips every year. The average church group in the mix spends $75,000 a year on travel programs annually. "These nonprofits are killing us," says Nancy Connair, general manager of Wisconsin Coach Tours in Waukesha, Wisconsin. "People who travel in my area will cancel my tours and go with a nonprofit group for as little as two dollars' difference in the price, and when my nonprofit competitors don't pay taxes and use volunteers and reduced postal rates to market their tours, I just can't keep up."

In October 1995 the IRS denied tax-exempt status for "sports ambassador" tours conducted by the People to People Program, organized in 1956 by Dwight Eisenhower as a nonprofit designed to supplement the U.S. Information Agency in its efforts to broaden understanding and friendship with people of other nations. In 1964 the group added golf and tennis tours to its programs; by 1987 (the latest tax year examined by the IRS in its action), more than four hundred supporters participated in four tennis tours and nine golf tours. The typical golf tour cost $7,000 to visit six cities in three weeks; at each destination, participants played in at least one golf match, required practice rounds, and official People to People receptions. In return, the supporters received letters thanking them for their "contributions" and a "tax receipt" for the full amounts paid. In its ruling, the IRS concluded that the golf and tennis tours "did not contribute importantly to [the nonprofit's] exempt purposes" and that the participants were not entitled to the "out-of-pocket" charitable-contribution deductions taken during the 1986 and 1987 taxable years.

"From antiquity to contemporary times, great art has followed the fabulous prosperity of Europe's maritime powers along the Continent's scenic shorelines and riverbanks. Marvelous manifestations of that creativity will be enjoyed in the glorious flowering of spring during this distinctive Metropolitan Museum of Art voyage of the gracious *Regina Renaissance.* I hope you will be aboard," wrote Emily Rafferty, the museum's vice president for development and membership in New York, in a four-color brochure sent to museum supporters under a nonprofit postal permit in 1995. Though the museum employed an independent travel consultant to handle reservations, its use of nonprofit postal rates lowered the marketing costs of the trip substantially.

In July 1996 the Small Business Administration (SBA) formally asked the Treasury Department to crack down on nonprofits selling tax-exempt tours to the public. "Rather than allowing nonprofits to serve traditional educational tour markets for which this exemption is appropriate, small businesses complain that this exemption has emboldened [tax-exempt organizations] to expand into those market segments with the highest disposable income, the largest number of professionals, the most educated customers, and the least need for tax exemption," wrote SBA counsel Jere Oliver in a letter to Donald Lubick, the acting assistant treasury secretary for tax policy. The letter follows an exchange of draft regulations—one version prepared by nonprofit educational organizations, the other by the travel industry—presented to the IRS for review and possible enactment in 1997.

Outpacing Bally's and other for-profit chains, the national nonprofit YMCA organization now holds claim to being the nation's largest operator of health clubs and one of the largest day-care providers. With more than $1.8 billion in annual revenues, the YMCA would be listed in the middle of the Fortune 500 rankings of major corporations if it operated as a for-profit concern. Figures cited by the Association for Quality Clubs, a national trade organization representing for-profit health-club owners, claim that the YMCA's tax-exempt operating privileges give the group a cost advantage over commercial competitors of as much as 30 percent. While the YMCA's membership numbers rose 22 percent between 1990 and 1993, the comparable numbers at Bally's—the country's largest for-profit health club operator—dropped 9 percent. The YMCA's day-care fees rose 17 percent per year during that period, while the fees at KinderCare Learning Centers doubled. "It's frustrating when taxpaying operations compete with tax-consuming ones," fumed Lynn White, president of the National Child Care Association when the study was conducted. "But taking on the 'Y' is like taking on God, country, and apple pie."

Kevin O'Connell owned a health spa in Oakland, California, that his family had operated since 1934. Today the building that housed O'Connell's spa sits empty. In 1995, O'Connell filed suit against the downtown Oakland YMCA, charging that the non-profit built a $10 million tax-exempt facility around the corner from his spa with the intention of running him out of business. "This Yuppie Men's Cash Association, as I call it, stole my best corporate clients, and I lost a third of my business in just one year," says O'Connell. Spokespeople on both sides of the debate claim pure motives. "We're just sticking up for our members," says John McCarthy, president of the Association for Quality Clubs. "Nonprofits are throwing up so many health-club facili-ties aimed at the upscale adult-fitness market for one reason— cash." "There are many different market segments in the fitness industry, and the YMCA serves a definite clientele," counters a YMCA spokesman. "Many of our facilities have for-profit clubs and spas operating nearby, and we're all managing to do well and take care of our own goals."

When the nonprofit Waukesha (Wis.) Memorial Hospital de-cided to build a $10 million, 72,500-square-foot health-and-fitness center to compete with nearby private health clubs, Rep. Jim Sensenbrenner (R-Wis.) and Rep. Gerald Kleczka (D-Wis.) intro-duced H.R. 3801, a bill that would make income from health-club operations taxable as unrelated business income for nonprofit hos-pitals and prohibit the use of tax-exempt bonds by nonprofits for creating nonprofit health clubs. The bill currently sits on the House Ways and Means calendar awaiting a hearing date. "Non-profit hospitals have recently expanded into the fitness-club busi-ness, where they plan to use their tax-exempt status to obtain the same advantages enjoyed by YMCAs and county recreation de-partments," Sensenbrenner said.

Associations representing small businesses packed a House Small Business Committee hearing in July 1996 to provide ex-amples of unfair competition from nonprofits. When a hospital in Illinois built an $8.3-million, tax-exempt health club in 1994, a nearby for-profit club lost two hundred members and declared bankruptcy, claimed Roger Ralph, director of the International Health, Racquet & Sportsclub Association. A spokesperson for the Textile Rental Services Association of America testified that nonprofit hospitals should be prohibited from entering into the commercial laundry business. Competition from nonprofit entities is a "growing problem," concluded committee chairman Rep. Jan Meyers (R-Kan.), because they have become "more entrepreneurial as their traditional sources of funding have dried up." Meyers acknowledged that "competing policy tensions pervade this entire issue," because many nonprofits also provide needed services to their communities.

Museums operating gift shops and other types of retail outlets and publishing catalogs received guidance from the IRS in December 1995 when the agency issued a private-letter ruling—not a legal precedent but a memorandum taxpayers can rely on for general advice—to the gift shop at a living-history museum explaining what is and what is not considered tax-free income. The sale of such items as books, tapes, toys, and mementos designed in the likeness of museum exhibits and pieces can be tax-exempt as long as the items "contribute to the educational mission" of the museum. Batteries, ponchos, and other products sold for visitor convenience also aid the mission, according to the ruling. However, magazines, pain relievers, and similar goods are taxable sales.

A 1995 lawsuit filed by two marketers of home-study courses alleges that Nursing Education of America, a nonprofit organization based in Ridgedale, Missouri, avoided paying $3.5 million in taxes and postage costs over the past three years by operating what is essentially a for-profit continuing-education company under the fraudulently obtained aegis of a nonprofit organization. The pending San Diego case illustrates a growing wrinkle in the unfair-competition issue: the illegal use of nonprofit status by what are actually for-profit companies. Given the enormous growth in small businesses offering services, experts say it has become much easier to claim nonprofit protection than in previous years. "It is really as simple as can be to become a nonprofit," claims Daniel Langan, a spokesman for the National Charities Information Bureau. "You write up a mission statement, you recruit a board of directors, you get a budget, and you send all of that to the Internal Revenue Service, and that's basically it."

"The government wants to make it relatively easy for new charities and philanthropies to get started," says Paul Streckfus, editor of *Organization Tax Review*, a trade journal based in Arlington, Virginia. "But the IRS definition of a nonprofit has become so broad that almost any entity that wants to become tax-exempt can find a way to do so." As stated earlier, in the fiscal year which ended September 30, 1994, the IRS approved more than 46,000 applications for nonprofit status and denied a scant 520.

In the Nursing Education case, William Keefer—the owner of the for-profit National Center of Continuing Education—filed a complaint against the nonprofit group more than a year earlier, but he decided to go to court when the IRS told him it could not comment on pending investigations. His suit charges that Nursing Education does not use its revenues for charitable purposes but instead has paid substantial salaries to its top officers and rented office space in houses owned by two top employees. Besides the illegal use of tax exemptions and nonprofit postal rates, the suit points out Nursing Education's unreasonable promotion of itself as a nonprofit, "attract[ing] customers who wish to support legitimate nonprofit organizations." Keefer's suit asks that Nursing Education be prohibited from calling itself a nonprofit and from paying employees excessive amounts in salaries and office rents.

Even when the nonprofit entity was created directly by an act of Congress, the line between unfair competition and commercialization that supports the group's tax-exempt purpose can become blurred. In 1987, Research Corp.—a Tucson, Arizona–based nonprofit foundation set up in 1912 to assist university scientists in funding research and taking their inventions to the market for applied scientific uses—created Research Corp. Technologies Inc. (RCT), a taxpaying entity, to take over its technology-commercialization programs. The parent company gave RCT a $35 million low-interest loan and a portfolio of inventions that produces tens of millions of dollars in steady income. John Schaefer, Research Corp.'s president and chairman of RCT, contends that the split—approved by a special act of Congress—was needed because federal restrictions on the commercial activities of nonprofits made it difficult for the foundation to continue commercializing inventions. "We were limited for the most part to securing a patent and licensing the patent to another company," he says. "Now we can act more like a venture-capital firm and support our inventions with our own funds."

However, Michigan State University went to court in 1995, alleging that the transfer of patents from the foundation to RCT—a move that included the rights to two extremely popular cancer medications developed by Michigan State scientists that have earned millions of dollars for RCT—amounts to an "unconscionable" amassing of wealth in a private firm where financial records are not readily available for review by the developers of the inventions. RCT posted retained earnings of nearly $43 million at the end of 1994, including $4.5 million set aside for "special compensation" for RCT's two dozen employees—a move needed, say RCT officials, to "attract and retain top people."

While the AARP, the ADA, and other national nonprofits bask in the glow of public approval and interest, a number of tax-exempt entities control huge business empires with little or no public notice of the breadth and depth of their assets and revenues. Known primarily for its image as a grassroots network of Catholics promoting the ideas of fraternity and good deeds—wearing plumed hats and cloaks in Columbus Day parades or volunteering in parish social-services programs—the Knights of Columbus is one of the country's most highly profitable life-insurance issuers, with $4.6 billion in assets and $24.5 billion in policies in force. The Knights is one of America's fastest growing life insurance companies, consistently outperforming averages for the top twenty-five insurance firms. With a surplus exceeding $600 million, the Knights boasts top ratings from Standard & Poor's and A. M. Best, the insurance industry's major rating agencies. The group stands in the top 1 percent of the more than seventeen hundred U.S. and Canadian life-insurance companies. Benefiting from one of the oldest clauses in the U.S. Internal Revenue Code, the Knights pays no federal taxes and very few state and local taxes and does not have to comply with many regulations that govern the group's for-profit competitors.

Though the Knights defends its record of doing good, tax returns for 1993 obtained by investigators from the *Boston Globe* revealed that the Knights contributed $9.1 million to charity that year, compared to $224 million in profits. The Knights incorporates the application form for life insurance into the basic membership application, and as many as one-third of the members sign up for the coverage each year.

Operating under a century-old tax exemption for mutual-aid societies that helped immigrants bury dead indigents and support the widows and children, more than 175 fraternal organizations like the Knights of Columbus have used their nonprofit privileges to launch commercial sidelines like insurance companies that provide steady competition for America's for-profit insurers. When Treasury Secretary Donald Regan introduced a proposal in 1984 to begin taxing fraternal organizations, treasury officials estimated that closing this loophole in the tax laws would raise $275 million a year in revenue within five to six years. In the proposal, the federal government argued that fraternal organizations had deserved tax exemption "when large parts of the United States were rural and agricultural and when many individuals and businesses were unable to obtain insurance from commercial companies. Today tax-exempt insurance companies are generally indistinguishable from their taxable counterparts. They sell the same products as taxable insurance companies and compete with taxable companies for business." Spending more than $200,000 alone on lobbying fees, the Knights banded with other fraternals to bury the proposal before it reached Congress.

Until 1934, the U.S. Internal Revenue Code required only that nonprofit organizations be organized and operated exclusively to further a specific tax-exempt purpose. A series of Supreme Court rulings from the 1920s through the 1940s held that the destination of income (the nonprofit purpose for which the money was eventually spent) rather than its source (the commercial activity that may have generated the funds in the first place) was the controlling element in determining an organization's right to a tax exemption. In the famous case of *C. F. Mueller Company v. Commissioner,* U.S. District Court judges in New York decided that a prosperous macaroni company that paid all of its profits to New York University was nevertheless exempt from taxes, based on the "destination of income" test.

The Revenue Act of 1950 introduced the concept of the unrelated business-income tax (UBIT) in order to prevent such organizations from competing unfairly with for-profit commercial enterprises. "The tax-free status of Section 501 organizations enables them to use their profits tax-free to expand operations, while their competitors can expand only with the profits remaining after taxes. . . . [The UBIT] merely impose[s] the same tax on income derived from an unrelated trade or business as is borne by their competitors," reads the *Congressional Record* from the Eighty-first Congress, describing the legislative history of the UBIT.

What constitutes unrelated business income? "Associations are continually confronted with the issue of whether nondues income from certain activities generates unrelated business income tax," wrote the late George Webster, longtime legal columnist for *Association Management* magazine. According to Webster, the Internal Revenue Code defines unrelated business income as gross income that meets three criteria: (1) The income is derived from a trade or business; (2) the trade or business is carried on regularly; and (3) the trade or business is not substantially related to the nonprofit's tax-exempt mission.

Many nonprofits license their name or logo to for-profit corporations to use in marketing certain products and services; if the nonprofit does not become actively involved in the commercial marketing, then income earned from the licensing agreements is generally considered royalty income and thus not subject to UBIT. IRS regulations hold that nonprofits earning more than $1,000 in unrelated business taxable income within a fiscal year must file a related return (Form 990-T) describing the unrelated business income generated during the year.

In recent years, only thirty thousand of the 1.1 million tax-exempt groups on the IRS master list (excluding churches) have filed unrelated business income tax returns (Form 990-T). After deductions, fewer than half of these returns reported any actual income, while the rest showed breakeven or losing results. The unrelated income tax bill from these 990-Ts totaled $120 million in 1987 and $137 million in 1988, but the IRS collected a paltry $116.9 million in 1991, the last year for which an accurate count is available. "That's not the direction that we should be going, especially when you consider the increasingly commercial nature of many nonprofits today," observes BCFC's Kenton Pattie.

In many cases, judging whether nonprofit revenues qualify as unrelated business income depends on what the tax-exempt organization has done to earn the money. Under a 1996 Ninth Circuit Court of Appeals ruling, nonprofits do not have to pay UBIT on income from renting their mailing lists unless they go beyond certain "minimal" activities loosely proscribed by the court. Affirming a 1993 U.S. Tax Court decision, *Sierra Club v. Commissioner/IRS*, the Ninth Circuit judges held that income from mailing lists constitutes royalties, not compensation for services, and is therefore expressly exempt from UBIT. The decision outlined services related to the renting of lists that were performed by outside vendors (mailing-list managers and computer-service bureaus) who were paid by the list renters. "A key element is that a nonprofit cannot perform these extensive services itself" without risking UBIT exposure, says Edward Coleman, an attorney with the Washington law firm of Webster, Chamberlain & Bean. Sierra Club attorney Holy Schadler noted that the decision means that nonprofits should retain outside vendors to handle mailing-list sales and rentals, the contract between the nonprofit and the vendor should state that the payments are royalties, and the nonprofit should not allow the vendor to use its offices and personnel to conduct the prohibited activities. (The IRS is currently weighing the decision to appeal the ruling to the U.S. Supreme Court.)

While some nonprofits learn the tricky rules for avoiding UBIT, others have bitten the bullet and formed taxable subsidiaries into which to fold their commercial activities. "One of the primary reasons for establishing a taxable subsidiary is where you are earning a degree of unrelated business income in your nonprofit that could potentially threaten your tax-exempt status," says Jeffrey Tannenbaum, an attorney with the law firm Galland, Kharasch, Morse & Garfinkle in Washington and a former manager of the legal section of the ASAE. Taxpaying subsidiaries can also be established to provide protection against legal liability (especially if a product is being sold), receive tax-deductible contributions, or in the case of 501 (c)(3) foundations, conduct unlimited lobbying activities. However, the subsidiary must be operated on an arm's length basis by the parent nonprofit. "You cannot be involved in the day-to-day management of the subsidiary," confirms Tannenbaum. "You have to organize the subsidiary with the honest intention of carrying out a real, substantial business." "Many associations that established taxable subsidiaries in the 1980s haven't kept up with the [record-keeping] detail that's required" by the IRS, reports David Duren, a partner with the Washington accounting firm Tate & Tryon. "They're in for a rude awakening if the IRS visits."

Even the most promising for-profit subsidiaries carry their share of problems for nonprofits, however, if a subsidiary's mission and operating philosophies differ sharply from the governing precepts of its tax-exempt parent. On Martin Luther King Day in January 1996, six leaders from America's largest and most powerful black church denominations gathered in Washington, D.C., for a press conference to launch the Revelation Corp. of America, a for-profit venture owned 70 percent by the denominations and 30 percent by John Lowery, a white businessman from Memphis, Tennessee, who founded the company. Through Revelation, more than 18 million churchgoers in forty-three thousand congregations around the country can take advantage of discounts and coupons for a dizzying range of products and services. Corporations named as category-exclusive sponsors of the venture—current sponsors include Hanover Direct for catalog marketing, BTI Americas for travel services, Norwest for mortgages, and Progressive Insurance for auto insurance—will close sales via a national toll-free call center or coupons distributed in churches. Sponsors will send rebates and commissions on each purchase to a trustee, who in turn pays 70 percent of the funds collected into a national housing fund (dedicated to support homebuyers and developers in traditionally black neighborhoods) and 30 percent to each buyer's church (two-thirds to the church's general fund and one-third to a ministers' profit-sharing fund). Lowery described the venture as "the black AARP." "If it's worth $40 million [to Pepsi] to sell only Pepsi at Dallas Cowboys games ten times a year," he told delegates at the National Baptist Convention USA's annual congress in St. Louis in June, "what's it worth to them if I place their coupons in forty-three thousand [black] churches fifty-two Sundays a year?"

On the surface, Revelation makes perfect marketing sense. African Americans control more than $340 billion in annual buying power, and this method of steering their shopping habits is designed ultimately to support black churches and promote home ownership in black neighborhoods. However, the deal does not ring true to critics who charge that Revelation's money-making mission trades on the credibility of America's black churches. "The church is not a Fortune 500 kind of operation," C. Eric Lincoln, professor emeritus of religion and culture at Duke University, stated in an interview in *Fortune* magazine. "It is the blackest institution we have, which means it has certain cultural investments that are important beyond the dollar." Lincoln observed that the church is in danger of losing its focus as the traditional catalyst for civil rights, trading historical highs, such as its support of the Underground Railroad and the 1960s civil rights marches, for immediate material gain. "The most credible institution we have left is the black church. The black church has a long history of vulnerability to rapacious individuals. When you start dealing in multiples, as will be the case here, involving many people and millions of dollars, the possibilities increase." "When the church leadership takes the initiative to deliver its constituency to the marketplace and in turn is generously rewarded, it creates a real moral crisis for some of us," notes John Hurst Adams, senior bishop of the African Methodist Episcopal Church.

Lowery pitched his plan initially in the spring of 1995 to the Congress of National Black Churches (CNBC), a traditional gathering of America's eight major black denominations. After Lowery's presentation, the CNBC board referred the plan to its legal counsel and accountants, who recommended that the churches not endorse the Revelation concept. The experts cited concerns about incomplete financial data as well as the ongoing fear that black churches would face enormous tax consequences if they participated in Revelation's revenue-sharing process. Under current IRS rules, churches can collect only $1,000 in income from business activities not related to their tax-exempt purpose before being subject to federal and state taxes. Lowery eventually began organizing Revelation with the individual cooperation of two denominations.

Church leaders also raised the prospect that Revelation is simply a front to exploit black Americans so that the white men behind the concept can become richer. "I'm far beyond being hung up about race in America, but I'm concerned because one of the things that's constantly being said is, 'Here is the strongest institution, the black church, coming together to empower black people [through Revelation],' " observed Calvin Butts, pastor of the Abyssinian Baptist Church in New York and one of the nation's best-known black preachers. "The symbolism is very important. These black convention presidents are out front, but a white man is really running things." Henry J. Lyons, head of the National Baptist Convention U.S.A., is the chief executive officer of Revelation, while Lowery holds the titles of executive vice president and chief operating officer. Lowery currently draws no salary—"I'll earn a salary only if the executive committee votes to give me a salary," he told one reporter—but will draw 30 percent of any interest and dividends paid by the housing fund (which will be invested by Prudential Securities in mortgage-backed certificates).

In April 1996, Revelation seemed to stray further from its declared mission of empowering black America when Lowery met with Jerry Falwell, one of the country's most conservative white pastors, at the Charlotte, North Carolina, airport. By the end of the meeting, Falwell had agreed to provide Revelation access to his 5-million-name mailing list. "The bottom line is that by using these coupons and catalogs, our people save money," says Falwell. Liberty University, his church-run college in Lynchburg, Virginia, will receive the same 30 percent share of Revelation sales as the black churches, while Falwell declares emphatically that he will not receive any benefits personally. "Falwell is so anti–affirmative action, so anti everything that represents the forward progress of blacks, that it's frightening to think that this could have happened," Butts says. Revelation's supporters disagree. "Theologically, I may not be on the same plane as Dr. Falwell, but greenologically we agree 100 percent," says Marshall Shepard Jr., a Revelation board member from the Progressive National Baptist Convention. "The KKK [Ku Klux Klan] can join if they are a bona fide organization. We want to be inclusive."

To avoid potential conflicts in their commercial activities, some tax-exempt groups avoid direct ownership of these ventures and choose instead to enlist the aid of for-profit companies to market and operate them. They accept direct payments from consumers and users and forward a share of the proceeds to the tax-exempt groups lending their name and credibility to the ventures. However, they do not always give up every competitive advantage in the process. The Capital District Kiwanis Foundation— organized in 1972 in Fairfax, Virginia, to promote Kiwanis-backed philanthropic activities in the District of Columbia, Delaware, Virginia, and Maryland—teamed with Vantage Travel, a for-profit travel agency, to offer "America's Magnificent National Parks," a fifteen-day tour, including stops at Yellowstone, the Grand Tetons, Monument Valley, and the Grand Canyon. "This trip offers *terrific* [emphasis theirs] value, a unique itinerary, and a wealth of features impossible to arrange on your own," declares Herbert Bauer, the group's travel coordinator, in the cover letter accompanying the four-color brochure in a mailing sent to prospective travelers. "Vantage Travel has arranged every detail of this extraordinary program: advance ticketing, registration at hotels, many meals, sightseeing, prepaid admission to all the parks."

While the selection of a for-profit travel company addresses concerns about unrelated business income, the foundation mailed the sales materials in its own envelopes (printed with nonprofit funds) at nonprofit postal rates (16.5 cents per piece, compared with 32 cents for commercial mail). "You can't go halfway in competing fairly," says Bob Everidge, president of Shenandoah Tours, a large tour company in Staunton, Virginia, who received the Kiwanis promotion in the mail. "This offer should have been sent at the same rates I have to pay every day to mail my catalogs to customers. I can't compete effectively against people who can bend the rules to cut their postage costs in half."

In the worst cases, the commercial activities of a tax-exempt organization turn from generating funds to consuming them, at the expense of the nonprofit's members, financial reserves, and public opinion. In the late 1980s, the AARP began hearing rumblings from its members about possible financial difficulties at RFD Travel Corp., a Kansas-based tour company that was one of the AARP's preferred vendors. Under this sales agreement, RFD paid a rights fee and a percentage of each tour sold to an AARP member in exchange for the use of the AARP's logo and the imprimatur of the organization as an AARP partner. Though the AARP largely refused comment on the incident, legal documents and court petitions relating to the RFD case show that the AARP apparently loaned the for-profit tour company at least $12 million in 1987 and 1988 to cover RFD tours purchased by AARP members but for which RFD did not have sufficient funds to operate the trips. When the funds were given to RFD, the AARP allegedly struck an agreement with RFD and its bank that future tour deposits and prepayments would be deposited into an escrow account, effectively preventing RFD from using the monies for any purpose other than paying for the actual components of the trips for which the deposits had been made.

The escrow agreement was apparently monitored on a regular basis until the early 1990s, when the bank allegedly began sweeping the funds from the escrow account into the tour company's operating account, giving the company access to the protected funds to pay general and administrative expenses unrelated to the actual tour products. When the AARP canceled its preferred-travel-vendor arrangements in 1994, that move caused tremendous financial strain for RFD, which had grown through the years mostly on the strength of the AARP account. Despite achieving $10.1 million in sales for 1994, laying off at least ten employees, and cutting other administrative costs, RFD ceased selling tours on September 12, 1995, and filed for Chapter 7 bankruptcy protection in the U.S. Bankruptcy Court for the district of Kansas on November 22. Records obtained from the bankruptcy court clerk list the AARP as the company's largest creditor holding an unsecured, nonpriority claim—making it effectively one of the last groups in line to collect any money from the bankruptcy estate, after eight creditors holding secured claims and 166 unsecured priority claims (mostly passengers who are owed a total of $939,542.08 in prepayments for future tours or other refunds).

On the court's "List of Creditors Holding 20 Largest Unsecured Claims," the AARP holds the top spot with a claim of $15,178,876.03, described euphemistically as "financial assistance." The AARP's claim equals 95 percent of the total amount of $15,975,733 in unsecured claims. Among the other 105 unsecured creditors, the next-largest claim is held by a consulting firm in Kansas City, Kansas, owed "trade debt" in the amount of $110,498.18.

AARP representatives refused comment on the claim, and the FBI has reportedly begun an investigation on possible charges of mail fraud in the case.

# 9

# *Too Much Time in Gucci Gulch*

ASK RALPH REED ABOUT THE MISSION of his nonprofit organization and he will give you a firm answer: "What we want is to see people who share our values . . . sitting in mayoralties, city council seats, county commissions, state legislatures, and Congress," Reed declared in a 1995 speech describing the Christian Coalition, a grassroots organization of religious conservatives.

Founded in 1989 by televangelist Pat Robertson to give Christians "a voice in their government" after Robertson's failed run for the presidency, the Christian Coalition now boasts 1.7 million members—some of whom pay $1,000 a year to become a "regent, or God's agent"—in seventeen hundred chapters spanning every state in the nation. The coalition, which wielded a $25 million budget in 1995 and commands legions of volunteers, dominates the Republican Party in at least eighteen states and exerts strong influence in more than ten other state organizations. Republican candidates for national offices clamor for the coalition's support, and local politicos push its agenda in school-board meetings and city-council chambers nationwide. As the group's executive director, Reed plies the political talk-show circuit touting the accomplishments of the coalition in strengthening America's moral fiber.

In the process, the Christian Coalition shares one risk with many other U.S. nonprofit groups: It engages in political advocacy that threatens to violate federal regulations governing the civic behavior of tax-exempt organizations. In August 1996 the Federal Election Commission (FEC) filed a suit accusing the coalition of spending thousands of dollars in direct promotion of the candidacies of Republican office seekers ranging from President George Bush to Sen. Jesse Helms of North Carolina and Senate candidate Oliver North of Virginia. Allegedly, the coalition carried out these activities in direct concert with campaign officials without reporting the expenditures as political contributions—an accusation that could lead to the revocation of the Christian Coalition's tax-exempt status. "This court case is our friend," Reed told reporters after the FEC suit was filed. "After we win, we will be in an even stronger position."

The Christian Coalition controversy highlights a long-hidden secret of inside-the-Beltway politics: Some of the country's largest nonprofit organizations have become accomplished power brokers, relying on their tax-exempt status as a key weapon to advance their political ends while avoiding the scrutiny given to political action committees (PACs) and other visible players in the arena of public affairs. The American Medical Association (AMA) spent more than $8.5 million in the first six months of 1996 alone in federal lobbying expenditures, for example, and the U.S. Chamber of Commerce invested $7.5 million during the same period, according to a September 1996 study coordinated by the Associated Press.

In some cases, these groups actually lobby the federal government on the one hand while at the same time receiving thousands of dollars in direct federal grants. Said Marshall Wittmann and Charles P. Griffin in a *Washington Post* editorial in September 1995:

> More than two hundred years ago, Thomas Jefferson wrote: "To compel a man to furnish funds for the propagation of ideas he disbelieves and abhors is sinful and tyrannical." To suggest that Jefferson, Madison and their colleagues would have condoned using taxpayer dollars to fuel special-interest lobbying is preposterous. Yet today's federal government does precisely that. Each year, American taxpayers provide

more than $39 billion in grants to organizations that could possibly use some of this money to advance their political agendas. Every such government subsidy favors one faction over all others, and taken together, they nourish a network of advocacy groups that, primarily, have a direct interest in the growth of the welfare state.

Under the restrictions outlined in the Internal Revenue Code, section 501, many nonprofits—particularly the tax-exempt groups that qualify as charities, educational organizations, and religious bodies—cannot participate or intervene directly in any political campaign for or against a candidate for public office. They cannot endorse candidates, contribute to political campaigns at any level of government, raise funds for political purposes, distribute issue statements, or "become involved in any other activities that may be beneficial or detrimental to any candidate," according to federal regulations. Penalties for breaking these rules include not only the loss of a group's tax-exempt status but also a stiff excise tax on the funds spent on the prohibited activities.

On the other hand, nonprofits are permitted to "instruct the public on matters useful to the individual and beneficial to the community," and many groups have learned the legal loopholes that allow them to throw their two cents into America's political debates. For example, many tax-exempt trade associations have formed PACs to funnel contributions to friendly candidates; conduct "voter education" marketing programs, such as debates and forums, to promote their positions on key issues; and coordinate "grassroots" opinion campaigns that use computer-generated letters and targeted mailing or telephone lists to inundate legislators with comments from their constituents.

Nonprofit lobbyists and government-relations directors often trip over the fine line separating legal political "instruction" from outright political intervention. The 1996 FEC suit challenging the tactics of the Christian Coalition revolves around charges that the group illegally arranged $1.4 million worth of telephone-calling banks and "voter guides" to get out the vote for Republican candidates, including almost $1 million alone to the 1992 Bush presidential campaign. While Reed argues that the guides in themselves do not advocate the election or defeat of candidates, many critics charge that they helped to orchestrate the GOP takeover of Congress in the 1994 elections; 198 of the 535 members of Congress scored 86 percent or higher on the coalition's 100-point scale of whether members vote the way the coalition thinks they should. "The coalition's influence in the Republican Party is seismic," says David Greer, a spokesman for the Log Cabin Republicans advocacy group.

Christian Broadcasting Network (CBN) founder Pat Robertson began his bid for political power in 1981 when he launched the tax-exempt Freedom Council. The organization fell apart five years later due primarily to tax-law problems related to its partisan activities on behalf of Republican candidates. Two years later, Robertson used the council's mailing list of 1.8 million households in his run for the Republican nomination for president. After his campaign collapsed, Robertson used the same list to found the Christian Coalition in 1989. Set up as a "social welfare" [Internal Revenue Code 501 (c)(4)] organization operating under temporary tax-exempt status (awaiting permanent approval by the IRS), the coalition cannot endorse candidates or engage in partisan politics unless those activities are carried out via a PAC that must report its income sources and expenditures. Also, while the coalition does not have to pay taxes on its revenues, its supporters cannot write off their donations as deductions.

In addition to the charges of illegal campaign financing, the FEC alleges that the coalition has attempted on occasion to circumvent the rule requiring nonprofits to report political contributions from their members. Judy Liebert—the Christian Coalition's chief financial officer, suspended in June 1996 from her $85,000-a-year job after discussing her concerns about the group's financial practices with federal authorities—told FEC investigators that Christian Coalition executive director Ralph Reed instructed her to treat a $60,000 gift from John W. Wolfe, a wealthy Ohio businessman, as an anonymous gift. In the 1992 letter accompanying his donation, Wolfe wrote to coalition founder Pat Robertson that a mutual friend "tells me your group is very supportive of President Bush and that you will be doing a massive distribution of literature on his behalf. . . . I am pleased to send you a contribution of $60,000."

Recording the donation as an anonymous gift appears to violate federal election rules. The coalition denies that it misused the funds and points out that Wolfe's name is typed beside the $60,000 gift on a secret list of donors attached to the group's 1992 tax returns. The lawsuit and the Wolfe allegations are "a completely baseless and legally threadbare attempt by a reckless federal agency to silence people of faith and deny them their First Amendment rights," says coalition spokesman Mike Russell.

Republicans have pointed to similar abuses of nonprofit political prohibitions by liberal organizations. The National Republican Congressional Committee filed a complaint in 1996 with the FEC charging the American Federation of Labor–Congress of Industrial Organizations (AFL-CIO) labor union with violating election laws in support of Democratic candidates. "Unions say they are simply involved in union activities, fighting for the rights of workers, but they're also deeply involved in political activity," claims Republican election lawyer Jan Baran. "Neither the law nor the First Amendment allows the government to regulate everything in politics."

However, the questions about the Christian Coalition have hit home harder. After five years of explosive growth, contributions to the coalition declined in 1995 for the first time, according to the group's tax records. The coalition reported $18.7 million in donations during that year, down 12 percent from the 1994 total of $21.2 million. Russell attributed the drop to 1995's being a nonelection year that allowed the group's state affiliates to focus more on their own fund-raising efforts. "We're on track for a $24 million budget in 1996," he predicts. (Other signs of trouble: While the coalition claims 1.7 million members nationwide, its primary publication, *Christian American* magazine, was sent to 310,296 people in September 1995, down from the previous year's "paid or requested" circulation of 353,703. Also, the FEC confirms that coalition chapters in as many as thirty-five different states are under investigation for using tax-exempt funds raised by the supposedly nonpartisan organization to support only Republican candidates publicly.)

The list of potential political abusers includes the usual cast of characters notorious for special-interest lobbying. In April 1996 the IRS launched a full-scale investigation of the financial records of the National Rifle Association (NRA), one of the country's best-funded nonprofit political players. Founded 124 years ago as an association representing the interests of hunters and competitive shootists, the NRA now has 3 million members. Its political subsidiary, the Institute for Legislative Action, is widely judged an extremely successful example of the strategies nonprofit groups can employ to advance their aims in matters of public policy. The NRA Political Victory Fund, the association's PAC, gave more than $1.8 million to federal candidates in 1993 and 1994 and invested another $1.5 million in advocacy commercials, phone banks, and direct mailings to influence various political battles. NRA affiliates raise funds for a number of public causes ranging from a national firearms museum to a civil-rights legal-defense fund for defendants in firearms-related cases.

Based in Fairfax, Virginia, the NRA holds its tax-exempt status under federal tax regulations that grant it the right to raise non-tax-deductible funds, usually in the form of membership dues and direct donations, that can be used to support political activities. The IRS audit is apparently focusing on the relationship between general NRA funds and monies raised by other NRA branches, such as the NRA Foundation, created in 1992 as a charity for educational causes under a different section of the tax code and empowered to accept tax-exempt donations and grants. In many instances, it is illegal to mix funds from charities that accept tax-deductible monies with funds from other types of nonprofits. "You cannot take the money in on a [charity] account and spend it on [other] purposes. This is something that the IRS is investigating very heavily right now," says Bennett Weiner, vice president of the philanthropic advisory service of the Council of Better Business Bureaus. "Two organizations existing side by side creates a very easy environment for

ganizations wield," testified Sen. John McCain before the Senate
Subcommittee on Social Security and Family Policy in June
1995. "I was surprised to find that some of these organizations
pursue a policy agenda that their own constituencies oppose.
While there are a number of organizations that fit this description, I am chiefly concerned about the growing trend among 'su-
perlobbying' organizations to disconnect their advocacy from the
interests of the people they purport to represent."

McCain's target during the hearing was the American Association of Retired Persons (AARP), the country's largest nonprofit organization after the Roman Catholic church. He cited
the 1988 debate on Capitol Hill over the Medicare Catastrophic
Act as a prime example of the AARP's legislative priorities. After
several failed attempts, McCain succeeded in 1989 in his efforts
to repeal certain unpopular portions of the bill. "[W]hen seniors
finally realized the impacts of the Catastrophic bill, a veritable
revolt among the 'beneficiaries' forced Congress to repeal the
act. What is less remembered is that the bill was, by and large,
conceived, written and sold to Congress by the Washington lobbyists of the AARP. . . . After the [bill] became law, when increasingly agitated seniors demanded it be revoked, the AARP
fought all efforts to repeal it. Local AARP chapters throughout
the nation repudiated the national AARP organization for continuing to support the Catastrophic legislation, but still the national AARP opposed repeal. . . . Forty-four national seniors
organizations, including the National Committee to Preserve Social Security and Medicare and the National Association of Retired Federal Employees supported repeal, but not the AARP."
McCain's explanation for the AARP's political reticence was that
the nonprofit's sideline business of selling prescription medications to its members stood to gain millions of dollars if these
drugs remained part of the bill's covered provisions—a "conflict
of interest," McCain said, that encouraged AARP to abandon its
tax-exempt mission of representing the best interests of Americans aged fifty and older. "Many seniors in Arizona mailed me
their AARP membership cards, denouncing their membership
from the AARP for endorsing President Clinton's health-care

bill. These seniors were appalled that their opinions were being blatantly ignored by an organization which promotes itself as an advocacy organization for the nation's elderly," he said.

In 1994, the AARP—widely acknowledged as one of Washington's most powerful lobbying organizations—received $74 million in government funds.

When it comes to protecting their tactical advantages in the world of politics, nonprofits have learned to be aggressive and preemptive. The Independent Sector, an alliance of America's leading nonprofit groups, unveiled its new five-year program plan in 1996, declaring that it hoped to respond to the challenge of nonprofits being "under siege" from federal budget cuts and attempts by Congress to limit nonprofit lobbying. The group's three main priorities are building public confidence in the nonprofit sector, assembling a national network of "partners" that can be mobilized quickly to lobby the government on nonprofit issues, and increasing the visibility of the coalition itself in the nonprofit community.

Many nonprofit executives hone their politicking skills through seminars and materials offered by the American Society of Association Executives (ASAE). Boasting more than twelve thousand members, the Washington, D.C.–based ASAE is the trade association for association managers and professionals. The ASAE employs a formidable staff of in-house lobbyists and outside political consultants to wage a pitched battle on many fronts for nonprofits, from defending reduced postal rates to urging more latitude in federal regulations governing the calculation of unrelated business income tax.

As an example of its tenacious defense of nonprofit political power, the ASAE refiled in 1996 a lawsuit against the U.S. government challenging a 1993 law that made lobbying a nondeductible business expense. In the suit, the ASAE alleges that the lobbying "tax" violates the speech, petition, and association clauses of the First Amendment and the equal-protection clause of the Fifth Amendment, and the litigation asks the U.S. District Court for the District of Columbia to declare the tax unconstitutional and to force the IRS to refund associations' initial tax payments. The ASAE and ten coplaintiffs filed an initial lawsuit against the tax in December 1994, asking the court to enjoin the IRS and the Treasury Department from enforcing the tax based on its alleged unconstitutionality, but one of the judges dismissed the case without a hearing. "In refiling the lawsuit, ASAE is finally able to challenge the lobby tax on its merits, rather than seeking an injunction to prevent the law from taking effect," reported *Association Trends* magazine after the new lawsuit was announced. A 1996 ASAE survey found that 54 percent of America's associations report being subject to the new lobbying law tax, reflecting a major new (and, in some cases, unbudgeted) expense item for trade organizations.

ASAE members attend educational sessions such as the February 1996 government-relations-section "roundtable" in Washington to learn new PAC management techniques and tips to prepare themselves for the volatile 1996 federal campaigns. Panelists for the roundtable included PAC directors and political consultants from the American Optometric Association, the National Federation of Independent Business, the National Association of Home Builders, and the Association of Trial Lawyers of America, among others. Attendees learned the ins and outs of direct mail, telemarketing, "high dollar" events, "peer pressure" events, and matching-fund initiatives to raise dollars from their members and supporters. One seminar focused on targeting direct-mail audiences properly; "direct mail doesn't have to be a megavolume campaign to work" in generating government-relations contributions, the speaker asserted.

"An intensive, year-long campaign to increase political awareness among direct-marketing companies has paid off for the Direct Marketing Association," read the lead paragraph in a page-one article in *Association Trends* magazine dated June 7, 1996. The DMA's PAC—dubbed "direct*voice"—had tripled its contributions to congressional candidates in a year's time. "Twelve months ago, DMA's direct*voice had seventeen authorized companies [that had given DMA written permission to solicit funds from them], fewer than fifty individuals to solicit, and generated $15,000 in contributions," DMA senior vice president for government affairs Jerry Cerasale Sr. said. The PAC now boasts 135 authorized member companies and 750 individual targets. In 1995 direct*voice gave money to more than fifty incumbent members of Congress—72 percent to Republican candidates and 28 percent to Democrats.

Like their partisan counterparts, nonprofit groups can fall into the familiar trap of bending the truth at times to mesh "public opinion" with their lobbying messages. For example, a recent direct-mail survey sent to AARP members polled rank-and-file members with questions like the following: "A Balanced Budget Amendment will mean cuts in your Social Security. Do you favor the Balanced Budget Amendment?" "With loaded questions like that, why even bother to mail the survey?" asks a senior Capitol Hill staffer.

Lobbying experts at an ASAE roundtable in July 1996 advised listeners that grassroots-style lobbying "is no longer a question of 'if' but 'when' for associations," according to Constance Campanella, president and chief executive officer of State-side Associates, a Virginia-based consulting firm. She told the crowd of nonprofit managers that term limits have produced enormous turnover at the state level. "Your ability to develop friends [in the states] and build support has been eradicated," she said, pointing out that there have been forty-eight new governors in the 1990s, compared to eleven in the 1980s. She countered the misperception that nonprofits could not afford to invest in grassroots lobbying campaigns. "Generally, you can get away with good grassroots with a small amount of money." Another speaker urged the crowd to "humanize" their grassroots letters, keeping the message simple and focused, and to include grassroots activities in a nonprofit lobbying campaign from the beginning.

In some cases, nonprofits have graduated from questionable surveying tactics to outright accusations of unethical or even illegal lobbying behavior. In February 1996 the U.S. attorney's office in Brooklyn, New York, reopened an investigation into whether major tobacco companies misled the federal government about the actual purpose and activities of the Council for Tobacco Research, a nonprofit research organization funded by the companies. First launched in 1992, the federal probe will examine thousands of documents subpoenaed from tobacco companies and the council itself (including files that the council argues are protected by attorney-client privilege). The prosecutors decided to reopen the investigation amid growing interest in tobacco-linked civil litigation and criminal cases. The investigation will focus on whether the tobacco companies and the council conspired to defraud the IRS by claiming nonprofit tax status for hundreds of millions of dollars spent on sympathetic tobacco-related research that claims there is no conclusive evidence that nicotine is addictive. Furthermore, prosecutors allege that the companies used the council—which supposedly funds only independent tobacco research projects—to hide negative research findings from Congress since the council's founding in 1954.

Sometimes allegations of abusing one's tax-exempt status turn on a single instance of alleged illegal behavior. In September 1996 the IRS began an audit of a college course called Renewing American Civilization taught by House Speaker Newt Gingrich at two Georgia colleges, Reinhardt College and Kennesaw State University. Gingrich taught the classes at Reinhardt, a small private college, in 1995 and 1996. He began the course—an ideologically conservative overview of American civilization financed by tax-exempt foundations—at Kennesaw in 1993.

A Reinhardt spokeswoman confirmed that the content of the course is the focus of the IRS investigation. "Have you ever, anywhere in your life, heard of one course being audited?" Gingrich complained to reporters following the announcement of the audit. "You call the IRS, ask them their guidelines, ask how many colleges they've audited one course in." The analysis of the course began as a result of ethics complaints filed by former Democratic representative Ben Jones of Georgia, a Gingrich rival who contended that the classes were not a legitimate tax-exempt educational activity but rather a political activity designed to recruit Republican activists.

In September 1996 the House Ethics Committee expanded its own inquiry to determine whether Gingrich misled the panel's investigation of charges that he improperly used ties with the tax-exempt groups for political purposes. The nonprofits involved in the probe were named as the Progress and Freedom Foundation, a think tank founded by Gingrich associates, and the Abraham Lincoln Opportunity Foundation, an entity used by Gopac (a PAC once headed by Gingrich) in the 1980s to support another Gingrich project.

At other times, the tactics involved may be correct in their legal interpretation yet questionable in their adherence to the spirit of the law. Critics charge that sponsorship of the Commission on Presidential Debates—the nonpartisan tax-exempt group charged with organizing debates for presidential candidates during an election year—by major U.S. corporations amounts to special-interest influence. National sponsorships of the three 1996 debates (ranging from $25,000 to $250,000 apiece) were purchased by tobacco company Philip Morris, frozen-foods giant Sara Lee, Sprint, Dun & Bradstreet, and Lucent Technologies, the AT&T technology spin-off. In addition, $1.5 million was raised from companies in the three host cities. "These corporations have no influence whatsoever or contact whatsoever with the commissioners or candidates about the debates," claimed Frank Fahrenkopf, cochairman of the commission. "It is their contribution to good government and nothing more."

Just as former members of Congress and presidential administrations have learned to turn their positions into lucrative launching pads for lobbying and consulting careers after their terms of public service have ended, nonprofits have learned the value of having close ties with current and former public officials and their families and friends. When Elizabeth Dole, a former cabinet secretary and the wife of Republican presidential candidate Bob Dole, became president of the American Red Cross in 1991, a foundation and other interests controlled by agribusiness executive Dwayne Andreas donated $3 million to the nonprofit, having given nothing to the charity during the previous five years. After contributing $500,000 during Elizabeth Dole's first year as president, the Andreas Foundation gave an additional half-million dollars in 1992 when Andreas's wife,

Inez, was named to one of twelve at-large seats on the Red Cross board of directors. In 1993, Archer Daniels Midland (ADM), the agriculture conglomerate that Andreas heads, donated foodstuffs valued at $2 million to help the Red Cross feed poor people in Haiti. During the same period of time, the Andreas interests gave more than $200,000 to Bob Dole's political campaigns or to the two private foundations set up by the former U.S. Senate majority leader. Other corporations that gave large donations following Elizabeth Dole's appointment as Red Cross president, after having given little or nothing before, include American Financial Corp. (headed by Carl Lindner, a close friend and longtime supporter of the Doles) and a foundation tied to the insurance conglomerate American International Group (AIG). In addition, AIG and ADM have put their corporate airplanes at Elizabeth Dole's disposal for Red Cross business trips, as they have for the Doles' political trips.

While federal election laws attempt to limit the influence corporations exert over political candidates, with restrictions on individual contributions and a ban on corporate campaign donations, corporate gifts to private foundations, charities, and the "soft money" funds of political parties have been viewed as a reliable means of currying favor with public officials by supporting their favorite causes. Elizabeth Dole's supporters point out that she takes meticulous care to separate her political life from her fund-raising work for the American Red Cross. "Company executives always wanted to talk politics when Elizabeth came to solicit donations," reports John Thomas, a former Red Cross fund-raiser who made corporate-giving presentations with Mrs. Dole. "She knew they were likely to have politics on their mind. When the subject came up, she would excuse me from the room at the end of the presentation so that she could discuss politics privately with the CEOs. I was very comfortable with that distinction."

. "That's no separation of interests at all," counters Ellen Miller, director of the Center for Responsive Politics, a Washington-based advocacy group that tracks political fund-raising trends. "It's two for the price of one, the charitable and the political. Whether she thinks she can separate the two, those who contribute will not do so." "Look at the confluence of interests when she solicits money from the same donors who support her husband's campaigns," notes Charles Lewis, director of the Center for Public Integrity. "The issue is that in Washington this is yet another way to get in the door and stay in the door. It doesn't exactly hurt your position with the Republican presidential nominee to give to her charity."

Elizabeth Dole's announcement that she had planned to continue in her post as Red Cross president if she had become the first lady "is a little bit troubling," says Marc Miller, the author of a book about politicians and their spouses' careers. "As the wife of the president of the United States, it's awfully hard to think that people will say no if you're soliciting them for the Red Cross."

# 10

## *Outright Swindles*

"THE ICY HAND OF WINTER is already reaching for Port Graham, threatening to strangle the little ones in a death grip," read a 1992 direct-mail appeal from the American Indian Heritage Foundation that was designed to solicit contributions to purchase food and supplies for the starving Paiute Indians in an Alaskan village. The letters were signed by Princess Pale Moon, the foundation's director.

But the residents of Port Graham had no idea they were supposed to be starving.

An investigation of the fund-raising appeal by reporters of the *Anchorage Daily News* discovered that the villagers knew nothing about the foundation or its fund-raisers. In fact, the Paiute Indian tribe is located in Nevada, not Alaska. Later that year, Port Graham officials refused a shipment of one thousand pounds of frozen beef livers that the foundation tried to foist on the community. The final affront in the affair, critics say, is that Princess Pale Moon—born Rita Ann Suntz—is an imposter. "She might as well be the queen of England," one Alaskan Indian leader said. For the record, Suntz replied that she can track Native American ancestors on both sides of her family, and foundation records claim that the group donated nearly $21 million to needy Native Americans in 1993, the year following the Port

Graham incident. Today the American Indian Heritage Foundation no longer exists.

The scams of hucksters like Rita Ann Suntz illustrate the ultimate in nonprofit abuses: using the "halo effect" of doing good for others to steal funds for one's own benefit.

Gilbert Peterson trusted in more than the halo effect when he invested money in the Philadelphia-based Foundation for New Era Philanthropy; he thought literally that his prayers had been answered. "It looked like a great answer to a need that we'd been thinking and praying about," says Peterson, president of Lancaster Bible College, a tiny school in the heart of Pennsylvania's Amish country with seven hundred students, an endowment of $1.5 million, and no debt. The foundation approached Peterson with an amazing offer: For every dollar raised and invested by Lancaster Bible College, the foundation's core donor base of 125 wealthy, anonymous benefactors would match it, allowing the school to double its money every six months. (Actually, New Era qualified as a charity, not a true foundation, because it engaged in fund-raising and held no endowment.)

Launched in 1989 by John G. Bennett Jr., a medical-school dropout who had drifted into the business of conducting training seminars for nonprofit managers, the Foundation for New Era Philanthropy began with a miraculous premise. Bennett told friends at the time that a wealthy, unidentified philanthropist had offered to stake $100,000 if Bennett could locate twenty other individuals to commit $5,000 apiece. In return for making the $5,000 donation, at the end of six months, the twenty individuals would each be able to designate a total of $10,000 to the nonprofit organization of their choice. After two rounds of successful matches in early 1991, Bennett offered the matching opportunity to a circle of fifty prominent nonprofit patrons, and eventually the matching invitations began arriving on a monthly basis.

By the fall of 1992, the charity moved to its new headquarters in Radnor, Pennsylvania, and set up an office in London. Ultimately, the group collected more than $350 million in donations. In 1995, Bennett purchased a home with cash and had a reported annual salary of $672,000. Besides the matching grants, Bennett made many charitable gifts from foundation funds with no conditions attached. When a troop of handicapped Boy Scouts requested a grant of a few thousand dollars, Bennett gave them $100,000. He donated the same amount to a youth-ministry program in Camden, New Jersey, when the director of the program mentioned in passing to Bennett that the group needed funds. Bennett found himself showered with praise, awards, and kudos from America's most prominent benefactors. "You, New Era, and the anonymous donors are gradually changing the face of Philadelphia and making it into a new kind of city," Vivian Weyerhauser Piasecki, a Philadelphia social doyenne, wrote to Bennett in 1995.

Lancaster Bible College's Gilbert Peterson felt the same good vibrations from New Era. With the unanimous approval of his board of trustees, Peterson sent New Era its first deposit, about $400,000, in 1993, following up thirty days later with an additional $400,000. As the tiny college watched its New Era accounts double, gifts in fiscal year 1994 jumped to $5 million, from $1.5 million in 1993. Many gifts were deposited directly with New Era (with the donors' permission). The college's 1994 tax forms show thirty-two different payments to New Era totaling $5 million, each deposit ranging from $5,000 to $2.4 million. In May 1995 the college planned to withdraw its $10 million balance—half of that amount in matching funds from New Era—to begin construction in earnest.

Then the ceiling fell in. On May 13, Bennett called his top six aides into his office; with a pastor standing by his side, the ashen-faced Bennett admitted that there were no anonymous donors. Instead, Bennett had designed and operated an elaborate Ponzi scheme in which the group solicited funds from one organization only to pay off another—until the money ran out. A few days later, New Era declared bankruptcy, listing assets of $80 million and liabilities of $551 million. (In May 1995 the trustee for the bankruptcy revised the liability estimate from $175 million to $225 million, far less than the original figure submitted by Bennett and his staff.)

When New Era collapsed, the news shook the nonprofit world and many of America's most well known financiers and charitable donors. More than 180 different nonprofit groups that had invested funds with New Era, hoping for a dollar-to-dollar match within six months, lost their entire stake. The Nature Conservancy stands to lose as much as $2 million. Young Life Inc., a Colorado Springs, Colorado–based group that fosters religion among adolescents, risked at least $2.5 million, money that had been earmarked for a new headquarters and for camp scholarships. United Way of Southeastern Pennsylvania lost $2 million. Among individual philanthropists, Laurance S. and Mary Rockefeller had net losses estimated between $3.5 million and $8 million. Famed stock expert Peter Lynch reportedly lost $517,000. Former treasury secretary William Simon paid New Era more than $3.2 million before the group went bankrupt.

The colleges and graduate schools listed in the bankruptcy filing as New Era creditors span the country, with a strong concentration in the Northeast (the figures in parentheses are the amounts owed by New Era to the schools, reflecting in most cases the school's original investment plus the promised 100-percent match):

Biblical Theological Seminary ($5.8 million)
Biola University
Boston College
Central College (Kans.)
Coalition for Christian Colleges and Universities ($350,000)
Covenant College ($5 million)
Drexel University ($6 million)
Fuller Theological Seminary ($1 million)
Gordon-Conwell Theological Seminary ($9.8 million)
Houghton College ($4 million)
John Brown University ($4 million)
King College ($5 million)
Messiah College ($2 million)
Moody Bible Institute
Philadelphia College of the Bible ($8 million)

United Theological Seminary ($1.75 million)
University of Pennsylvania School of Nursing
University of Pennsylvania Cancer Center
Westminster Theological Seminary
Wheaton College (Ill.) ($4.6 million)
Whitworth College ($7 million)
(Several institutions have disputed the court filing amounts, saying they are owed less.)

Gilbert Peterson had planned to use the proceeds from his college's New Era investments to build a new library, a graduate center, and a thirteen-hundred-seat chapel—the first in the bible college's sixty-two-year history—that would allow students and faculty to worship in a sanctuary instead of the gymnasium that had to be set up with seven hundred folding chairs every day. Instead, the college lost an estimated $16 million—the worst loss attributed to the New Era bankruptcy—even though Peterson had done his homework beforehand, reviewing New Era's records and seeking recommendations from other small colleges.

When the story of New Era's closing its doors broke, a friend called Peterson. " 'Have you seen the *Wall Street Journal*?' my friend asked," Peterson remembers. "I said, 'No, I've read my Bible, but I haven't read the *Wall Street Journal*.'" Hours after the story broke in that newspaper, Peterson called his college's board of trustees and began reassuring students that the school would not be forced to close. He has vowed to reconstruct the building fund "one donor at a time, one dollar at a time."

When news of the collapse spread to Bristol, Tennessee, Richard Stanislaw—president of King College, a 560-student religious institution in Appalachia—began checking his records and breathed a sigh of relief. The college had received a check from New Era in April, one month before the end, equaling "every penny" that King had invested in the charity (despite the bankruptcy-court filing that asserts King is on the hook for an estimated $5 million). "We're one of the lucky ones in that when the music stopped, there was a chair for us," Stanislaw says. At the very least, however, the college lost whatever interest it might have accumulated on the money sent to New Era.

In November 1995, Bennett produced a videotape for distribution to New Era donors, telling them that he accepted full responsibility for the demise of the charity. "Please hear me when I say I never intended to hurt any of you," he said in the videotape. "I know that I've done that, however, and I'm so sorry." Some donors expressed anger and disappointment at Bennett's remarks. "The tape doesn't clear up what happened," says Paul Nelson, head of an ad-hoc coalition of 184 Christian nonprofit groups that gave money to New Era. "Whatever was in his mind from the very beginning or somewhere midway or near the end, we still don't really know. His video is repentant, and he's sorry, but there's a lot of folks who are sorry. We all live with things that we're sorry for."

A U.S. bankruptcy court judge approved a settlement with Bennett at the end of 1995 in which Bennett agreed to surrender $1.2 million in property, cash, and securities, including his $620,000 house, a $249,000 house belonging to his daughter, and the 1992 Lexus which Bennett drove personally. The settlement represents a small portion of the adjusted estimate of $100 million owed to approximately three hundred creditors and a fraction of the $9 million Bennett allegedly steered from New Era accounts into a number of unrelated business ventures. In addition to Bennett's funds, a number of nonprofit groups that had received early payouts from New Era agreed to return the funds to the bankruptcy trustee so that the monies could be shared equally with all of the defrauded charities. The University of Pennsylvania turned over $2.4 million, Princeton University gave up $2.1 million, and Harvard University will pay $467,000. (Only Penn had sent funds to New Era; Princeton and Harvard received designated gifts from philanthropists participating in New Era.) Under the terms of the trustee's proposed settlement, the victims of the scam would receive a minimum of 62–64 cents on the dollar of their losses, provided that most of the early participants put back at least 65 percent of their gains. Participating philanthropists would not receive a refund, although they would have a say in which charities received their money.

In May 1996 a group of thirty nonprofits sued Prudential Securities for $90 million, contending that the brokerage firm was a coconspirator in the New Era fraud. The lawsuit followed earlier litigation by two small nonprofits in Syracuse, New York. The suits charge that Prudential "represented and assisted New Era's representations to charities . . . that the funds [given to New Era] were being safely held in 'escrow' or 'quasi-escrow' accounts." Prudential denies the allegations.

One day after the New Era bankruptcy trustee filed his proposed settlement offer, he sued Prudential, alleging that the brokerage firm overlooked repeated and obvious signs that the charity was fraudulent out of a desire to earn commissions and excessive interest. The suit seeks the return of $160 million in funds that Prudential loaned New Era or held for the charity in a brokerage account and asks further that the court list Prudential behind all other creditors in the case. "Prudential knew, should have known, or had a reasonable basis to suspect that New Era was operating . . . a scheme to defraud its creditors," the suit says. According to the suit, while New Era participants were told that their funds were being held in an escrow account—in fact, some of them received confirmation letters from Prudential to that effect—the money was actually funneled to a single brokerage account which New Era tapped frequently for payouts. At some point, the account allegedly became a margin account, allowing New Era to borrow funds against the account while paying interest to Prudential for that privilege. By the time of New Era's collapse, Prudential had earned $740,293 in interest from millions of dollars in loans against the margin account.

Amazingly, the trustee's suit claims that a Prudential vice president in Detroit learned that the Detroit Institute of Art—a museum on whose board the executive had recently served—had sent $1 million to New Era, to be doubled in six months, and had a copy of a Prudential letter stating that the funds were being held in escrow. The vice president notified other Prudential officials about the possibility of a Ponzi scheme being operated by New Era, but the warning went largely unheeded.

Adding insult to injury, the suit cites records showing that Prudential continued to accept deposits from charities and philanthropists into New Era's account, even after it had been notified of the U.S. Securities and Exchange Commission (SEC) investigation. In fact, on the same day that Prudential sued New Era for $45 million owed in loans, the firm deposited $1.8 million from Laurance Rockefeller and $85,000 from his wife, Mary, and applied those funds to the debit balance in the account.

Meanwhile, the Pennsylvania attorney general has sued New Era for operating a Ponzi scheme to defraud investors, and Prudential has filed suit to recover $44.9 million that New Era had borrowed against its margin account with the company. Additionally, the SEC is suing Bennett for a number of violations, including diverting at least $4.2 million from New Era coffers for his own use, and a class-action suit was filed by the Museum of American Jewish History against New Era on behalf of all investors.

On September 27, 1996, John G. Bennett Jr. was charged with eighty-two criminal counts, including mail fraud, wire fraud, bank fraud, and money laundering, in a $135 million case described by prosecutors as the biggest charity fraud in U.S. history. Bennett pleaded not guilty and was freed on $100,000 bail. He faces the possibility of $28 million in fines and a 907-year prison sentence.

Monday-morning quarterbacks in the nonprofit sector questioned how professional nonprofit managers were duped by a charity that had produced only one annual report in six years, did not have audited financial statements, did not register with the state of Pennsylvania as a charity until three years into its existence, required participants to send checks payable directly to itself instead of an escrow account, and sometimes asked investors to funnel money through an intermediary. "Maybe this scandal will do some good, because it shows the volatility and frailty of nonprofit institutions," asserts Richard Ray, a member of the King College board of trustees, "at a time when the government is trying to kill off the National Endowment for the Humanities and other sources of federal funds."

"The investments in New Era are going to be costly for some, but they will have done a favor if they cause [nonprofit] boards to be more vigilant in protecting their assets," predicts Nancy Axelrod, president of the National Center for Nonprofit Boards. "Also, I believe there are nonprofits out there that had the chance to invest in New Era but turned it down. I hope that list is much longer than the list of those that participated."

Nonprofits skirting the edges of the law do not target only the rich and famous, of course. The Jewish Educational Center (JEC) of San Francisco, a tax-exempt group that funds the eighty-four-student Beth Aharon Day School, has become one of the biggest used-car dealers in the country by soliciting cars as donations and then auctioning them. From its threadbare beginnings in 1991, the charity expects to earn $7.3 million in car sales in 1996.

Rabbi Bentziyon Pil, a thirty-seven-year-old Russian immigrant, started soliciting donated cars for the JEC in 1991 by running newspaper advertisements, but the tactic never worked well. Two years later, he borrowed $25,000 from a friend to run radio spots asking for car donations to help needy immigrants and promising hefty tax deductions in return. Now running on nine radio stations on both coasts, the ads bring in an estimated two hundred cars per week. In San Francisco alone, the JEC car auction involves forty-eight different phone lines and a two-and-one-half-acre car lot.

The first complaint filed by the JEC's critics is that the car donors are misled into thinking that their cars have been given directly to needy families, not sold. "I would not have given away my car in that case," says Gene Tamayo of Vallejo, California, who donated his 1983 Buick Skylark. "My impression after hearing the ads was that the car would be used by an immigrant from the Jewish community. That's the reason I donated it." Rabbi Pil responds that a small number of cars are still given away as direct gifts instead of being sold.

Some donors have questioned the actual value of the tax deductions credited by the JEC for the gift of a car. One radio ad promises "full Blue Book value," even for cars that have been damaged or totaled. Several former JEC employees made public claims that they regularly inflated the value of donors' cars to give bigger tax writeoffs. Pil says he never encouraged his employees to inflate deductions and that the JEC, in an effort to be legitimate, now avoids writing values on the receipts, allowing donors to decide how much they want to deduct.

More serious concerns have arisen about the group's excessive overhead costs. A review of the JEC's finances by the National Charities Information Bureau, a New York–based watchdog organization, found that the JEC spent $1.75 million in the fiscal year that ended March 31, 1995 but only $365,755 (21 percent) of those funds went into charitable activities. The bureau recommends that nonprofits commit at least 60 percent of their revenues to charitable programs. Pil disputes the bureau's figures and notes that selling donated cars naturally requires greater overhead expenses than the average charity. He cites the purchase of advertisements and start-up costs, such as new computers. While overhead costs have soared, the condition of the Beth Aharon school remains poor; it is so small that the principal works out of a shack near the playground. While the JEC advertises its support of programs for children in Bosnia, Rwanda, and Lebanon, Pil admits that the group has never helped children directly in any of these countries.

Meanwhile, the Pils themselves have done well by the charity's success. Once encouraged by his in-laws to "get a real job and become a taxi driver," Pil and his wife now live in a rented house valued at $472,000, he and his wife earn a combined annual salary of $84,000 from the charity, and he drives a donated 1990 Cadillac. "Sometimes I have to pinch myself," Pil admits.

These apparent abuses of nonprofit privileges finally drew the attention of tax officials in California. The state suspended the JEC's tax-exempt status in 1990 because the group failed to file required state forms and pay the filing fees; Pil says he did not think the JEC had earned sufficient revenue to be required to file the forms. The state attorney general's office says that the JEC's corporate status and tax-exempt status were stripped at the same time, while the JEC's lawyer claims that his client only learned in 1994 that there were problems with the charity's registration. (The tax-exempt status was restored in 1995 retroactively.) During the period in which the JEC did not have the necessary tax-exempt status, the charity should technically have paid state taxes on its car sales, but it did not, and the car donors were never affected because California law allows them to take state tax deductions as long as the charity in question is considered a tax-exempt group by the IRS. An IRS spokesperson confirmed that the JEC is now tax-exempt but refused to comment on prior years.

The charity continues to have problems satisfying legal requirements to operate as a nonprofit in various jurisdictions. The JEC registered as a charity in Los Angeles in early 1996, after receiving a warning letter from the city because the group had been running car-donation ads in the city since late 1994. In 1995, the JEC opened a branch in Jersey City, New Jersey, to serve donors in New York and New Jersey, but the JEC is not currently registered as a charity in either state. (An attorney for the JEC stated that he believes the charity is not yet required to register in New York, and Pil said that he is in the process of filing in New Jersey.)

Pil admits readily that he operates the multimillion-dollar charity by the seat of his pants, but he says that his intentions have always been good and that any errors can be chalked up to inexperience. "We were like blind cats" in starting a charity, he says. "We didn't know why it was so important to be so particular." "My question remains: What is their philanthropic work?" counters Wayne Feinstein, executive vice president of the Jewish Community Federation of San Francisco, a major Jewish charity in the region. "These folks are imperceptible in terms of service to immigrants in this area. They're not even on the radar screen."

While Rabbi Pil attributes his legal troubles to naïveté and ineptitude, Robert Johnson allegedly continues to control the business operations of several nonprofit groups after serving time in 1993 for perjury and illegal contributions to George Bush's 1988 presidential campaign. Johnson organized the illegal donations through two of his associations, the International Real

Estate Institute and the National Association of Real Estate Appraisers. Sentenced to six months in prison and fined $30,000, he served sixty days before a U.S. district court judge in Scottsdale, Arizona, freed him on appeal, ruling that the composition of the FEC was unconstitutional and therefore the FEC did not possess the proper authority to obtain the deposition from Johnson that resulted in his conviction.

Many observers in the nonprofit world assumed that Johnson would simply fade away. However, a year after his sentence, Johnson was accused by the International Association of Convention & Visitors Bureaus (IACVB) of implying that IACVB president Stephen Carey had endorsed Johnson's International Society of Meeting Professionals (ISMP). "IACVB denies implied endorsement of ISMP or any of its programs or activities," read an article in IACVB's membership newsletter. In December 1995, Johnson's son Troy gained considerable attention in the meetings industry when he refused to pay a convention bureau's bill for $450 for services it provided one of Johnson's associations for an overseas meeting. "They are still swindling money out of us," fumes one bureau staffer who refused to be identified. "Dealing with them has been a complete nightmare."

In media interviews, Troy Johnson upholds the image of a nonprofit executive on the defensive. After claiming that he and his father manage fifteen different trade associations, with members in 112 countries around the world, he refuses to disclose the names of the associations. "Why should I tell you?" he answers.

How easily can nonprofit swindles become established cons in the marketplace? Consider the case of a U.S. Tax Court petitioner (identified as "Mr. Helin") who applied for tax-exempt status to establish the International Postgraduate Medical Foundation (IPMF) for the stated purpose of providing continuing medical education to physicians. Helin listed himself as a trustee of the foundation as well as president of "H&C Tours," an independent, for-profit travel agency selected to arrange three-week tours built around the foundation's seminars in Russia, India, Egypt, Kenya, and other exotic destinations. The foundation's brochures mentioned that medical educational seminars were provided during the tours, but they did not describe the actual curricula for the seminars and symposia. The tour itineraries made it clear that educational activities accounted for less than half of the time on a given trip (average duration: 4.5 hours per day). The IRS ruled that a significant amount of the foundation's operations was used simply to increase the income of H&C Tours; for example, approximately 90 percent of the foundation's revenue in a given year was spent on producing and distributing tour brochures. Furthermore, the foundation did not solicit competitive bids from other travel agencies for the tours, giving H&C Tours more than $339,000 in gross revenues for air fares and land arrangements as a direct result of the foundation's tours. The application for tax-exempt status was denied.

# PART III

# OVERSIGHT AND REFORM

# 11

## *Starting at the Top: Congress and the States*

DURING HIS TERMS IN CONGRESS representing one of the poorest rural districts in Texas, J. J. Pickle earned a reputation as one of the most populist members of the U.S. House of Representatives. He was known for cutting through Beltway rhetoric with his down-home humor and commonsense answers to public-policy issues.

Even today, however, Pickle—who retired from Congress in 1993—admits that he met his match battling nonprofits over suggested reforms in the laws governing tax-exempt organizations. "We held a number of hearings on nonprofit abuses over the years, and I worried most about these problems because nonprofits threatened to get bigger than the government if they kept growing the way they were," he remembers. "Once a tax-exempt organization gets on the books, it normally stays there forever. They last longer than the stars. This business of examining nonprofits and massaging them and reordering the foo-foo of the issues is not going to do it. We've got to do something about it rather than just say it."

Congressional hearings held by Pickle and other legislators—who exhibited considerable bravery in addressing the subject, given the enormous lobbying clout of many nonprofits and the

political liabilities inherent in being perceived as "against the
Boy Scouts and the churches," as one staffer described it—
turned up a number of promising solutions to rectify the abuses
practiced by some nonprofit groups that mix personal gain with
their tax-exempt missions:

STEP 1:   *Make it harder for organizations to claim tax-exempt
and nonprofit status.*

"Getting federal approval to start a new nonprofit organization is like getting your driver's license," said Ted Chapler, executive director of the Iowa Finance Authority, a state-chartered
body that arranges tax-exempt financing for nonprofit groups.
"Until I looked, I thought being declared a nonprofit was pretty
difficult. Then I found that something like ninety-five or ninety-
nine percent of the groups that apply get approved." In 1994
(the last year for which reliable data are available), the IRS
turned down only 520 applications for starting a new nonprofit
organization while approving 46,887 applications; the organizers
of a new charity therefore faced 60–1 odds of winning their case
before the IRS in 1994, compared to 27–1 just ten years earlier.

Form 1023, the official IRS application to secure approval
for a new tax-exempt organization, asks for only the most rudi-
mentary information about the structure and purpose of a proposed nonprofit: the names and addresses of the group's
incorporators and a description of the charitable activities in
which the group intends to engage. An IRS spokesman confirms
that if the application does not raise serious questions at first
glance and includes the $425 filing fee, the applicants stand very
little chance of being rejected.

In almost every U.S. legal jurisdiction below the federal level,
the awarding of an IRS tax exemption leads virtually automatically to exemption from local property taxes, state corporate income taxes, state and local sales taxes, and many other levies
that are normally assessed on for-profit, private corporations.
"We don't ask for more than the federal government requires itself, in most cases, unless specifically required by state statute,"
admits Bob Babbage, Kentucky's secretary of state, describing
the state's process in determining whether a group deserves tax-

exempt status. "As long as the applicant can provide evidence of the federal exemption, we accept that standard."

Recommended improvements in the federal application process include a more detailed IRS form for filing to be considered a tax-exempt group. The current form, for example, does not ask whether the principal organizers of a new charity or philanthropy have ever been convicted of a crime. (Following the 1991 revocation of the tax exemption of a children's charity whose president—sentenced to federal prison in 1988 for fraud—bilked the nonprofit for hundreds of thousands of dollars in personal expenses, the leading IRS official in charge of non-profit exemptions said that the form did not ask about criminal history because he felt that few criminals actually apply for non-profit exemptions.) "How difficult can it be simply to ask a few more questions on the form that gives a nonprofit virtually un-ending freedom from taxes and many regulations?" asks Kenton Pattie, executive director of the Business Coalition for Fair Competition (BCFC), a lobbying alliance of more than twenty small-business trade associations. "Even if you don't catch many crooks in the beginning, you can catch them lying later."

"Tax exemption should be granted conditionally based on a charity's actual performance," maintains Richard Blumenthal, former Connecticut attorney general. "Tax exemption is not a right, it's a privilege, and charities should have the burden of justifying themselves from time to time."

STEP 2: *Police nonprofits on a more frequent basis.*

Critics wag that nonprofit managers may be more fearful of being struck by lightning than being audited by the IRS. Currently, the IRS employs only a few hundred field examiners to review the nation's 1.2 million nonprofit groups. In 1993, in fact, the IRS examined 5,472 tax-exempt organizations, less than 0.5 percent of all nonprofits and substantially fewer than the 6,708 groups examined in 1988. As a result, some groups do not bother to file the required Form 990 annual tax return; in 1989, the last year accounted for in IRS reports, only 133,157 non-profits filed the proper federal tax returns. An investigation by the *Philadelphia Inquirer* in 1993 estimated that if the IRS began auditing every nonprofit group in the United States today, it would take seventy-nine years to complete the examinations, given current staffing levels.

Faced with these criticisms, the IRS launched its Coordinated Examination Program (CEP) in 1992. To better understand how nonprofits operate and how to police their fund-raising activities more carefully, the IRS has been sending specialized teams of agents to conduct line-by-line examinations of tax-exempt groups' ledgers. Besides finding potential errors in tax-exempt accounting, the exams are designed to teach agents clues in non-profit bookkeeping that will enable the IRS to audit such groups more efficiently. "We realized we were faced with an exceedingly sophisticated group of organizations," said Marcus Owens. "There was some reason to be concerned with what the ultimate goal of the organization was—whether we were really looking at a tax-exempt [group] anymore." Thirty percent of Owens's department—which boasts a thousand staffers and a $125 million budget—is devoted to CEP audits.

The CEP audits target the 15 percent of America's tax-exempt organizations that account for half of the sector's revenues, with a special focus on hospitals and universities. The IRS also decided to examine two high-profile national nonprofits known for their political activism and commercial ventures: the National Rifle Association and the American Association of Retired Persons. IRS agents have closed thirty-five CEP audits, including twelve health-care providers and three educational institutions; in each case, according to Owens, the nonprofit was forced to adjust its books, and some groups reported reduced operating losses (resulting in higher tax payments).

A 1995 report by the General Accounting Office (GAO) confirmed that tougher IRS efforts to audit nonprofits' books carefully yield greater results in collecting unpaid taxes and controlling nonprofit abuses. The report found that between 1992 and 1994, the IRS revoked the tax-exempt status of sixty-seven organizations and audited thirty percent fewer nonprofits but earned 200 percent more in back taxes and penalties from the nonprofits that were examined. "For too long we have been too reluctant to look into many nonprofit, tax-exempt organizations," stated Sen. David Pryor (D-Ark.) when the GAO study was released.

STEP 3: *Make nonprofit tax returns more easily available to the public.*

Learning the reported details of a tax-exempt group's finances and corporate structure can be as easy as writing a letter to the IRS. Federal tax law requires any nonprofit group to show to anyone who asks for it their original application for tax-exempt status (Form 1023) as well as the last three years' worth of their annual tax returns (Form 990). These papers must be kept on file at the nonprofit's primary offices for public inspection, although the nonprofit does not have to make photocopies for people requesting the inspection. The reason for the disclosure rule? The federal government believed that the measure would serve as a public check on the oversight of nonprofit groups. "There will always be more organizations than the IRS and state attorneys general can keep tabs on," said Owens. "By making the 990s available, it was hoped that the spotlight of publicity would serve to throw the spotlight on the structure and commercial activities of nonprofits." Unfortunately, many nonprofits have learned the loopholes of the system, such as leaving certain portions of the form blank with the knowledge that few forms are checked for accuracy and completeness. In 1988 the GAO issued a report showing that 48 percent of all 990s filed with the IRS lacked at least one of the required reporting schedules. "We routinely attend health-law seminars throughout this country," IRS associate chief counsel James J. McGovern told a congressional subcommittee during a 1991 hearing. "We have on many occasions listened to presentations from tax practitioners advising those who attend the seminar how best to avoid the [disclosure] requirements."

Of course, some nonprofit managers honestly do not understand the legal disclosure requirements. "Thank you for making us aware of the law," the treasurer of the National Football League told a newspaper researcher in 1993. "No one ever asked us [for the forms] before. We really didn't know what we were required to do. Now we know."

Copies of these forms can also be requested directly from the IRS, usually at no charge. However, filling such requests can take several months and may depend on the timing of filing-deadline extensions granted to a nonprofit organization by the IRS. The procedure involves writing the IRS regional office that covers the state in which the nonprofit is headquartered, listing the group's name and address (and, if known, the federal employer identification number). (See Appendix B for an address list of IRS regional centers.)

While nonprofits must keep their applications for tax-exempt status and their 990s on file, they are not required to share their Form 990-Ts, the annual tax return reporting unrelated business income. Every nonprofit with unrelated revenues exceeding $1,000 in a given year must file Form 990-T.

Several pending congressional bills would streamline the process for collecting nonprofit tax information. A Democrat-sponsored bill introduced in 1996 would create a national clearinghouse offering copies of nonprofit tax returns for a reasonable fee. Another provision—included as part of a sweeping taxpayer protection bill that passed both houses of Congress and awaits President Clinton's signature—would require nonprofits to send copies of their tax forms within thirty days of receiving a written request for the forms. Groups would not have to respond to such requests if the IRS agrees that the requests represent harassment or if a group already makes the forms widely available through other means.

To offer a format that makes for easy review by consumers and taxpayers, the federal government should investigate alternative formats like the one-page "Fact Sheet" of financial statistics required by the Connecticut attorney general's office from each charity doing business in the state, based on their tax filings. Also, the IRS and Congress should review the paltry penalties in place for failing to file a timely, complete, and accurate 990: $10 per day that the failure continues, not to exceed $5,000, or 5 percent of a nonprofit's annual gross receipts, whichever is smaller.

Whatever the case, the federal government should avoid snafus that undermine the serious nature of nonprofit tax filings. In

1994 the IRS extended the Form 990 filing deadline for non-profits from May 15 to July 15—giving them, in effect, an across-the-board two-month extension—because of a delay in the printing of new 990s. According to one IRS spokesman, the delay was no big deal: "We are talking 990s. We are not talking about taxable returns. It just doesn't have the same significance."

STEP 4: *Expand the range of penalties for nonprofit abuses and publicize instances of such abuses.*

Under current law, the only recourse available to the IRS to punish nonprofit groups that abuse their privileges is the "death penalty": removal of an organization's tax-exempt status. However, this sanction is viewed as such an extreme measure that the IRS rarely invokes it. Throughout the 1980s the IRS removed tax exemptions from an average of thirty nonprofits each year while approving about thirty thousand new nonprofits annually. "The threat of revocation [of the tax exemption] was just that—a threat," noted Congressman Pickle in a 1993 congressional hearing.

One solution advocated by the IRS is giving the agency power to impose sanctions less drastic than the full revocation of tax-exempt status. "Revocation of an exemption is a severe sanction that may be greatly disproportional to the violation in issue," argues IRS commissioner Margaret Richardson. "Revocation of an organization's exemption, which at first blush might seem appropriate in these situations, is often a step that could adversely affect innocent parties in the very community that the charity seeks to serve."

A bill pending currently in Congress would allow the IRS to impose stiff excise taxes on offending nonprofits (referred to by committee staffers as an "intermediate sanction"). While a similar proposal stalled in 1995 as the victim of other congressional debates, this measure has been attached to the popular taxpayer-protection bill that also streamlines public access to nonprofit tax returns. The Senate passed this intermediate sanctions bill in July 1996, with the provision that the IRS can now impose excise taxes against 501 (c)(3) or (c)(4) organization managers and other "insiders" who participate in illegal financial transactions.

(The IRS can impose the tax on individuals but not the nonprofit groups themselves.) The House passed an identical bill in April, and President Clinton signed the measure.

Some nonprofit-sector leaders have questioned the propriety of the new excise-tax provisions. "You can be penalized by the IRS for being paid too much," claims H. Thomas Davis Jr., with the accounting firm Carter, Ledyard & Milburn in New York. The new law would allow the IRS to levy an excise tax on a "disqualified person," defined as an individual who is in a position to exercise substantial influence over the affairs of a public charity and who receives excessive compensation from the charity or conducts a transaction in which he or she receives an economic benefit worth more than the goods or services provided to the charity. The excise tax is 25 percent of the amount of the excess benefit, and the disqualified person must return the excess benefit to the charity or risk an additional 200 percent tax. A 10 percent tax may be charged to directors and trustees who knowingly participated in the incident.

"Suppose a public charity paid its chairman a salary and benefits package equal to $200,000 per year when the fair-market value of the services he performed was only $150,000," Davis offers. "The new excise tax rules would require the chairman to pay a 25 percent excise tax on the $50,000 in excess benefits as well as return the $50,000 to the charity. The directors of the charity would each owe $5,000 personally if they approved the compensation knowing that it was excessive." Davis cautions that nonprofit managers will be forced in the future to rely on a compensation committee of objective trustees or credible market data on comparable salaries to avoid being hit with the excise taxes.

By publicizing such penalties, the federal government plays into a notion widely held among disaffected taxpayers: "Give me my tax dollars that are being spent on these nonprofits groups that are making trouble and I will spend the money on charity myself." In 1996, Republican presidential candidate Bob Dole floated the idea of giving federal tax credits equal to the donations made to private charities. "[The credit] would present America

with a stark choice," Dole said. "Give your money to the Department of Housing and Urban Development or give it to Habitat for Humanity ... to big government or to Big Brothers and
Big Sisters." The idea originated with Sen. Dan Coats (R-Ind.),
who proposed a $500-per-person tax credit for donations to char-
ities caring for the poor. "Individual Americans who pay taxes,
not federal bureaucrats, should decide which good deeds deserve
their support," Coats says. "This proposal would give 100 percent
tax relief on a $500 gift instead of the 20 percent to 40 percent
people get now, depending upon their tax rates." The Coats proposal—which Budget Committee Chairman John Kasich (R-Ohio)
sponsored in the House—requires that only charities devoting at
least 75 percent of their programming dollars to the poor would
be eligible. Federal researchers estimate that half of the 70 million
Americans eligible for the credit would use it, by writing checks
to their favorite charities and claiming the deductions when they
file their federal-income-tax returns.

Critics point to several flaws in the Coats plan. The stronger
competition for donations would increase charities' fund-raising
costs, leaving relatively fewer dollars to care for the poor. (Backers of the credit have already counterproposed a 25-percent limit
on an eligible nonprofit's administrative costs.) The new pressure
to raise funds would "add substantial costs to the local homeless shelter or soup kitchen, and it may not provide a terrific return," points out Virginia Hodgkinson, research director for
Independent Sector. "It would be a paperwork nightmare," predicts James Bausch, president of the watchdog agency National
Charities Information Bureau, because nonprofits would be
forced to track the income of their beneficiaries in order to qualify for the credit.

While supporters of the tax credit say that private nonprofits do a better job than government agencies at fighting poverty,
Lester Salamon points out that 61 percent of government spending on human services programming is already routed through
the private sector in the form of grants and awards. "This is just
one of those convenient myths that cloud our understanding,"
he says. Helmer Eckstrom, president of the American Associa-

tion of Fund-Raising Counsel, asserts that expanding the existing federal tax deduction for charitable contributions and allowing taxpayers who do not itemize their returns to claim the charitable deduction anyway would boost charitable giving without the additional hassles of a charity tax credit. "That idea has the potential to be a terribly inefficient system for raising money," he concludes.

STEP 5:   *Place reasonable limits on nonprofit salaries and perks.*

Most of the abuses uncovered by IRS field agents auditing nonprofit groups fall within the arena of executive excess: enormous salaries, no-interest loans, luxury cars, and even yachts and expensive vacations that clearly have no relevance to the nonprofit's stated missions. Under one measure discussed in the House Ways and Means Oversight Subcommittee in 1993, charities would be forced to seek IRS approval for pay packages above a standard level or pay an excise tax for exceeding the limits. The Tax Exemption Accountability Act, introduced in the House of Representatives in 1996, calls for caps on the compensation of officers and directors of tax-exempt organizations at the salaries currently received by U.S. cabinet members (exempt from the capping: salaries of clergy or "high cost" medical professionals, such as surgeons). "In defining what pay is reasonable, we encourage our clients to look at comparable private-sector firms as well as other tax-exempt groups in their field," advises Peter L. Faber, a tax attorney at McDermott, Will & Emery in Washington, D.C.

STEP 6:   *Require nonprofits to reapply for their tax exemption on a regular basis.*

Once a tax exemption is granted by the IRS today, that privileged status remains intact virtually forever, barring a major instance of abuse by the nonprofit group. However, asking tax-exempt groups to complete a new Form 1023 every five or 10 years would force them to report major changes in their corporate structure, operations, staffing, and mission statements.

Moreover, the "sunsetting" of a nonprofit's tax exemption would serve to keep the group mindful of the need to focus on its tax-exempt purposes to avoid the danger of straying from these missions and thus endangering the exemption when the IRS reviews the renewal application. Today a charity can spend virtually all of its money on fund-raising and administrative costs and still retain its tax-exempt status. Federal law should require instead that a set percentage (say, 60 percent) of a nonprofit's revenues be spent only on programs related to its charitable purpose. If federal audits uncover nonprofits that fall short of the marks, their tax exemption could be placed in jeopardy. "Some of the more egregious abuses would cease if public charities had to spend even as little as half of their income on purposes other than management salaries and payments for fund-raising," observed former Connecticut attorney general Richard Blumenthal.

States and cities find the federal challenges in recognizing and policing nonprofit groups magnified at their levels. Every state has its own set of laws governing the activities of nonprofits, but most states defer to the federal government's awarding of tax exemptions as the primary criterion for a group to qualify for state exemptions as well. Other than scattered attempts by revenue departments or the offices of attorneys general, state-level audits and enforcement efforts leave much to be desired in terms of their scope and effectiveness. Blumenthal watched the time he spent on nonprofit abuses double during his tenure. "One person who set up charities for causes such as drug-abuse prevention and soldiers of the Gulf War openly bragged that he only wanted to make a living," he remembers. "There is a need for a greater federal role. Bad charitable operations can continue to operate in many states in the absence of a coordinated national approach."

When states attempt to strengthen their oversight of nonprofit groups, the nonprofit community relies on its grassroots network of volunteers and donors to apply political pressure that far exceeds the responses faced on Capitol Hill by federal legislators. A recent attempt by Colorado to tax the property of nonprofit groups, for example, led to recall petitions aimed at the bill's sponsors and widespread accusations that the legislators supporting the bill were "out to get the good guys." The bill is certified for the November 1996 ballot, but a court challenge to the vote is pending.

However, as tax revenues remain tight and as a growing array of needs clamors for those dollars, many states have grown more aggressive in their efforts to collect more money from nonprofits. In April 1996 the U.S. Supreme Court agreed to hear a case that underscores the growing trend among state and local governments to find ways to collect revenues from traditionally tax exempt organizations. *Camps Newfound/Owantonna Inc. v. Town of Harrison* involves a Maine summer camp attended mostly by residents of other states. A recently passed Maine statute denies the state's charitable property-tax exemption to organizations that primarily serve residents of other states. The camp's attorneys argue that the law represents an illegal state-level regulation of interstate commerce. "If the Supreme Court upholds the Maine statute, then that gives legislators considerably more room to maneuver in granting tax exemptions," said Janne G. Gallagher, a partner in the Washington-based firm of Harmon, Curran, Gallagher & Spielberg who specializes in representing nonprofit organizations. "There would be nothing to stop states from limiting exemptions for all kinds of organizations that serve out-of-state people, most notably colleges and universities."

A bill that would require tax-exempt groups to make payments to the state in lieu of taxes passed the New Hampshire senate in early 1996 and was sent to the state house for approval before being sent to Gov. Stephen Merrill. House Bill 345 would give cities the authority to collect payments from nonprofits through local ordinances or ballot initiatives. While some groups could be granted exemptions, most would be asked to pay an amount based on factors such as the amount of services they offer free to the community, the relief to local governments provided by those services, the cost of government services (such as police and fire protection) to the group, and its sources of income. "There's been an effort under way in New Hampshire for some time to provide a mechanism for getting money out of charities," observed attorney Janne Gallagher. "New Hampshire remains the only state that continues to rely upon property taxes as the primary mechanism for financing government." (In Nebraska a legislative committee has reported a similar bill to the floor that is predicted to lapse without a vote in 1996 but will be introduced again in 1997 because of property tax limits that are scheduled to take effect in 1998.)

Facing declining tax bases and federal cutbacks, many major cities around the country have begun investigating the wisdom of widespread tax exemptions for nonprofit groups. In Syracuse, New York, the mayor has proposed charging nonprofits a "core service fee" that would ostensibly cover the costs of basic city services, such as road maintenance and police and fire protection. "We don't have a choice anymore," Mayor Roy Bernardi told the *New York Times*, citing an expected $16 million shortfall in a budget of $160 million for a city in which 58.7 percent of the property is tax-exempt. "It's either A, find added revenue, or B, we don't provide the services we have in the past. And no one wants to hear B." The corporate counsel for Syracuse advised the mayor that the fees would be legally permissible, given recent findings that fees directly attributable to specific city services do not conflict with the laws granting tax-exempt status. However, given the constitutional protections separating church and state, it is likely that churches could not be compelled to pay the fees.

Throughout New England, cities have developed creative means of securing more money from nonprofits. In Connecticut the state reimburses municipalities for a portion of the taxes lost due to tax exemptions, and the cities have clamored for an increase in the reimbursement rate. In Maryland and Delaware, cities have been permitted to form "special benefit" districts in their downtown areas that require all legal entities within the districts, including nonprofits, to pay fees for services like street cleaning. In New York City a city-council proposal to remove tax exemptions given to "elite nonprofit institutions," defined as groups with executives earning more than $130,000 annually, died recently. In many jurisdictions, nonprofits that are engaged in commercial ventures often receive only partial exemptions, with the business portion of their property placed on the tax rolls along with other types of profit-making companies.

In 1995 the Washington, D.C., city council began deliberations to institute a study of all property, income, and sales-tax exemptions in the city. "I am aware of the state of finances for nonprofits," council member Kathleen Patterson stated during one "town hall" meeting on the issue. "A nonprofit is a nonprofit because it has no profit. That has not escaped me. But we could use this study to help plot a strategy for the city's recovery [from a 1995 shortfall of $722 million]." Pending city-council legislation would revoke the tax exemptions of the Federal National Mortgage Association, the Student Loan Marketing Association, and the Federal Home Loan Mortgage Corporation.

Philadelphia mayor Edward G. Rendell issued what amounted to an ultimatum to nonprofit institutions in his city in 1994: Pay the city one-third of what they would have paid in property taxes without a tax exemption or face court challenges to their entire tax-exempt status. Rendell based his call on a Pennsylvania Supreme Court ruling that limited state and local tax exemptions to groups that can demonstrate they are a "purely public charity," such as those that provide aid to the poor. The city stands to collect $33.2 million annually if all nonprofits voluntarily participate in the program; they can finance a portion of the charge by donating services to the city and its public schools. While Rendell declared in a public statement that the program recognizes "the vitality of Philadelphia's nonprofit institutions," many tax-exempt groups have disagreed. "The university believes it deserves its tax-exempt status," grumbled a spokesman for Pennsylvania State University.

Two key strategies would allow states and cities to improve their oversight of nonprofit groups in crucial ways:

STEP 1: *Consolidate the oversight of nonprofit groups from many different agencies and commissions into a single statewide source.*

Unlike the federal government, which relies primarily on the IRS to grant exemptions and regulate nonprofits' activities, most states divide these responsibilities among different agencies and boards. For example, the secretary of state might be in charge of applications for tax-exempt status and nonprofit incorporations, while the revenue division would be responsible for reviewing annual state tax returns for tax-exempt groups. Adopting the federal model of consolidating oversight in one place—preferably the revenue division, which has enforcement authority to collect taxes and levy fines—would greatly streamline the state's ability to police the nonprofits within its boundaries. The same principles apply to cities, especially large metropolitan areas that have both large local and state nonprofits and the regional offices of national nonprofits.

STEP 2: *Match state and local nonprofit rules with federal regulations.*

While the majority of state and local officials rely primarily on the IRS to determine the eligibility of a nonprofit group for tax-exempt status—honoring the federal exemption as well for state and local taxes of all sorts—they do not always follow suit in matching other federal laws and regulations. The result is a mishmash of conflicting requirements that can complicate enforcement efforts. For example, the calculation of state corporate income taxes on a nonprofit's commercial sidelines should be combined with the assessment of federal unrelated business income tax (UBIT) on the venture, so that state and municipal tax collectors could focus instead on more critical compliance issues.

Other state-level actions could include the following:

*Establish a private-enterprise review commission.* A review commission should be set up by the state legislature to hold hearings and receive testimony, specifically to make legislative recommendations based on the group's findings in the arena of unfair competition and nonprofit abuses. For example, Arizona established a commission composed of representatives from the legislature, small businesses, state agencies, the board of regents and the state board of directors for community colleges, nonprofit health care institutions, and other tax-exempt groups. The commission was given the task of reviewing situations in which state rules, regulations, or laws give an edge to nonprofits competing with private businesses. In addition, the commission had to evaluate the costs of government programs to determine whether privatizing certain functions made sense.

*Apply the "maximum separation" doctrine in state laws governing nonprofits.* This legal doctrine requires that a person or company doing business in two separate markets maintain appropriate separation between the two in order to avoid the unreasonable transfer of economic power from the primary market to the secondary market. By incorporating this doctrine into state laws and regulations governing nonprofits, the result will be the encouragement of nonprofit groups to form for-profit subsidiaries to carry on their commercial activities.

*Incorporate the UBIT into the state's revenue scheme.* Too often, states lose revenues by not pursuing the business profits of nonprofit organizations. States should review their tax structure to determine a method of strengthening their ability to collect taxes on net income from nonprofit business ventures. At a minimum, states should enact laws that tax the unrelated business income of nonprofits in the same way as for-profit businesses. In this way, fair compensation to the state is assured.

*Set a higher tax rate for nonprofits that fail to disclose income.* The IRS and the states should examine more closely the tax returns of nonprofit organizations to identify those sources of income on which tax should be collected. State laws related to the taxation of unrelated business income should be changed to set higher rates for unrelated revenues that are not voluntarily disclosed. When a nonprofit voluntarily reports and pays taxes on all of its income from unrelated business ventures, that income would be taxed at normal corporate rates. However, in the event that state audits reveal that a nonprofit has concealed unrelated income, a trigger effect would be implemented, and the tax rates would automatically be much higher. This recommendation would force nonprofits to consider carefully the tax consequences of their business ventures before they are launched.

With higher rates plus penalties facing those who deliberately decide to avoid voluntary payment, nonprofits are more likely to decide from the beginning of a venture to expose themselves to the proper taxes, just as any small business would have to do.

*Establish a commission to review the state corporation counsel's criteria for the chartering of nonprofit organizations.* A thorough review of state nonprofit corporation laws is needed to determine whether amendments or new rules are needed to preclude the granting of charters that are so broad that business ventures appear to be authorized. In most cases, organizations seeking a nonprofit charter are required to submit a statement of purpose. Vague wording in the statement of purpose can lead to abuse by allowing commercial ventures that are construed as related to their tax-exempt purposes. If the state's criteria for granting charters were more stringent and subject to regular review or legislative oversight, nonprofits would be required to offer the state corporation counsel precise information concerning the purpose of, and specific details of, the nonprofit's sales income. A temporary commission established by the state legislature could undertake such a review and report its findings back to the legislature, with suggestions for amending the state's laws governing incorporation of nonprofits.

*Establish a formula to determine whether unrelated business activities take precedence over tax-exempt purposes.* Current laws permit substantial commercial activities by nonprofits as long as the nonprofits also fulfill their tax-exempt purpose. An amendment might be adopted stating that if a nonprofit engages in a specified amount of business activity (e.g., taxable sales equaling more than 25 percent of total operating revenues), then nonprofits would be presumed to be operating for other than tax-exempt purposes and be required to refile with the state corporation counsel, thus reopening the question of its eligibility for tax-exempt status. Furthermore, the state corporation counsel should publish an annual report on all nonprofits whose charters are under review. This information would help donors in the state to know if their contributions were in danger of being ineligible as tax deductions.

*Tax factors should be reflected in state solicitations.* By statute or governor's executive order, it should be established that in all state contracts, cost comparisons of competitive bids from nonprofits and for-profits should be adjusted to reflect the fact that nonprofit bidders will not generate tax revenue for the state. For example, a nonprofit bid of $100,000 might be equal to (not lower than) a for-profit bid of $115,000 because of the $15,000 in taxes that the for-profit bidder will pay.

*Establish a permanent, independent state commission to investigate complaints about nonprofits.* The commission would have permanent authority to conduct investigations of fact whenever a private business in the state files a complaint about a nonprofit group. It would serve as a neutral meeting ground for the two parties, would have clear legal authority to conduct a full investigation of facts, and would report its findings to the governor and the appropriate legislative committees. The commission need not be a large bureaucracy and, in fact, could contract out with private firms for any specific investigations, using its own staff for coordination only. The intent of the commission would be to serve as an early warning system for the legislature and perhaps act as an ombudsman for small businesses.

*Develop data concerning nonprofit income within the state.* A legislator, legislative committee, or the governor's office could request the state bureau of revenue to develop figures indicating the amount of sales revenue collected by, and the amount of taxes paid by, nonprofit organizations. These figures will help paint a better picture of the impact of nonprofit activity within a given state. The data from such a study could help the legislature or governor develop policies to address pressing nonprofit concerns.

Many legal observers and, interestingly, nonprofit managers agree that some or all of these suggested federal, state, and local changes should be implemented to provide more oversight of the nonprofit community and, in fact, blunt the growing negative perceptions of America's tax-exempts. What stands in the way of these changes? The largest obstacle by far is the enormous halo effect, the aura of doing good under which many nonprofits operate with seeming impunity. "Most of these groups have strong, direct access to Congress, the state legislature, and the city council," observed one Capitol Hill staffer who asked not to be identified. "Your typical politician doesn't want to take on nonprofits. You don't score any points doing that."

# 12

## Nonprofits, Police Thyselves

CALLING FOR NONPROFIT MANAGERS and volunteer leaders to shoulder more direct responsibility for their actions generates swift responses from many segments of the nonprofit world.

Stronger tax laws and higher postal rates for nonprofits "just make it harder for those of us in the nonprofit sector to do the kind of thing that the [federal government] calls us to do—that is, contribute in a voluntary way to the moral character of the country," grumbled John Stapert, executive director of the Association of Church Presses, at an association meeting in 1991. "Clearly, something is wrong when churches must work as hard to please the IRS as they do to please God," echoed an anonymous colleague who spoke to a reporter covering the session.

Like many of their counterparts in the business world, nonprofit leaders understand the psychological and political benefits of appearing proactive, rather than reactive, in the move toward greater oversight of America's tax-exempt economy. In some arenas they have made great strides toward effective, wide-reaching self-regulation. Two watchdog agencies—the National Charities Information Bureau (NCIB) and the Council of Better Business Bureau's Philanthropic Advisory Service (PAS)—enforce performance standards for member nonprofits and communicate those standards to the public at large.

Based in New York City, the NCIB gauges the relative efficiency and trustworthiness of almost 370 major charities that operate throughout the United States, from CARE and the Salvation Army to the Billy Graham Evangelistic Association and the American Red Cross. Using a comprehensive rating system and a series of generally accepted operating ratios, the NCIB issues regular reports on the relative health of individual charities. For example, the NCIB standards hold that a national philanthropy should devote at least 60 percent of its gross revenues to the philanthropy's stated tax-exempt mission, leaving the remainder for fund-raising and administrative costs. The NCIB's comments and ratings are reported heavily in consumer media ranging from evening television news broadcasts to *Money* magazine.

As a unit of the Council of Better Business Bureaus, the PAS provides more hands-on assistance and advice directly to the chief staffers and volunteer leaders of nonprofit groups. At the same time, the agency issues alerts to the consumer media when a sufficient number of complaints have been posted against a particular tax-exempt organization. Like the NCIB, the PAS survives mainly from the dues paid by member nonprofits.

Despite the extensive records maintained by these watchdog agencies, however, critics charge that they do nothing more than sound the alarm after the fire has already claimed the house. "The two traditional independent watchdogs, the National Charities Information Bureau and the philanthropy division of the Better Business Bureau, rarely scrape underneath the gloss," says David Shenk, a reporter for the *Washington Monthly* who has written about nonprofit excesses in Washington, D.C. "Here, for example, was the official word from the Better Business Bureau in the wake of the United Way [of America] fiasco: 'In past years, the national office, United Way of America, has met our standards, based on the reviewed materials they provided.' That guard dog needs a set of dentures."

For many tax-exempt organizations, however, the buck of accountability for governing the structure and operations of the group rests finally with the board of directors. The articles of incorporation for a nonprofit generally prescribe the format and conduct of the board, from the qualifications of individual directors to the specific management tasks and powers given to the board directly. How many directors typically serve on the board of the average nonprofit? The answer varies depending on the style of the association: Is it driven largely by professional staff members or by the volunteer leaders and members themselves? "A comparison of the size of governing boards of trade and professional associations shows that the boards of volunteer-driven associations are, on average, 18 percent larger than those of staff-driven associations," observes association management consultant James Dunlop in *Leading the Association: Striking the Right Balance Between Staff and Volunteers*, a study conducted for the Foundation of the American Society of Association Executives. "The median size of boards in volunteer-driven associations is 18.25 members and in staff-driven associations 15.5 members. Larger boards in volunteer-driven associations may reflect emphasis on including as many elements of the membership as possible, whereas in a staff-driven association, the emphasis may be on greater efficiency. The same relationship holds for the boards of philanthropic associations. The median board size for a volunteer-driven association is 35.9 members and for a staff-driven association 31.4 members."

Regardless of their numbers and qualifications—in fact, seemingly in spite of these factors—nonprofit boards of directors today tend to be lax or downright negligent in exercising their oversight powers to keep their groups on track with their stated missions and inside the boundaries of the law. In a recent survey of local United Way affiliates, the Not For Profit Leadership Project at Baruch College in New York found that only a third of the nonprofit executive officers questioned believed that their board members fully understood the mission of their particular organization.

An in-depth examination of major nonprofit scandals like the case of United Way of America chief executive officer William Aramony yields an interesting portrait of the ways in which tax-exempt groups' boards of directors exercise their authority. Despite public statements by board members that Aramony had made "poor judgments" that damaged the reputation of the venerable charity, Aramony's excessive salary and perks had been reviewed and approved annually by the United Way of America board. His exorbitant travel and expense reports detailing overseas junkets were made available periodically to the board for review. The three allegedly illicit for-profit spin-offs that first broke the scandal in the public eye were created by the express approval of the board. Since the United Way of America board at the time included the chairman of IBM, the presidents of several unions, the commissioner of the National Football League, and the chief executive officers of Microsoft, Exxon, Johnson & Johnson, J. C. Penney, and Sears, it can hardly be argued that the directors lacked the management ability to rein in Aramony's errors in judgment.

Why do nonprofit boards sometimes fail to keep control of their groups? "The more successful a nonprofit organization is at raising money, the more corporate the board is going to act," contends Robert Bothwell, executive director of the National Committee for Responsive Philanthropy. "In other words, the more it's going to let the charity alone. The corporate model says that the board chooses the next executive and then steps back unless things aren't working out right." Even in cases of the most egregious abuses of power, however, some board members do not notice what is happening around them. A 1992 investigation by the *Washington Monthly* reviewed the records of the Community Foundation of Greater Washington, a nonprofit coalition that attracted support from dozens of Beltway power brokers. When staffers were accused of spending more than $250,000 on travel and meeting costs while the association's reserves were running dry and fund-raising was falling off, many board members confessed that they had no idea what was happening until reports of the profligate spending appeared in the local media, even though the foundation's annual tax returns clearly indicated the disproportionate expenses. "When you meet maybe twice a year, you don't do a lot of micromanagement," said board member Eleanor Holmes Norton, the nonvoting representative in Congress from the District of Columbia. Another board member, an executive at the Washington Post Co., claimed that he thought he had been taken off the board roster several months before the scandal broke.

Compounding the challenge of directing the affairs of a nonprofit organization for directors is that so many of them serve on a multitude of different nonprofit boards. While full-time jobs are generally limited to one per customer, business executives and politicians often view nonprofit board seats as positions of honor that can be accepted two or three at a time. When the United Way story surfaced, a scan of *Who's Who* for United Way of America board members revealed that Ralph Larsen, the CEO of Johnson & Johnson, sat on five other nonprofit boards. Monsanto's Earle Harbison Jr. served on six other boards; the National Association of Letter Carriers' Vincent Sombrotto, on 10 others; and The Limited's Leslie Wexner, on thirteen others. The logical question arises whether any executive responsible for the success of his or her own business can do more than scan the books briefly of several nonprofit groups with board meetings scheduled once a quarter or once a month apiece.

In light of the perceived gaps in oversight among members of nonprofit boards, what stance does the National Center for Nonprofit Boards—the professional society representing the interests of directors of tax-exempt organizations and dedicated to the mission of training directors to carry out their assigned responsibilities—take on the issue? "There is absolutely nothing wrong with the system as it stands," claims Maureen Robinson, the center's executive director. "Most board members provide excellent volunteer service—not perfect but pretty damned good." Robinson says the practice of serving on several nonprofit boards at once gives a volunteer new perspectives and ideas that in turn benefit each group. She describes the question of whether United Way of America board members unknowingly contributed to the charity's problems as a concern over "appearances," not an actual instance of managerial sloppiness on the part of board members.

To exert the proper influence on a nonprofit group's activities and strategic plans, organizational consultants recommend that the board of directors concentrate on ten key tasks:

1. *Hiring and firing the chief staff officer.* "This duty is clearly recognized as the most important job of any association board of directors," asserts David R. Bywaters, president of Lawrence-Leiter & Co. management consultants in Kansas City, Missouri. "Ultimately, the evaluation of the board, its overall reputation, probably rides on that one decision alone."

2. *Determining and setting broad policy for the nonprofit.* "This function is paramount," Bywaters says, "because the directors are the people charged with setting the overall strategic direction of the group. Once they've set the direction and tone, then it's up to the staff and the rank-and-file members to make those things happen." The greatest hazard to setting policy at the board level is that boards tend to use policy discussions as a means of micromanaging the nonprofit.

3. *Establishing the mission and strategy of the nonprofit.* "No other body can clearly articulate why the nonprofit exists and the purposes that it should fulfill to achieve its tax-exempt mission," Bywater notes. "Since the board approves the budget, it must also figure out how to pay for the mission and strategies."

4. *Establishing challenging performance criteria for staff.* Staff performance evaluations should be scheduled at least annually, and the members of the board should personally judge the work of the chief staff officer.

5. *Representing all members effectively and equitably.* "This task ensures that no one vested interest becomes too strong," advises Bywater. "Sometimes boards get into trouble if they believe that the profile they fit as individuals should be considered the pattern for the average member. An equally devastating tendency is for a board member to identify with a given constituency and try to vote the opinion of that constituency, even if it conflicts with his or her own good judgment. Directors represent all members, the entire association, and not simply one segment of it."

6. *Asking good, penetrating, and insightful questions.* Board members should use their meetings as opportunities to test the risks of potential actions, and they can ask the hard questions without seeming antagonistic.

7. *Representing the nonprofit to its members and constituents, not simply the other way around.* Board members are part of the nonprofit's public image. They are expected to represent the nonprofit to every group with whom they come into contact, including the members who pay dues and the constituents who receive the benefits of the nonprofit's services.

8. *Sharing knowledge and expertise with the rest of the board.* Board members should be selected for what they bring to the table in terms of direct experience or education. They may not know in the beginning how to run a nonprofit, but they should be expected to know a great deal about their own profession or industry and to apply that knowledge to the challenges facing the nonprofit.

9. *Monitoring the implementation of action items, the work plan, or the projects that match the nonprofit's strategic plan and mission.* Board members cannot be expected to monitor the day-to-day workings of a nonprofit group, but they should set in place reporting systems that keep them apprised of the progress of the day-to-day workload in moving the nonprofit toward its stated goals.

10. *Making sure that the fiscal integrity of the nonprofit is guarded and its assets protected.* For example, the auditing certified public accountant or firm that examines the nonprofit's financial records annually should report directly to the board rather than the chief staff officer. In addition, it is the board's ultimate responsibility to ensure that the nonprofit adheres to applicable laws and regulations governing the financial stability and health of the nonprofit.

Also, the board of directors must be viewed as the last word on ethical conduct within the nonprofit group. The examples set by board members should serve as models for the nonprofit's staff members and volunteers.

In the eyes of many brand-new nonprofit executives, altruism and fiscal health are not mutually exclusive. While recent financial scandals have pushed many nonprofits to strengthen their accounting safeguards, they have also fostered a growing sense of doing good for others among "social entrepreneurs"—business-oriented nonprofit managers who are mixing their moneymaking techniques with new ideas about helping others. After ten years as a manager at Polaroid and five years designing employee-training games for Fortune 500 companies, Joline Godfrey of Ojai, California, founded An Income of Her Own in 1992. Her program taps the skills and experiences of businesswomen in teaching teenage girls how to become entrepreneurs. Nearly half of the high school girls who have attended Godfrey's weeklong workshops in Palm Springs now run businesses of their own, and the group is lining up sponsors for its fourth annual Business Plan Competition for young women, with the help of teen magazines and women's business publications.

Robbie Pentecost, a nun who returned to St. Louis University in Missouri to pursue her master's degree in business administration, is seeking corporate financial support for community-based projects, such as her business plan for McMurphy's Grill, a restaurant run by Catholic charities that employs mentally ill homeless people and gives them on-the-job training. Named Humanitarian of the Year in 1991 by a national association of colleges, Michael Canul founded a program while he was still in college to help young Latino and African-American students prepare for university studies. The twenty-five-year-old Canul now owns a holding company with five partners, with the goal of buying small companies via leveraged acquisitions; he plans to take them public and use 20 percent of pretax profits to support a new foundation, called Fulfill the Dream, to invest money in nonprofit ventures. "If we're going to get serious about bringing more resources to our most pressing social problems, we have to go to the boldest terrain," says Canul of his groundbreaking strategy.

Whatever ideas might be involved in the operation of nonprofit groups, observers in the nonprofit sector offer several concrete suggestions to improve the health of tax-exempt groups and their boards. First, *nonprofits must identify and recruit the best candidates for board seats rather than focusing on social connections or perceived fund-raising ability.* "While CEOs and lawyers can bring in the bucks, the priority in a search should be the quality and commitment of the individual," says Pablo Eisenberg of the Center for Community Change. "You need good working people. Some can be prestigious, but the board is not there just for fund-raising." "If the board isn't diverse, giving won't be significant for underrepresented constituencies," adds Beth Daley, spokesperson for the National Committee for Responsive Philanthropy.

Second, *nonprofit board members should understand their roles and their commitments up front, before agreeing to serve.* Bylaws of the nonprofit should spell out the duties and responsibilities of board members as well as the rules regarding a director's serving on more than one nonprofit board simultaneously. Some tax-exempt groups create honorary categories so that people simply seeking name recognition can lend their support to the groups without committing their time and energy as directors.

Finally, *nonprofits should emphasize the legal liabilities facing members of the board of directors.* "Officers and directors of a nonprofit ordinarily serve voluntarily without pay. They accept the positions, whether received by election or appointment, because of their interest in the trade or values represented by the nonprofit and because they desire to see those goals enlightened and advanced," explains Jerald Jacobs, author of *Association Law Handbook* and an acknowledged legal expert on nonprofit issues. "Despite the generosity they display in accepting the positions and agreeing to serve, nonprofit officers and directors should understand that there is at least a possibility of personal liability stemming from their activities. The successful lawsuit invoking personal liability against nonprofit volunteers is rare, but the consequences are drastic enough that nonprofits should apprise them of the possibility and take steps to guard against it."

According to Jacobs, the basic rule of liability for nonprofits is the same as the rule applied to for-profit companies: As long as an officer or director exercises ordinary diligence and care, no personal liability will arise, even when actions or decisions made in poor judgment cause injury or damage. However, nonprofits bring added risks in the areas of antitrust concerns and activities that are beyond the nonprofit's appropriate sphere of authority. Many nonprofits purchase insurance to cover these risks for their directors and officers, "but it's a good tactic to make sure that new leaders know firsthand what they're getting into before they agree to serve a year or two or more on your board," Jacobs recommends.

In a 1991 speech at the Colorado Association of Nonprofit Organizations Ethics Conference, Colorado governor Richard Lamm outlined what he called "five additions to the Ten Commandments" for nonprofit groups to improve their self-regulation:

Addition 1: *Not only to thy institution, but to thy self be true.* It is clearly not enough to say that you work for a good cause and justify bad actions in the pursuit of a good cause [he told the crowd of nonprofit managers in Denver]. Much of the evil in this world is committed by people who are absolutely certain that they know what they are doing and that somehow it is "right" because it meets some larger purpose. Certitude can be very reinforcing, but it can also be very corrupting. People too often think that because they are doing the Lord's work the Lord will excuse the way in which it is accomplished. . . . Being nonprofit does not lower ethical standards; it raises them.

Addition 2: *Practice what you preach and make sure your organization does also.* Nonprofits set their own yardsticks. They are set up to do good and given a tax exemption because they perform some manner of good works. Not only are you judged by higher standards, but your organization is judged by higher standards. In any organization, high moral standards are the key to creating long-term legitimacy, but particularly in nonprofit organizations. Setting the examples which gain the confidence of the community and the endorsement of your followers is of more importance than in the profit sector.

Addition 3: *It is not enough to mean well; one must also do good.* It is often said that the hardest thing to change in public policy is a policy that was once successful but no longer meets its purpose. I think that clearly applies to non-profit organizations. . . . There are few nonprofit organizations that can assume that the "good" they performed in the 1960s continues to be relevant in the 1990s. . . . [T]here are a large number of us nationwide who are looking at the reasons why we give tax-exempt status to organizations. America is filled with nonprofit hospitals that give practically no charity. Certainly they give far less charity than their tax exemption is worth to them. As my colleague [Jeff O'Connell, a professor at the University of Virginia] says, "So here they are: charities which provided almost no charity receiving extravagant charitable and commercial support from others, with no or few strings attached earning huge sums with no liability for taxes, tort, labor laws, or social security and ignoring the most important, if less dramatic, tasks of health care."

Addition 4: *Beware of small-"c" corruption.* In my experience, individuals must worry most about large-"C" corruption. Whereas organizations must fear more subtle corruption, that of small-"c" corruption. Institutes don't have to worry about honoring their mother and their father or lusting for their neighbor's wife. They do have to worry about a more subtle form of corruption. . . . It is very easy to be corrupted by your source of money. It is very easy to be influenced by old friends and connections against your better judgment.

Addition 5: *The ultimate challenge of a nonprofit organization is to create a good society.* You ultimately cannot have a successful organization in a corrupt society. Nonprofits must not only work for successful specifics; they must work for a successful society.

# 13

## *Protecting Yourself*

IN 1994, U.S. NONPROFITS received more than $129 billion in charitable donations, up 3.6 percent from the previous year, according to the American Association of Fund-raising Counsel Trust for Philanthropy. Of that total, individual donors—people mailing in checks for $10, $25, $50, and $100 at a time—account for almost 81 percent.

When those generous donors write out their checks, says Irvin Alexander, director of the Philanthropic Advisory Service (PAS) of the Council of Better Business Bureaus in Arlington, Virginia, many of them make one serious mistake. "People who send money to any charity before they check out the group—its mission, its history, its spending habits—are putting the cart before the horse. They give, then they call us to check, when they should really call us first." The PAS logs calls from every corner of the United States each year complaining about nonprofit fund-raising practices and operations (the most common complaint: fund-raisers for local police and firefighter groups, especially campaigns in which donors are actually promised preferential treatment by these taxpayer-supported agencies if they give money).

Whether you simply write checks to your favorite charities at Christmas or serve as a volunteer or director for one or more nonprofit organizations, you must become more vigilant about protecting your rights and your assets from the threats of scams, legal liabilities, and sloppy management practices. The following recommendations will guide you in the proper direction:

ASSIGNMENT 1:   *Investigate the background and practices of the nonprofits you support.*

Several national watchdog groups—ranging from the PAS to the National Charities Information Bureau—devote their time and energy to tracking nonprofits, from reviewing their federal tax returns to compiling complaints from individual citizens and law-enforcement agencies around the United States. Your first step is tapping into the records of these groups to learn their impressions of a targeted nonprofit organization. The PAS and another watchdog group called the American Institute of Philanthropy (AIP) actually grade nonprofits based on their compliance with rigorous financial standards. For example, how much money does a nonprofit spend on programs to fulfill its tax-exempt mission, as opposed to general and administrative expenses? How much money goes to the actual fund-raising effort? (The St. Louis–based AIP requires charities to spend no more than \$35 of every \$100 raised on direct fund-raising costs, such as postage, telephone calls, and fund-raising consultants.) Does the nonprofit attempt to hide certain costs using joint allocations, such as a letter sent to potential donors that gives them facts about the nonprofit's mission and asks for money at the same time, with all of the expenses of the letter-writing campaign recorded on the books as "program costs" because the letter helps to raise public awareness of the nonprofit's tax-exempt mission? How much money does the nonprofit spend on administrative costs, such as the salaries of its key administrators (data that the PAS lists on its annual Charity Index)? Has the charity adopted a name similar to a better-known nonprofit, riding on the coattails of the other organization's reputation in order to enhance its own fund-raising efforts? (Philanthropies like the American Cancer Society have actually taken "competitors" with similar names to court to protect the goodwill generated by their names.) Many nonprofits cooperate with these watchdog agencies, even to the point of registering their fund-raising campaigns with the PAS's Solicitation Advisory Program, which sets standards for fund-raising, financial accountability, and other areas.

Depending on the level and type of information supplied to watchdog representatives, nonprofits sometimes receive widely varying grades from different agencies. The Greenpeace Fund, for example, does not currently meet the standards of the PAS, while the group earned an A– ranking from the AIP. In this instance, Greenpeace did not supply the PAS with enough financial data during the review process to earn a recommendation. The Christian Appalachian Project (CAP) in Lancaster, Kentucky, satisfied the PAS requirements but received a D from the AIP, which penalized the charity for spending a lower percentage of money on direct programs than recommended. The AIP sets its target for direct charitable spending at 60 percent of revenues (the national target for the PAS rankings is 50 percent), but the calculation does not include in-kind, noncash donations, explains CAP's director of national direct-response fund raising; if in-kind contributions had been included in the total, CAP would have been shown to spend 79 percent of donation on direct charitable projects instead of the range of 44 percent to 57 percent reported by the AIP. "We still focus on the monetary donations," replies Daniel Borochoff, the AIP's director. "If I give CAP $100, I want to know how that cash is spent."

To request the rankings for a particular nonprofit, consult these watchdog organizations:

Philanthropic Advisory Service
Council of Better Business Bureaus
4200 Wilson Blvd., Suite 800
Arlington, VA 22203-1804
tel.: (703) 276-0100

(*Annual Charity Index* for $14.95 plus $2 shipping, or the free annual holiday editions of *Give But Give Wisely*, a list of national charities that generate the most calls to the PAS)

American Institute of Philanthropy
4579 Laclede Ave., Suite 136
St. Louis, MO 63108

($3 for the AIP charities report)

National Charities Information Bureau
tel.: (800) 501-6242

ASSIGNMENT 2:    *Get proper tax records for your donations.*
You should always determine the exact federal tax classifi-
cation of a nonprofit organization you are supporting with monetary contributions or in-kind donations. "Tax exempt" does not
always means "tax-deductible"; "tax exempt" refers to the fact
that a nonprofit organization does not itself pay taxes, while
"tax deductible" means contributors can deduct donations on
federal (and many state) tax returns. The most common tax clas-
sification for nonprofits that accept tax-deductible donations is
the one describing private foundations: 501 (c)(3) (referring to
the applicable section of the U.S. Internal Revenue Code).
When you make a tax-deductible donation, you must ensure
that the nonprofit is following new tax rules on substantiating
donations. Many unsuspecting donors lose major gift deductions
because nonprofits do not comply with a provision of the 1993
federal tax act that makes canceled checks insufficient proof of
gifts to charity. Instead, taxpayers who donate $250 or more
must get written acknowledgments that report the gift's size, the
inclusion of noncash property in the gift, and the provision by
the nonprofit of any goods or services in return for the gift. In
the latter case, the nonprofit must describe the goods or services
and estimate their value, which is then subtracted from the
claimed deduction, for every donor who contributes more than
$75. Taxpayers must get the letters before the due date (includ-
ing extensions) for filing tax returns for the year in which the
gifts were made. "Don't wait until the IRS calls you or audits
you to go back to the charity and ask for your letter. It will be
too late," warns Laurence Foster, a partner with the accounting
firm KPMG Peat Marwick in New York. Based on concerns ex-

pressed by nonprofits that the new rules are difficult to administer, the Treasury Department relaxed several provisions. For example, contributors may generally ignore small gifts from nonprofits, such as coffee mugs or parking validations. In another example, a museum that awards gift-shop discounts to the employees of a corporate donor does not have to value the discounts in its tax-deductibility letter for the company. "These changes are major improvements for many nonprofits," says Peter Faber, a partner at the law firm McDermott, Will & Emery in New York. "They have been very concerned about how to comply with the new law."

One area in which nonprofits sometimes let the law slip is benefit dinners and galas. As stated, the IRS requires charities to provide a receipt for the value of a donation (e.g., tickets to a benefit dinner) when the donor is given something in return (e.g., the meal itself). A $250 dinner ticket may net the donor a $150 tax deduction, less the cost of the food and dinner favors. However, if the donor buys the ticket and then tells the charity to keep the ticket or sends it back before the event, the donor earns the $250 deduction. In some cases, businesses have skipped buying dinner tickets in lieu of ads in the dinner program or other types of direct expenses; by doing so, a corporate donor changes the purchase from a charitable deduction to an allowable business expense so that the full amount of the ad can be deducted. In 1996, for the first time, the federal-tax-return form for nonprofits (Form 990) asks nonprofits if they have complied with "quid pro quo" disclosure rules.

ASSIGNMENT 3: *Gauge the risks you assume when you volunteer for a nonprofit group.*

When you agree to work a shift at the fund-raising carnival for a local charity or take a seat on a statewide nonprofit's board of directors, you may not realize that you have left yourself open to legal liabilities on behalf of that tax-exempt group. "Association officers and directors, even though they serve voluntarily and without pay, may be exposed in some circumstances to personal criminal or civil liability for acts they perform on behalf of the association," reports attorney Jerald A. Jacobs in his book *Association Law Handbook*. "Ordinarily, an association officer or director who acts in good faith—using ordinary diligence and care—will not be found liable. Even incompetence or bad judgment will not generally be enough upon which to make a case for liability against an officer or director. Bad faith or fraud are tests for liability."

What types of nonprofit activities can lead to personal liability for a volunteer?

- Participation in acts that are beyond the nonprofit's corporate power and authority (or, in fact, the approval of such acts if the approval is given with full knowledge of the nature of the activity and of the fact that it lies outside the power and authority of the nonprofit)
- Activities which intentionally cause injury or damage to persons or property (called torts), even if the activities were carried on at the behest of the nonprofit (e.g., slander, negligence, interference with contract rights)
- Criminal activities of the association, such as violations of antitrust laws, where the volunteers participated in or knowingly approved the activities
- Failure to carry out the duties of a volunteer leader as described in the nonprofit's charter or articles of incorporation

Normally, liability does not result on the basis of torts committed by the employees or past leaders of a nonprofit (unless the volunteer knew about the activities) or the performance of contracts entered into by the nonprofit (unless fraud is involved).

Fortunately, you can take several steps to protect yourself against the possibility of claims for personal liability:

1. *Be a conscientious volunteer leader.* If you sit on a nonprofit's board or serve as an officer, attend all applicable nonprofit meetings and read the group's publications and correspondence carefully to remain up-to-date on the nonprofit's programs and policies.

2. *Read the fine print.* Take time to request copies of, and read cover to cover, the nonprofit's articles of incorporation,

bylaws, tax returns, financial statements, and other governing documents.

3. *Keep your own nose clean.* Disclose fully any potential conflicts affecting your volunteer service and avoid conflicts of interest in any dealings with the nonprofit (e.g., serving as a vendor or supplier to the nonprofit during your service on the board of directors).

4. *Read and approve meeting minutes.* If you offered comments or opposing ideas during an official meeting, make sure that the minutes of the meeting reflect those points clearly and attribute them to you by name.

5. *Ask for legal advice.* Request a lawyer's expert opinion (preferably, from the group's designated counsel) on any matter that has the potential to affect the operations or leadership of the nonprofit.

6. *Look carefully at the financial audits.* Make sure that the nonprofit is audited by independent, certified accountants annually and review the results cover to cover. Also, monitor more frequently issued financial reports (e.g., monthly income statements) to spot negative or questionable trends before they show up in the annual audit.

Many states have enacted laws allowing nonprofit corporations to indemnify their officers and directors against claims made against them, provided that the claims are based on the volunteers' activities on behalf of the nonprofit. Obvious exceptions to these laws include criminal complaints or accusations involving fraud or gross negligence. Check the specific laws in your state for the extent of the legal indemnification allowed and the procedure for claiming it. (In many cases, the nonprofit's board of directors simply adopts a resolution awarding indemnity to the volunteer leaders, or the motion is attached to the nonprofit's bylaws.)

Also, many jurisdictions permit nonprofits to purchase officer and director liability insurance to protect volunteer leaders in the event that they are required to pay claims or that the nonprofit must defend officers and directors who have been indemnified in the group's bylaws. You should review the policy personally, since many policies have detailed limitations and qualifications. They vary widely in terms, coverages, exclusions, conditions, definitions, deductibles, premiums, and endorsements.

Basic officer and director liability insurance covers errors and omissions by a nonprofit's volunteer leaders acting on behalf of the organization. The coverage provides payment for damages and costs of legal defense in claims against these individuals. Frequently excluded items include liability resulting from fraud or dishonesty, unjust enrichment, gross negligence, personal injury and property claims, fines imposed by law, claims based on activities which occurred before the insurance was purchased, and deductibles paid by the insured nonprofit organization. Some policies exclude coverage for antitrust claims, either entirely or when the antitrust liability exceeds a specified amount. Also, the policy may cover not only payment of claims in matters involving officers and directors but also those involving the nonprofit itself as a legal entity or the staff of the nonprofit (called an "association professional liability" policy). As you check the limits and qualifications of the coverage, you should also determine whether the policy requires an indemnification clause in the nonprofit's bylaws for volunteer officers and directors.

In February 1996 the House Judiciary Committee held hearings on nonprofit volunteer protection legislation that would encourage states to enact laws to provide protection from litigation to volunteers acting in good faith who donate their time to tax-exempt organizations. The National Coalition for Volunteer Protection, an issues coalition composed of leading national nonprofit organizations, drafted the federal bill. Testifying for the bill was a parade of nonprofit leaders, including John H. Graham IV, chief executive officer of the American Diabetes Association; Sister Christine Bowman, a spokeswoman for the Catholic Health Association; and Chris Franklin, vice president of the American Red Cross. Despite general agreement by members of the committee, the House has failed to act on the legislation in its current form.

ASSIGNMENT 4:  *Ask lots of questions.*

When a nonprofit organization approaches you in the future with a donation request or a volunteer assignment, consider this list of questions your starting point for finding out as much as possible about your potential commitment and liability:

### *Twenty-five Questions You Must Always Ask When You Deal With a Nonprofit Organization*

1. When was the group founded, and where is it currently headquartered or incorporated?
2. Has the group filed federal and state applications for tax-exempt status as well as any required articles of incorporation and bylaws? (Ask for copies.)
3. What is the group's tax-exempt mission, in plain English?
4. What are the group's primary nonprofit programs?
5. How does the group govern itself: a board of directors, committees, etc.?
6. How do members and constituents of the group provide input for its operations and long-term direction?
7. How many staff members work for the nonprofit (on a full-time or part-time basis)? How many reliable volunteers does the group count in its membership base?
8. What is the relationship between the group's officers and directors and its chief staff members?
9. Does the nonprofit have any parent organizations?
10. Who are the nonprofit's primary competitors (for-profit or nonprofit)?
11. What are the group's primary sources of funding?
12. If the nonprofit conducts direct fund-raising programs, who is responsible for carrying out these programs? What are the target audiences for the solicitations? What techniques are involved: direct mail, telemarketing, special events, etc.?
13. In the group's annual budget, what percentage of revenues goes toward fund-raising expenses? What percentage pays for general and administrative costs, including salaries and headquarters expenses?
14. What percentage goes directly toward the nonprofit's core charitable programs? What are the largest categories of expenses in this area?

15. Does the group arrange for an independent annual audit by a credible, certified accountant?

16. Has the group filed the proper federal, state, and local tax returns on a regular basis? Are the federal returns made easily available for public inspection, as required by law?

17. Does the nonprofit conduct unrelated business activities to raise funds? If so, has the group paid unrelated business income tax properly?

18. Has the group submitted the proper data to national nonprofit watchdog organizations, such as the Philanthropic Advisory Service of the Council of Better Business Bureaus, the National Charities Information Bureau, and the American Institute of Philanthropy?

19. Does the group receive government funds or grants? If so, what are these monies used for, and is there any possibility that the dollars are used in turn to lobby the federal government on behalf of the nonprofit's key issues?

20. Who is chiefly responsible for the group's lobbying campaigns, and what are its key issues?

21. What complaints have been lodged against the nonprofit within the last year by consumers, volunteers, government officials, or law-enforcement agencies? Has the group been sued within the last year, and if so, why?

22. Does the nonprofit have a policy on handling such complaints?

23. Does the nonprofit indemnify its officers, directors, and volunteers?

24. Does the group carry liability insurance to protect its officers, directors, and volunteers against claims?

25. What sort of resistance or reluctance do the nonprofit's staff members or volunteer leaders offer when answering questions 1–24?

Question 25 provides a litmus test for evaluating the overall level of comfort you may experience when working with a nonprofit organization. The adage "Where there's smoke, there's fire" applies especially well in this case. If you cannot get straightforward answers at the beginning of the relationship, you may find unpleasant surprises down the road when that good cause turns into a lost cause. Given current disturbing trends in America's nonprofit community, those lost causes spell growing concerns for the "do-good-until-it-hurts" spirit that sets the United States apart as the land of givers.

President Harry Truman never took full credit for his reputation as a man who did not shy from speaking his mind. "I never did give anybody hell," he said once. "I just told the truth, and they thought it was hell."

*For a Good Cause?* poses disturbing questions about the future of America's nonprofits—and if history proves prescient, those questions will likely fall on deaf ears. Federal, state, and local government may not be willing to tackle politically sensitive examinations of the role nonprofits play in our lives so that we can decide whose job it is to take care of many basic social, physical, and spiritual needs that are not being fully met today. Nonprofit leaders may argue that a closer look at how tax-exempt organizations operate will result in more burdensome regulations for the nonprofit community. Rank-and-file citizens may not think the issue is worth the bother.

However, like other great concerns facing our society—from immigration and Social Security to the whole arena of family values—the growing influence and pervasiveness of America's nonprofits cannot be ignored. Hundreds of thousands of dedicated volunteers and staffers do good for their fellow men through these groups, but their good deeds do not outshine the bare-faced need for review and reform.

"It takes two to speak the truth—one to speak and one to hear," Henry David Thoreau wrote. *For a Good Cause?* contains not answers but questions that America must resolve soon in order to preserve its nonprofit sector.

# Nonprofits: How Do They Rate?

This table shows whether national nonprofit organizations met Better Business Bureau (BBB) standards and provides the grade each organization received from the American Institute of Philanthropy (AIP) on a scale of A (excellent) to F (abysmal).

| National Nonprofit Organization | Met BBB Standards? | % Spent on Programs | AIP Grade |
|---|---|---|---|
| American Cancer Society | Yes | 75 | B + |
| American Civil Liberties Union | NA | 65–74 | B – |
| American Heart Association | Yes | 76–78 | B + |
| American Humane Association | No | 76 | A – |
| American Lung Association | Yes | 85 | A |
| American Red Cross | Yes | 93 | A + |
| Center for Science in the Public Interest | NA | 41–83 | D |
| Children's Defense Fund | NA | 82 | A |
| Christian Appalachian Project | Yes | 44–57 | D |
| Christian Children's Society | NA | 80 | A |
| Cousteau Society | NA | 82 | B + |
| Disabled American Veterans | Yes | 55–66 | C – |
| Goodwill Industries International | NA | 81 | A |
| Greenpeace Fund | No (1) | 86 | A – |
| Humane Society of the United States | Yes | 61–78 | C + |
| Just Say No International | NA | 21–67 | F |
| Mothers Against Drunk Driving | Yes | 48–76 | D |
| NAACP Legal Defense & Education Fund | NA | 76 | B + |
| National Abortion & Reproductive Rights Action League | NA | 40–60 | D |
| National Association of Chiefs of Police | NA (2) | 27–57 | F |
| National Association of Police Organizations | NA | 8 | F |
| National Audubon Association | Yes | 65 | C + |
| National Council on Crime and Delinquency | NA | 74 | B + |

| National Nonprofit Organization | Met BBB Standards? | % Spent on Programs | AIP Grade |
|---|---|---|---|
| National Law Enforcement Officers Memorial Fund | NA (3) | 65–72 | B − |
| National Organization for Women | NA | 62–69 | B − |
| National Right to Life Committee | NA | 44–53 | D |
| Nature Conservancy | Yes | 81 | A − |
| Planned Parenthood Federation of America | Yes | 72–76 | B + |
| Public Citizen | NA | 52–75 | D |
| Salvation Army | Yes | 86 | NA |
| Sierra Club Legal Defense Fund | Yes | 73–75 | B + |
| Southern Poverty Law Center | NA (4) | 40–66 | D |
| United Negro College Fund | Yes | 80 | A − |
| Vietnam Veterans of America Foundation | NA (5) | 82 | A |
| World Vision | NA | 65 | B |

**Notes:**

1. Inadequate financial data given to BBB
2. Did not supply data to BBB
3. Did not supply data to BBB
4. BBB review in progress
5. Did not supply data to BBB

# IRS Regional Centers

### New England/Mid-Atlantic States
Maine, New Hampshire, Vermont, Michigan, Massachusetts, Rhode Island, Connecticut, New York, and New Jersey

Internal Revenue Service
Brookhaven Service Center
P.O. Box 400
Holtsville, NY 11742

### Mid-Atlantic/Puerto Rico/International
Pennsylvania, Delaware, Maryland, District of Columbia, Puerto Rico, and International

Internal Revenue Service
Philadelphia Service Center
11511 Roosevelt Blvd.
Philadelphia, PA 19154

### Midwest
Ohio, West Virginia, Indiana, and Kentucky

Internal Revenue Service
Cincinnati Service Center
P.O. Box 145500
Cincinnati, OH 45214

### Midwest Plains
Missouri, Illinois, Iowa, Wisconsin, Minnesota, Montana, Nebraska, North Dakota, and South Dakota

Internal Revenue Service
Kansas City Service Center
P.O. Box 24551
Kansas City, MO 64131

**South**
Alabama, Arkansas, Florida, Georgia, Mississippi, North Carolina, South Carolina, Tennessee, and Louisiana

Internal Revenue Service
Atlanta Service Center
P.O. Box 47421
Atlanta, GA 30362

**Southwest/West**
Texas, Kansas, Oklahoma, Utah, Arizona, Wyoming, Colorado, and New Mexico

Internal Revenue Service
Austin Service Center
P.O. Box 934
Austin, TX 78767

**Far West/Alaska/Hawaii**
California, Hawaii, Alaska, Oregon, Washington, Idaho, and Nevada

Internal Revenue Service
Fresno Service Center
P.O. Box 12866
Fresno, CA 93779

# Internal Revenue Code Categories of Nonprofit Organizations

(The figures cited refer to specific sections of the U.S. Internal Revenue Code applying to distinct categories of nonprofit organizations, distinguished by the types of services offered or the constituencies served.)

| Section Number | Topic |
|---|---|
| 501 (c)(1) | Corporations organized under an act of Congress (U.S. instrumentalities) |
| 501 (c)(2) | Single-parent title-holding companies |
| 501 (c)(3) | Charitable, educational, literary, religious, and scientific organizations |
| 501 (c)(4) | Social-welfare organizations |
| 501 (c)(5) | Labor, agricultural, and horticultural organizations |
| 501 (c)(6) | Business leagues, boards of trade, trade associations, chambers of commerce, real estate boards |
| 501 (c)(7) | Social and recreational clubs |
| 501 (c)(8) | Fraternal beneficiary societies |
| 501 (c)(9) | Voluntary employees' beneficiary societies |
| 501 (c)(10) | Domestic fraternal beneficiary societies |
| 501 (c)(11) | Teachers' retirement funds |
| 501 (c)(12) | Benevolent life insurance associations; mutual cooperative telephone companies |
| 501 (c)(13) | Cemetery companies; burial associations |
| 501 (c)(14) | Credit unions |
| 501 (c)(15) | Mutual insurance companies |
| 501 (c)(16) | Corporations to finance crop operations |
| 501 (c)(17) | Supplemental unemployment benefit trusts |

| 501 (c)(18) | Employee-funded pension trusts |
| 501 (c)(19) | War veterans' organizations |
| 501 (c)(20) | Legal-services organizations |
| 501 (c)(21) | Black-lung benefit trusts |
| 501 (c)(22) | Multiemployer benefit trusts |
| 501 (c)(23) | Veterans associations (formed before 1880) |
| 501 (c)(24) | Employee benefit trusts |
| 501 (c)(25) | Multi-parent title-holding companies for pensions |
| 501 (d) | Religious and apostolic organizations |
| 501 (e) | Cooperative hospital service organizations |
| 501 (f) | Cooperative service organizations of operating educational organizations |
| 501 (j) | Amateur sports organizations |
| 501 (k) | Child-care organizations |

# Internal Revenue Code Sections Dealing With Nonprofits

In his seminal textbook *The Law of Tax-Exempt Organizations* (New York: John Wiley & Sons, 1991, 6th ed., cumulative supplement), noted nonprofits attorney Bruce Hopkins identifies the various provisions of the Internal Revenue Code which comprise the statutory framework for the field of tax-exempt organizations:

| Section Number | Topic |
| --- | --- |
| 41 | Tax credit for increasing scientific research activities |
| 74(b) | Rule concerning prizes and awards transferred to charitable organizations |
| 84 | Tax on appreciated property gifts to political organizations |
| 103 | Exclusion for interest on governmental obligations |
| 115 | Exclusion from gross income for revenues of political subdivisions and the like |
| 117 | Exclusion for qualified scholarships from gross income |
| 120 | Exclusion from gross income for value of repaid group legal services |
| 162 (e) | Denial of business expense deduction for expenses of most lobbying and political campaign activities, flow-through rule relating to dues; "anti-cascading rule" that operates to ensure that lobbying expense disallowance rule results in denial of deduction at only one level |

| | |
|---|---|
| 168 (h) | Tax-exempt entity leasing rules |
| 170 | Income tax deduction for charitable contributions |
| 170 (b)(1)(E)(ii) | Pass-through foundation rules |
| 170 (b)(1)(E)(iii) | Conduit foundation rules |
| 192 | Deduction for contributions to black lung benefit trusts |
| 274 (a)(3) | Denial of business expense deduction for payment of club dues |
| 277 | Treatment of deductions incurred by certain non-exempt membership organizations |
| 337 (b)(2) | Recognition of loss or gain for property distributed to tax-exempt parent in liquidation of subsidiary |
| 401 (a) | General rules for qualified pension, profit sharing, and like plans |
| 401 (k)(4)(B) | Prohibition on maintenance of 401 (k) plans by tax-exempt organizations |
| 403 (b) | Treatment of certain annuity contracts provided by charitable organizations to their employees |
| 457 | Deferred compensation plans of tax-exempt organizations |
| 501 (a) | Source of tax exemption for nearly all exempt organizations |
| 501 (b) | Tax-exempt organizations subject to tax on unrelated business income |
| 502 | Feeder organizations |
| 503 | Denial of tax exemption to certain organizations engaged in prohibited transactions |
| 504 | Rules as to status of non-exempt charity because of lobbying or political campaign activities |
| 505 | Additional requirements for certain employee benefit funds |
| 507 | Rules by which the private foundation status of charitable organizations is terminated |
| 508 | Special rules for charitable organizations, including notice requirements |
| 509 | Description of charitable organizations that are not private foundations |
| 509 (a)(1) | Rules as to certain charitable institutions and donative publicly supported charitable organizations |

| 509 (a)(2) | Rules as to service provider publicly supported charitable organizations |
| 509 (a)(3) | Rules as to supporting organizations |
| 509 (a)(4) | Rules for organizations that test for public safety |
| 511 | Imposition of tax on unrelated business income |
| 512 | Definition of unrelated business income |
| 512 (b) | Various modifications in computing unrelated business income |
| 512 (c) | Special unrelated business rules for partnerships |
| 513 | General unrelated business rules |
| 513 (c) | Definition of "trade or business" |
| 513 (d) | Trade show and like activities rules |
| 513 (e) | Rules as to certain hospital services |
| 513 (f) | Rules as to bingo games |
| 513 (g) | Rules as to certain pole rentals |
| 513 (h) | Rules as to rentals of lists and distribution of low-cost articles |
| 514 | Rules as to unrelated debt-financed income |
| 521 | Tax-exempt farmers' cooperatives |
| 526 | Tax-exempt shipowners' protection and indemnity associations |
| 527 | Tax-exempt political organizations and tax on political activities |
| 527 (f) | Tax on political expenditures |
| 528 | Tax-exempt homeowners' associations |
| 642 (c)(5) | Qualifying pooled income funds |
| 664 | Qualifying charitable remainder trusts |
| 2055 | Estate tax deduction for charitable contributions |
| 2501 (a)(5) | Gift tax exemption for transfers to political organizations |
| 2522 | Gift tax deduction for charitable contributions |
| 3121 | Employment tax definitions |
| 3306 (c) | Employment tax definitions |
| 4462 (h) | Exemptions from labor maintenance tax |
| 4911 | Excise tax on excess lobbying amounts by public charities under expenditure test |
| 4912 | Excise tax on excess lobbying amounts by public charities under substantial part test |
| 4940 | Excise tax on investment income of private foundations |
| 4940 (d)(1) | Exempt operation foundation rules |

| | |
|---|---|
| 4941 | Private foundation self-dealing rules |
| 4942 | Private foundation mandatory distribution rules |
| 4942 (j)(3) | Private operating foundation rules |
| 4943 | Private foundation excess business holding rules |
| 4944 | Private foundation rules concerning jeopardizing investments |
| 4945 | Private foundation rules concerning taxable expenditures |
| 4946 | Private foundation rules definitions |
| 4947 | Application of private foundation rules to certain non-exempt trusts |
| 4948 | Application of foundation rules to foreign organizations |
| 4951 | Taxes on self-dealing with black lung benefit trusts |
| 4952 | Taxes on taxable expenditures by black lung benefit trusts |
| 4953 | Taxes on excess contributions to black lung benefit trusts |
| 4955 | Taxes on certain political expenditures |
| 4961 | Abatement of private foundation additional taxes |
| 4962 | Abatement of public charity and private foundation initial taxes |
| 4976 | Taxes with respect to funded welfare benefit plans |
| 5276 (c) | Exemption from occupational tax for U.S. instrumentalities |
| 6012 | Requirement of income tax returns |
| 6031 | Requirement of partnership tax returns |
| 6033 | Requirement of filing of annual information returns |
| 6033 (e)(1)(A) | Dues nondeductibility disclosure rules for associations; imposition of proxy tax |
| 6072 (e) | Time for filing returns |
| 6104 | Required publicity of information from certain exempt organizations and trusts |
| 6110 | Rules as to public inspection of written determinations |
| 6113 | Disclosure as to nondeductibility of contributions |

| 6154 (h) | Estimated unrelated income and foundation investment income quarterly tax payments |
| 6501 (1) | Limitations on assessment or collections; special rule for Chapter 42 taxes |
| 6651 (a)(1) | Addition to tax for failure to timely file annual information return |
| 6652 (c)(1)(A),(B) | Penalties for failure to file annual information return |
| 6652 (c)(1)(C) | Penalties for failure to provide public access to annual information return |
| 6652 (c)(1)(D) | Penalties for failure to provide public access to application for recognition of exemption |
| 6655 (g)(3) | Penalties for failure by a tax-exempt organization to pay estimated unrelated business income taxes; penalties for failure by a private foundation to pay estimated net investment income taxes |
| 6684 | Penalties with respect to liability for Chapter 42 taxes |
| 6710 | Penalties for failure to disclose that contributions are nondeductible |
| 6711 | Penalties for failure to disclose that certain information or service is available from federal government |
| 6852 | Termination assessments for flagrant political expenditures by public charitable organizations |
| 6901 | Rules as to transferred assets |
| 7409 | Action to enjoin flagrant political expenditures by public charitable organizations |
| 7421 (a) | Prohibition of restraint on assessment or collection of taxes |
| 7428 | Declaratory judgment provision for charitable organizations |
| 7454 (b) | Burden of proof in foundation manager cases |
| 7611 | Church audit rules |
| 7802 (b)(1) | Authorization, within IRS, of an Assistant Commissioner (Employee Plans and Exempt Organizations) |
| 7871 | Rules as to Indian tribal governments |

# Tax-Exempt Status for Trade Associations

Given the generally accepted definitions of the terms "nonprofit" and "tax-exempt," nonprofit organizations are expected not to realize any excess receipts over expenditures and not to pay taxes. However, these generalizations are not entirely warranted.

This observation arises most clearly in the case of trade associations—nonprofits formed primarily to advance the interests of members engaged in a particular business or industry. Trade associations can ordinarily generate greater income than expenses at the end of a fiscal year and still remain nonprofit (the excess amount is more appropriately called "surplus" rather than "profit," but the financial effect is similar). The determination under state law of an association's *nonprofit* status focuses primarily upon the reasons for which it is organized and operated rather than the actual year-to-year financial condition of the nonprofit. Also, even though it may be tax-exempt, a trade association may occasionally be required to pay taxes. A determination by the Internal Revenue Service of a group's *tax-exempt* status generally permits the group to realize and accumulate income without paying federal income taxes. However, it may be subject to federal income taxes when it has realized income from activities not related to the purpose for which tax exemption was originally granted (called "unrelated business income"). Some local jurisdictions enforce tax laws that may require associations to pay local taxes on real estate or personal property, sales taxes on goods and services, and certain other miscellaneous taxes.

Generally speaking, the statutory and regulatory criteria for tax-exempt status awarded to trade associations have been listed by courts and commentators to include the following:

1. *The trade association must not be organized for profit.* For the most part, this condition applies more to the legal foundation of a

group rather than its day-to-day operations. It can usually be met by writing the association's incorporation papers according to the language found in a state's nonprofit corporation law so that the papers spell out clearly that the group is not being created to generate profits for its members or founders. Some groups fail this test because they do not ensure that this "nonprofit" language is used throughout their formal organization papers. For example, even though an association's mission statement in its articles of incorporation states that the group has been created to support the interests of florists, the group can run into trouble later if other portions of the articles include items such as "the association will be managed to generate maximum excess revenues to be used for other projects as deemed proper by the board of directors" that may lead to questions about the actual nonprofit-oriented operations of the group.

Keep in mind that the nonprofit incorporation under state law does not lead automatically to tax-exempt status under federal requirements. The U.S. tax code includes other criteria that must be met before any association can claim exemption from federal income taxes and other levies.

2. *No shareholder, founder, or other individual may benefit from the earnings of the association.* Known as "private inurement," this concept holds that no person involved in the creation or operations of a nonprofit may in turn reap rewards for what is supposed to be charitable behavior. The nonprofit cannot distribute its earnings or surplus revenues to individual members, cannot pay cash dividends, and cannot offer services to these people at less than the actual cost. The most dangerous practice is actual cash payments, since a number of cases demonstrate that even the smallest payments may result in challenges to the group's tax-exempt status. However, small instances of services, such as a trade association staffer giving advice to an association member, are generally not considered inurement.

What types of inurement have actually led to the loss of a nonprofit's tax exemption? Examples include the routine payment of legal fees for members, the distribution to members of shares of income received from copyrights owned by the association, the elimination of dues paid by members based on the profits earned by the association from commercial activities, and rebates of shares of net earnings paid by an association sponsoring a trade show to its members who exhibited at the show. Some associations attempt to bypass the inurement test by requiring in their bylaws that, if the group is dissolved, the remaining funds will be paid to a charity or other tax-exempt groups not directly related to its members.

3. *A membership-based trade association must generally be an association of people with common business interests.* This provision applies mostly to trade associations and business leagues, where the members engage in the same business or profession (e.g., the American Medical Association) or share common business interests (e.g., the local chamber of commerce or convention and visitors bureau). Federal courts and the IRS interpret this criterion very strictly. For example, pipefitters in a union have been judged to be members of a tax-exempt group, while dealers of a certain make of automobile have not been found to meet the "line of business" requirement.

4. *The nonprofit must have as its purpose the promotion of a common business interest of its members.* In its articles of incorporation, bylaws, and other governing documents, the nonprofit should ensure that its central mission is described in terms of the common interests of its members. This mission must be carried out in the day-to-day operations of the nonprofit; for example, a group formed to promote the business interests of printers cannot spend the majority of its budget and activities in social functions.

5. *The association's activities must be directed to the improvement of conditions in one or more lines of business.* What constitutes a "line of business"? Supreme Court rulings have drawn a line separating actual categories of business activity from simply the marketing of a certain brand or product line *within* an actual line of business. This criterion trips some associations with a fatal flaw: Promoting an entire line of business can mean making products and services available to members and nonmembers alike. For example, an association for travel agents cannot generally publish and sell research that is not available (at a cost or at no cost) to agents who do not belong to that organization. In many instances, the association can charge nonmembers more for the same products and services delivered to its members—as much as an entire year's worth of dues, in some cases, no matter the cost of the actual item in question.

6. *The association cannot engage regularly in a business or commercial activity that is ordinarily carried on for profit.* Called the "similarity to business" requirement, this provision does not carry the weight that seems obvious on its face. Many associations conduct activities that are on their surface commercial in nature, but these activities are designed to improve conditions for members within a line of business and, therefore, can be justified as proper activities for a trade association to conduct. Early Supreme Court rulings held that it is the *destination* of the extra income, not its source in a commercial activity, that affects a group's tax-exempt status. In other words, some lim-

ited business activities of a tax-exempt group would be allowed, as long as the activities are "incidental" to the main purpose for which tax exemption was granted. However, the group may be forced to pay unrelated business income tax on the earnings from those activities.

Trade associations should take care that they do not spend inordinate amounts of time and attention on such commercial enterprises. A famous case involving an association of barbers and beauticians resulted in the loss of tax exemption, when the court concluded that the association spent so much time selling insurance programs as a member benefit that it could not concentrate on its actual tax-exempt mission!

7. *The association's activities cannot be confined to the performance of certain services for individual members.* The IRS has defined the "particular services for individuals" prohibition to cover any activities that serve as a convenience or economy to members of an association rather than as a means of promoting or improving the overall industry represented by the association. For example, the IRS has denied tax exemption to proposed nonprofits organized to test products for hazards or to publish a used car guide, because the primary purpose of these groups was to provide certain services to key individuals. Associations must gauge their services in light of whether they could be considered simply a service for certain people rather than a means of improving the industry or line of business as a whole. The courts have generally not revoked tax exemptions on the basis of this rule unless the services in question have proved not to be merely minor or incidental.

8. *The trade association must be generally considered a "business league," in the same vein as a chamber of commerce.* Obviously, most trade associations exist primarily to promote their members' business and professional interests and, in the end, those of the entire industry or profession in question. Therefore, the IRS generally considers "trade association" and "business league" to be synonymous terms.

Given the sometimes complex, convoluted nature of these eight criteria for tax exemption, why do trade associations and other nonprofits work so hard to win exemptions?

- Tax exemption allows a group to receive dues and other types of related income without having to pay taxes on those funds. (In the case of unrelated business income, a tax-exempt group can avoid paying tax on the first $1,000 of that income—an advantage not enjoyed by non-exempt groups.)
- The federal tax exemption leads in almost all cases to similar exemptions from state and local levies such as sales and property taxes.

- Operating as a nonprofit can give the association additional clout when dealing with government officials, the media, and the general public.

While no one can claim to make completely accurate predictions as to whether a certain group will be judged worthy of tax exemption, the general rule of thumb follows: Is the group organized and operated not to make money but to advance the business interests of a trade or profession without giving significant services and benefits to individual members and without giving certain members a financial return? If the group can answer yes, then tax exemption is generally a foregone conclusion under current IRS practices.

# IRS Forms and Procedures

Amazingly, U.S. tax law does not actually require, in plain and simple language, that a nonprofit organization seeking federal tax exemption under Internal Revenue Code Section 501 (c) secure written confirmation from the IRS that it is indeed exempt from taxes.

Getting the exemption in writing from the IRS definitely helps, however. Groups seeking exemption as scientific, educational, or similar types of nonprofits file Form 1023, while trade associations and other business leagues use Form 1024. These forms must be sent to the IRS district office having jurisdiction over the state in which the nonprofit group will have its headquarters office. By filing in writing, the nonprofit gives the IRS adequate information to determine whether the exemption will be considered retroactive to the date on which the group was actually created (since IRS rulings can sometimes take months to process).

What if the IRS turns down a group's request for exemption? The nonprofit may protest the district office's decision with the IRS regional appeals office responsible for that district, via a written protest filed within thirty days from the date of the "determination letter" sent to the nonprofit by the district office. The next level of appeals is a "technical advice" procedure with the IRS national office in Washington, D.C. Once a nonprofit has exhausted these administrative avenues, it may sue the IRS in a federal district court (generally by filing a tax refund suit alleging that the refusal to award an exemption was incorrect) or file a petition in U.S. Tax Court claiming tax-exempt status. (Groups claiming exemption under I.R.C. Section 501 (c)(3) can sue for a declaratory judgment in the U.S. Tax Court.)

Until new "intermediate sanction" rules are approved by Congress, the IRS processes revocations of tax-exempt status in roughly the same manner as it issues adverse rulings on tax-exempt applications: by sending a "determination" letter to the nonprofit. The district offices generally announce revocations, and appeals may be made to the regional appeals office and the national office (as well as through the courts as described above).

Nonprofits that are declared exempt from federal taxes must file annual informational returns, unless they do not have gross receipts exceeding $25,000 in each taxable year. Tax-exempt groups file Form 990 as the current version of this return. (An abbreviated form is available for the smallest nonprofits to complete.) Even those groups that have not yet received an official exemption letter from the IRS should file Form 990 if they are already operating as a tax-exempt group (noting on the return that the exemption request is pending), because the filing will protect them from possible penalties and interest for failing to file the return once the exemption is approved.

Exempt organizations that earn unrelated business income exceeding $1,000 in a taxable year must file Form 990-T in addition to the annual informational return. If the group has undergone a dissolution, termination, or other major disposition of its assets, it should file Form 966-E, due within thirty days after the group's board of directors has adopted a resolution approving the change in assets.

Failing to file these returns on time can result in stiff penalties, ranging from $10 per day of delinquency to a maximum penalty of $5,000.

# Notes

## Introduction

Locating and vetting reputable sources of historical data about the rise of nonprofit organizations in the United States proved more challenging than one might think. The background sections contained within *Giving in America—Toward a Stronger Voluntary Sector*, the final report issued by the 1973 Commission on Private Philanthropy and Public Needs, became my starting point. Backgrounders supplied by the public relations department at the American Society of Association Executives (ASAE), the "associations' association" in Washington, D.C., rounded out my basic understanding of the philosophical underpinnings of America's nonprofit sector.

The examples of nonprofit groups that affect the daily life of an average citizen grew from profiles listed in *Associations: A Family Portrait*, a promotional brochure published by the ASAE as part of its "Associations Advance America" campaign.

I compiled the statistical portrait of nonprofits from various sources, including the Internal Revenue Service, current editions of *Statistical Abstract of the United States*, and the Independent Sector (a roundtable of major national charities and nonprofits based in Washington, D.C.).

The most egregious examples of "commercialized" nonprofits—tax-exempt groups that one might never identify as such, based on their outward appearance and action as capitalistic businesses—came to light as a result of exhaustive and daring investigations undertaken by noted reporters Gilbert Gaul and Neill Borowski at the *Philadelphia Inquirer*. These hard-nosed business journalists spent the greater part of two years poring over tax returns for more than fifteen hundred different nonprofit groups, distilling their findings into a series of front-page articles for their newspaper. (The articles were later collected and published as *A Free Ride: The Tax-Exempt Economy* [Andrews &

McMeel, 1993].) The *New York Post* followed with a three-part series in September 1995 on nonprofit groups and their excesses and abuses.

### Chapter 1   Charity, American Style

One of the most comprehensive yet lucid histories of the development of America's nonprofit sector can be found in Eleanor Brilliant's book *The United Way: Dilemmas of Organized Charity*. An associate professor of sociology at Rutgers University, Brilliant devotes the bulk of her book to an examination of the degrees to which the organizational structures and day-to-day business practices of United Way of America contributed in large part to the recent financial debacle involving William Aramony, United Way's president. However, she also documents the social forces that turned the United States from a nation where most good deeds were performed by local volunteers and churches into a nation ringed with hundreds of thousands of organized nonprofits.

Alexis de Tocqueville, the French nobleman who documented his impressions of nineteenth-century America during a string of visits, recorded several notes about the American propensity to band together into associations in his journal *Democracy in America*.

For the legal and historical setting in which U.S. nonprofit law grew, I turned to Bruce R. Hopkins, one of the nation's foremost experts on tax-exempt statutes and regulations. Besides his regular articles in tax law journals and magazines, I relied primarily on *The Law of Tax-Exempt Organizations* (John Wiley & Sons, 1992) and subsequent updates for both the historical patterns of nonprofit law (from the rise of specific tax exemptions for certain organizations in the Sixteenth Amendment to the U.S. Constitution and the Revenue Act of 1913 to the current application of unrelated business income tax regulations) and the political and social contexts in which these rules arose.

Besides his insider's view of the United Way scandal, former United Way of America executive John Glaser provided a succinct overview of the current state of nonprofit work in the United States in his book *The United Way Scandal: An Insider's Account of What Went Wrong and Why* (John Wiley & Sons, 1994).

### Chapter 2   The Nonprofits Explosion

Burton Weisbrod, a professor of economics at the University of Wisconsin, presented one of the first comprehensive examinations of nonprofit organizations and their financial conditions in his book *The Nonprofit Economy* (Columbia University Press, 1990). Additional insights on the economic strength and variety of nonprofits came from *Free Ride* by Gilbert Gaul and Neill Borowski and reports prepared by the American Society of Association Executives and Independent Sector.

Specific details about the inner workings and commercial activities of the American Association of Retired Persons were gleaned from Charles Morris's excellent *The AARP and You* (Times Books, 1996).

The American Association of Fund-Raising Counsel (AAFRC) studies the collective giving of businesses, foundations, and individuals for charitable purposes each year and publishes the results as *Giving USA 1996*. Besides ample statistical data to document the relative health of various niches of the nonprofit community, this index includes detailed background material on the suspected causes for changes in U.S. giving patterns from the previous year. Survey results provided by empty tomb, a religious research organization in Champaign, Illinois, that tracks charitable and benevolent contributions in twenty-nine Protestant denominations around the country, proved helpful in explaining trends in religious donations.

To explain widely held misconceptions in giving patterns for America's richest households, I turned to *Why the Wealthy Give: The Culture of Elite Philanthropy* (Princeton University Press, 1996) by Francie Ostrower, a sociologist at Harvard University.

Explaining the impact of the 1996 federal welfare reform acts required a study of commentaries produced by several noted nonprofit experts, including Rev. Stephen E. Burger, executive director of the International Union of Gospel Missions, and Kimberly Dennis, executive director of the Philanthropy Roundtable. Both commentaries in question were published in *Policy Review: The Journal of American Citizenship* by the Heritage Foundation.

To illustrate the contention that not every segment of America's nonprofit community has been hit by the downward trend in giving, I employed data from the latest annual membership survey of the Association for Healthcare Philanthropy, the Falls Church, Virginia–based alliance of nonprofit hospitals and health-care institutions.

Unearthing concrete examples of the rampant commercialism infecting nonprofit organizations today proved in some cases a simple task, as the Small Business Administration and the Business Coalition for Fair Competition (an advocacy group in Arlington, Va.) were eager to supply me with transcripts from congressional hearings on the subject dating throughout the 1990s. In other instances, confirming examples of unfair competition required examination of the federal tax returns of targeted nonprofits. Other sources included "War Among the Nonprofits" (*Financial World*, September 1, 1994) and "Healing for Dollars" (*Lexington [Ky.] Herald-Leader*, July 7, 1996).

The Congressional Research Service shared statistics relative to the construction of public sports stadiums and arenas in the United States with tax-exempt financing instruments.

## Chapter 3   What Do a Thousand Points of Light Really Cost?

To decipher current thinking in the nonprofit community on the politics and philosophy of the concept of philanthrophy—what President George Bush called "a thousand points of light" in the United States—I turned to noted management consultant and educator Peter Drucker, whose book *Managing the Nonprofit Organization: Principles and Practices* is still considered the basic text outlining management practices among tax-exempt groups. Drucker values the contributions of nonprofits to life in the United States very highly; he describes them, in fact, as "central to the quality of life in America, central to citizenship, and indeed carr[ying] the values of American society and of the American tradition."

The public affairs office of the Internal Revenue Service (IRS) supplied the statistical analysis of the impact of tax exemptions on the national economy, while a *Prime Time Live* (ABC-TV) investigative report (April 10, 1960) and "War Among the Nonprofits" in *Financial World* magazine (September 1, 1994) provided examples of the fiscal largesse evident in some juggernaut nonprofits like the Bishop Estate in Hawaii. The IRS also pointed me to several relevant congressional hearings on tax exemptions, including a 1991 House Ways & Means Committee session in which an IRS commissioner estimated that only one of the nation's 3,200 nonprofit hospitals has lost its exemption within the past twenty years.

*The Complete Guide to Nonprofit Corporations* by attorney Ted Nicholas guided me to a better understanding of the statutory and regulatory requirements affecting the operations of the average tax-exempt organization.

John Patrick Michael Murphy and the Freedom From Religion Foundation in Colorado, as well as the Colorado Association of Nonprofit Organizations, gave me the background on Colorado's proposed constitutional amendment that would allow the state to tax property owned by churches and other nonprofits.

As I tried to map the maze of issues surrounding the question of tax-exempt financing for public stadiums and arenas, aides in the

Washington office of Sen. Byron Dorgan (D-N.D.) gave me information about the senator's outspoken opposition to the practice, including a Congressional Research Service study on the subject requested by
Dorgan. Erik Brady and Debbie Howlett of *USA Today* discussed the
exhaustive results of their three-month look in 1996 at sports facilities
across the United States financed in part or in whole by tax-exempt
bonds and public financing instruments.

The murky subject of nonprofit postal subsidies and mail classifications became clearer under the tutelage of Lee Cassidy, executive director of the National Federation of Nonprofits, and the reporting of
*Association Trends* magazine on the 1996 U.S. Postal Service plan to
reclassify nonprofit mail categories. The Council of State Governments
provided an explanation of state statutes that effectively exempt nonprofits from union collective-bargaining rules.

### Chapter 4   What Do You Think We Are— A Charity?

The Foundation Center, a national organization that studies and
tracks private foundations, gave me a clear picture of the operations
and legal structures of these nonprofit groups that manage endowments
and trusts to fund programs deemed in the public interest. Transcripts
of congressional hearings delving into the administrative costs of foundations threw further light on the subject, particularly a 1972 review
by the House Banking Committee.

*Time* carried an article in its March 29, 1993, issue about alleged
excesses in overhead expenses at the Freedom Forum, the Arlington,
Virginia–based nonprofit foundation run by former *USA Today* publisher Allen Neuharth.

Rev. Pat Robertson's launching and continuing control of the
Christian Broadcasting Network and the Family Channel have been
documented extensively in several investigative articles, including "The
Man Who Would Be King" (*Out*, March 1996). *Advertising Age* supplemented these pieces with ongoing coverage of the Family Channel's
programming and its potential sale.

Public-relations managers at the American Hospital Association
submitted materials on the subject of nonprofit hospitals, and the law-
review writings of Henry Hansmann, a Yale University economist and
attorney, outlined the case for removing tax exemptions from hospitals
altogether. The transcript of a 1991 House Ways & Means Committee
hearing on the "community benefit" standard for tax-exempt hospitals
proved helpful.

The eighteen-month investigation of U.S. nonprofit hospitals by Gilbert Gaul and Neill Borowski of the *Philadelphia Inquirer* unearthed concrete examples of the fiscal excesses of tax-exempt health-care facilities, and the pair's reporting led me in turn to key court decisions, such as Judge George Levin's written opinion in a tax case involving Hamot Medical Center in Erie County, Pennsylvania.

Knowing that someone must have written a guide to help eager nonprofits explore their commercial potential, I continued to search libraries and databases until I found *Filthy Rich & Other Nonprofit Fantasies* by Dr. Richard Steckel, who, having dubbed himself an "enterprise coach," teaches tax-exempt groups how to raise funds by starting business sidelines and moneymaking activities. For example, he encourages hospitals—never known as the nonprofits responsible for gourmet cuisine—to launch catering services from their cafeterias.

### Chapter 5   Over-the-Top Overhead

Few of the nonprofit organizations that I contacted while researching the book wanted to answer my questions about the salaries, bonuses, retirement plans, and perquisites given to their chief staff officers or other senior managers. To secure the actual amounts involved, I turned to the next best source: the annual Form 990 federal information returns required for every nonprofit group earning at least $25,000 in revenues and available for public inspection at each nonprofit's headquarters or through district offices of the Internal Revenue Service.

To gauge the overall condition of nonprofit executives' pay relative to their counterparts in corporate America, I secured the latest installments of ongoing salary surveys conducted by several national consulting firms and publications, including a 1996 survey of 184 nonprofits by the trade bible *Chronicle of Philanthropy* and the 1996 Cordom Salary Survey of Nonprofits produced by Cordom Associates. Additional comparative details came from the National Charities Information Bureau, the National Committee for Responsive Philanthropy, the Council on Foundations, Hay Associates, the *Philadelphia Inquirer*, and the book *Unhealthy Charities: Hazardous to Your Health and Wealth* by James T. Bennett and Thomas J. DiLorenzo.

Similarly, descriptions of the pay and benefits given to members of nonprofit boards of directors were compared to the average compensation for outside directors of industrial corporations compiled by Hewitt Associates. Data on deferred-compensation practices among nonprofit managers were gathered from surveys completed by Hay Associates,

Towers Perrin, and William M. Mercer Inc., as well as the government-affairs section of the American Society of Association Executives.

I relied heavily on "To the Rationalizers Go the Spoils" by Holman W. Jenkins J. (*Wall Street Journal*, July 30, 1996) to explore the $17 million payout to various executives at Blue Cross & Blue Shield of Ohio, in the wake of the nonprofit health-care organization's impending sale to Columbia/HCA.

"Old Money" by Christopher Georges (*Washington Monthly*, June 1992) and *The AARP and You* by Charles R. Morris (Times Books, 1996) described in great detail the conditions under which the American Association of Retired Persons spent as much in recent years to furnish its offices as it did on programs to help the elderly. The expensive relocation of the Freedom Forum was chronicled in a *Time* article on March 29, 1993. A three-part series in the *New York Post* in September 1995 by Jonathan Karl and Alex Monsky uncovered other examples of the tremendous overhead expenses incurred by national nonprofit organizations.

Showing that even America's churches struggle with the temptations of mammon in the form of excessive salaries, perks, and overhead demands, I included the story of the divisive court battle pitting the former chief executive officer of the Evangelical Lutheran Church in America's publishing house against the firm's board of directors, described in "Augsburg Fortress, Aamodt Sue Each Other" by Edgar R. Trexler (*The Lutheran*, September 1996).

### Chapter 6   Robbing Peter to Pay the Fund-Raisers

While public-relations professionals and senior managers at the New York headquarters of the Girl Scouts of the U.S.A. were understandably reluctant to offer much in the way of additional comment on the almost apocryphal stories of young Girl Scouts selling cookies and making little money, I began my research on this chapter by referring to two outstanding reports in the *Wall Street Journal*: "Thin Rewards: Sprawling Bureaucracy Eats Up Most Profits of Girl Scout Cookies" (May 13, 1993) and "Cookie Price War Sends Adult Troops Into Marketing Battle" (March 8, 1996). Beth Denton's struggles against the national hierarchy of the Girl Scouts was documented in the transcript of the January 27, 1994, edition of *Eye to Eye With Connie Chung*.

Additional examples of problematic fund-raising by nonprofits came from "Cancerous Growth" (*Financial World*, September 1, 1994) and "Other People's Money" (*Newsweek*, March 16, 1992), as well as from discussions with officials at the National Charities Information Bureau.

Offering discursive explanations of the roles played by professional fund-raisers and fund-raising companies in the nonprofit community today were Russell Lemieux, executive director of the American Association of Fund-Raisers and Direct Sellers, and Patricia Lewis, president of the National Society of Fund-Raising Executives.

The Direct Marketing Association completed an exhaustive study of donor attitudes and behaviors among generation groups, with the assistance of the Russ Reid Company, a national fund-raising agency.

Regarding the legal rules governing fund-raising activities, the American Institute of Certified Public Accountants, the Direct Marketing Association, and the Federal Trade Commission provided voluminous packets of background materials describing the strictures that supposedly keep professional dunners in check.

Two articles that pointed me in the proper direction on specific fund-raising points were "For Charity Groups, 'Tis a Prime Season for Sending Lots of Direct-Mail Appeals" (*Wall Street Journal*, December 23, 1993, holiday charity solicitations) and "A Higher Power of Fund-Raising" (*Lexington [Ky.] Herald-Leader*, March 9, 1996, church fund-raising drives).

### Chapter 7  Donations Gone Astray

Though the major national media covered the saga of United Way of America president William Aramony and his fraud trial to an ad nauseam level, I found the most balanced, in-depth reporting in the trade magazines devoted to nonprofit organizations, particularly *Association Trends, USAE, Association Management,* and *Chronicle of Philanthropy*. Also, two books followed the crisis with detailed analyses of the causes and effects of the United Way case: *The United Way Scandal: An Insider's Account of What Went Wrong and Why* (John Wiley & Sons, 1994) and *The United Way: Dilemmas of Organized Charity* (Columbia University Press, 1993). Nationally syndicated columnist Jack Anderson's column in February 1992 titled "Charity Begins at Home for United Way" broke the scandal initially and provided me a good starting point for my research.

Many of the other examples of nonprofit chicanery found in chapter 8 were unearthed at first in back issues of *Association Trends* and *USAE*, such as "Convicted Assn Executive Still Involved in Controversial Activities" (*USAE*, March 14, 1995); "Wilhoit gets 5 yrs in prison; to pay $960K restitution" (*Association Trends*, September 8, 1995). *Fortune* reporter David Stipp revealed in "I Stole to Get Even: Yet Another Charity Scam" (October 30, 1995) that American Parkinson's

Disease Association executive director Frank Williams had embezzled about $80,000 a year for ten years. Ellen F. Cooke's arrest and trial were covered in various issues of *The Lutheran*, including the September 1996 issue.

Michael Gartner's incisive commentary on United Way of America president Elaine Chao's eventual decision not to accept a $292,500 "payment" upon resigning her post in the summer of 1996 appeared in *USA Today* ("Aborted United Way Deal Failed Smell Test," June 4, 1996).

### Chapter 8    Crossing Into Profitable Territory

Bill Shore's commentary on the "entrepreneurial bankruptcy" of nonprofit groups in the United States appeared in *USA Today* ("Charities Change Roles By Turning a Profit," March 26, 1996).

Many examples of unfair competition highlighted in chapter 8 were identified to some extent by discussions and readings orchestrated by the Business Coalition for Fair Competition, an Arlington, Virginia–based advocacy group of small-business trade associations, and its executive director, Kenton Pattie. Other organizations that helped to give me a balanced view of the issue included the National Tour Association (Jim Santini), the National Child Care Association, the Association for Quality Clubs, the International Health, Racquet, & Sportsclub Association, the Textile Rental Services Association, the 1995 White House Conference on Small Business, the American Society of Association Executives, and the Greater Washington Society of Association Executives. Staffers in the offices of Rep. Jan Meyers (R-Kans.), chairman of the House Small Business Committee, helped me to locate critical hearing transcripts.

Steven D. Simpson's comments regarding the "myth" of unfair competition and the history of the unrelated business income tax appeared in his monograph *Income-Producing Activities of Tax-Exempt Organizations: The Myth of Unfair Competition*. Another monograph that proved helpful was *Profit Through Non-profits: Creating Strategic Alliances With Non-profits*, written by Alan Andreasen of Georgetown University and nine colleagues from marketing consultancies, the Arthritis Foundation, and the American Cancer Society. Additional data on the legal nature of the tax and its application under current laws were found in *Law of Associations* by George D. Webster and *The Law of Tax-Exempt Organizations* by Bruce R. Hopkins.

The Philanthropic Advisory Service of the Council of Better Business Bureaus gave me detailed background on the ways in which major charities are rated by national watchdog agencies relative to their commercial activities and subsidiaries.

"Profits at the Altar" (*Fortune*, September 9, 1996) provided the bulk of the details about the launch of Revelation Corp. of America. A two-part series in the *Boston Globe*, on April 2–3, 1995, by James L. Franklin, Meg Vaillancourt, and Patricia Wen alerted me to questions about the enormous insurance interests of the Knights of Columbus and pointed me in the right directions for further investigation.

In no particular order, the following articles piqued my attention to the point that these examples of unfair competition merited further study: "More Small Firms Complain About Tax-Exempt Rivals" (*Wall Street Journal*, August 8, 1995); "Church-Run Tours Collide With Travel Agents" (*Wall Street Journal*, March 4, 1996); "Nonprofit Group's Name to Go on For-Profit Pills" (*Wall Street Journal*, July 13, 1994); "National Geographic Society Pact" (*Wall Street Journal*, June 21, 1993); "As Nonprofits Add Sidelines, IRS Takes Aim" (*Wall Street Journal*, May 3, 1996); "How the YMCA Got So Healthy" (*New York Post*, September 6, 1995); "Cancer Group Endorses 2 Products" (Associated Press, August 17, 1996); "Non-Profit Health Groups' Corporate Ties Alarm Some" (Knight-Ridder News Service, December 4, 1994); "AARP Will License Name to HMOs" (New York Times News Service, April 29, 1996); "Uncle Sam Wants Nonprofit Profits" (*Fortune*, November 14, 1994); "Nonprofit Groups Targeted by SBA" (*Travel Weekly*, August 1, 1996); "IRS Keeps Critical Eye on Educational Travel" (*Tax Notes*, April 6, 1992); "Increasing Assn Revenues Can Be IRStressful" (*Association Trends*, March 15, 1996); "What Constitutes Unrelated Business Income?" (*Association Management*, March 1995); and "Priest's Company Triples Revenues" (*Belleville [Ill.] News-Democrat*, May 9, 1993).

I tracked down bankruptcy records open to the public through the offices of the U.S. Bankruptcy Court for the district of Kansas to research the financial underpinnings of the RFD Travel Corp. bankruptcy that left the American Association of Retired Persons holding the bag for more than $15 million in 1995.

### Chapter 9    Too Much Time in Gucci Gulch

To substantiate my initial impressions of the lobbying clout of major U.S. nonprofits on Capitol Hill, I relied on the results of an Associated Press study of the first six months of 1996 that delved into the Federal Election Commission reports filed by nonprofits (as well as for-profit corporations and individuals) that dedicate funds and people to lobbying the federal government on various issues.

Also, these "roundup" articles describing the amounts of money being spent by nonprofits to influence government actions, especially while some of them were accepting federal grants at the same time, pointed me in the correct direction for further investigation: "Spending Bill Deadlocks Over GOP Proposal to Restrict Nonprofits," *Washington Post*, Sept. 14, 1995; "Gov't Grant$ Galore for Lobbying Groups," *New York Post*, Sept. 7, 1995; and "There's No 'Gag Rule' on Nonprofits," *Washington Post*, Sept. 1, 1995.

In addition to responses and materials provided by the Federal Election Commission (FEC) and Christian Coalition representatives, the following articles and editorial commentaries supplied background details on the Christian Coalition's recent struggles against an FEC lawsuit and allegations that the coalition violated its tax-exempt mission by supporting Republican candidates: "Contributions to Christian Coalition Dip," *Lexington* [Ky.] *Herald-Leader/Associated Press*, Sept. 13, 1996; "The Clue in the Letter," *Newsweek*, Aug. 12, 1996; "Lawsuit singles out Christian Coalition," Los Angeles Times Syndicate [Cal Thomas], Aug. 4, 1996; "Religious Organization Fails the Duck Test," New York Times News Service [John Young], Aug. 4, 1996; "Christian Coalition Accepted $60,000 from Bush supporter," *Washington Post*, Aug. 3, 1996; "Christian Coalition Sued for Vote Efforts" and "Suit Puts Group's Tax Status at Risk," *USA Today*, July 31, 1996; and "Christian Coalition: Tax-free Conservative Political Machine or Religious Advocate?" *Lexington Herald-Leader/Associated Press*, July 8, 1996.

The National Rifle Association's downsizing efforts and the ongoing success of its federal and state lobbying machine have been well documented through the years. Two articles that assisted me in formulating questions for NRA spokespeople were "NRA Must Decide Whether to Refocus Its Aim As Its Membership Shrinks to Smaller Caliber," *Wall Street Journal*, April 12, 1996, and "NRA Says IRS Is Reviewing Its Tax Status," *Boston Globe*, June 3, 1996. Kimberly Dennis, executive director of the Philanthropy Roundtable, contributed commentary on the topic as well to *Public Review: The Journal of American Citizenship*, published by the Heritage Foundation.

Sen. John McCain (R-Ariz.) presented his opinions about the Washington strong-arm tactics of the American Association of Retired Persons during hearings held by the Senate Subcommittee on Social Security and Family Policy on June 20, 1995 (transcript provided by Federal News Service). Helpful articles describing AARP's lobbying record included "Buying Off the Elderly," *Newsweek*, Oct. 2, 1995; "AARP's Non-Profit Status Focus on Senate Hearings," *Lexington Herald-Leader/Associated Press*, June 14, 1995; "Simpson Prods Congress to Stand Up to AARP," *USA Today* [Linda Chavez commentary], June 28, 1995; "Grappling with AARP," *Providence* [R.I.] *Journal*, June 26, 1995; "Senator blasts AARP's profit-making, calls group 'vast business empire'," *Lexington Herald-Leader/Knight-Ridder Washington Bureau*, June 21, 1995; "Financial Dealings Spur Probe of AARP Empire," *USA Today*, June 13, 1995; and "GOP at Odds With AARP," *USA Today*, May 4, 1995.

*Wall Street Journal* staff reporters Laurie P. Cohen and Milo Geyelin provided the most comprehensive picture of the resumption of a criminal investigation of the industry-funded Council for Tobacco Research in "Probe Reopens Into Nonprofit Tobacco Group," Feb. 8, 1996.

These articles gave me the primary details regarding major instances of alleged nonprofit lobbying violations or ethical questions: "Gingrich College Course Under Review by IRS," *USA Today*, Sept. 5, 1996; "Dole Brought Husband's Contributors to Red Cross," *Washington Post*, May 1, 1996; and "The Man Who Would Be King," *Out*, March 1996 [Rev. Pat Robertson].

Finally, editors and reporters at two major nonprofit trade publications—*Association Trends* and *Association Management*—gave me background information and referrals to track recent developments in nonprofit lobbying regulations and practices. To flesh out those leads, I relied upon information gleaned from these stories: "An IRS Memo Underscores the Need for Charities to Stay Far Away From Politics," *Wall Street Journal*, July 31, 1996; "Grassroots Lobbying: Now's the Time," *Association Trends*, July 26, 1996; "DMA Increases PAC Contributions by 300% in a Year," *Association Trends*, June 7, 1996; "Roth's Counsel Says 'Never' to ASAE's Lobby Tax Challenge," *Association Trends*, May 17, 1996; "Raising Funds? One-to-One Is Key, PAC Mgrs Tell Assn Roundtable," *Association Trends*, Feb. 23, 1996; and "Consumer Groups Assail Bill Curbing Political Advocacy," *Wall Street Journal*, Nov. 8, 1995.

## Chapter 10   Outright Swindles

The astounding story of Princess Pale Moon (née Rita Ann Suntz) and the American Indian Heritage Foundation was broken in various installments throughout 1992 by reporters at the *Anchorage Daily News* (and later reported by *Newsweek* and other national media).

Likewise, enterprising reporter Steve Stecklow at the *Wall Street Journal* dedicated the bulk of his professional attention in late 1995 and most of 1996 to the ongoing story of the Foundation for New Era Philanthropy in Pennsylvania. At times, it seemed that he uncovered weekly bombshells about the "too-good-to-be-true" record of this charity and its eventual decline into bankruptcy and (for New Era founder John Bennett Jr.) fraud trials. The newspaper's most helpful installments on the New Era debacle included "Not So Simple: William E. Simon Is Kinder and Gentler, But Investments Lag," Sept. 15, 1995; "Bennett, in Videotaped Talk, Accepts Responsibility for New Era Collapse," Nov. 1, 1995; "Payback Time: New Era's Bennett Took Others' Millions; Now He's Giving Back," Jan. 24, 1996; "Nonprofits Sue Prudential Over New Era," May 9, 1996; "Trustee's Filing Identifies 46 Creditors That Made Money Before New Era's Fall," June 19, 1996; and "Trustee for New Era Is Suing Prudential," June 27, 1996.

Articles in other publications that provided details on the New Era case were "PA Attorney Genl Will Sue Charity for Ponzi-type Scheme," *Association Trends*, May 26, 1995; "Heaven Can't Help Them," *Newsweek*, June 5, 1995; and "Separating Rich People From Their Money" [Michael Lewis's "The Capitalist" column], *New York Times Magazine*, June 18, 1995.

In addition to data and interviews provided by the Jewish Community Federation of San Francisco and the attorneys general offices in California and New Jersey, "Wheeler-Dealer: How A Tiny Charity Transformed Itself Into a Used-Car Giant" by Edward Felsenthal in the *Wall Street Journal* (April 23, 1996) documented the incredible chutzpah of Rabbi Bentziyon Pil and his wife, Mattie, and the activities of the Jewish Educational Center of San Francisco.

Giving me leads for tracking down details on nonprofit executives who are paying for their misdeeds with massive fines and jail time were "Convicted" [former Maine Grocers Association executive director John Joyce], *Association Trends*, June 14, 1996, and "Convicted Assn Executive Still Involved in Controversial Activities," *USAE*, March 14, 1995.

I gleaned the example of the International Postgraduate Medical Foundation from testimony given by John C. Bennison, vice president of the American Society of Travel Agents, before the House Small Business Subcommittee on Procurement, Taxation and Tourism on May 11, 1993.

"Charities' Coffers Easily Become Crooks' Booty" (*Wall Street Journal*, June 5, 1995) introduced me to the work of nonprofit watchdog agencies such as the Philanthropic Advisory Service of the Council of Better Business Bureaus and the National Charities Information Bureau.

### Chapter 11    Starting at the Top: Congress and the States

The Internal Revenue Service's public affairs office in Washington, D.C., and field offices around the country responded to numerous requests for analyses and tallies for this chapter, particularly questions about the numbers of tax exemption applications received annually, the numbers of these applications that are approved or turned down, and the number of audits performed on nonprofits regularly.

Besides the IRS, the Business Coalition for Fair Competition gave me steady streams of background material on suggested reforms in federal and state statutes and regulations to police nonprofit abuses more fairly and completely. I want to acknowledge their assistance especially in formulating model reforms on the state level contained in this chapter.

General Accounting Office reports in 1988 and 1995 proved helpful in establishing the results of IRS oversight and enforcement efforts in the nonprofit community. While the former report discovered that almost half of the annual tax forms filed by nonprofits are incomplete, the latter found that the IRS revokes the tax exemptions of fewer nonprofits and audits fewer groups than in the past but earns much more in back taxes and penalties from the nonprofits that are examined.

Other organizations that reacted to queries or submitted research materials for my review included the Independent Sector, the National Charities Information Bureau, and the American Association of Fund-Raising Counsel.

To secure a general grounding in current federal proposals to regulate nonprofit business activities and tax exemptions, I culled details from many news reports, with a focus on the following: "The Senate ..." [brief news item on an intermediate IRS sanctions bill], *Association Trends*, July 26, 1996; "GOP Proposal Would Let Charity Begin at Home With Taxpayers Choosing Their Favorite Causes," *Wall Street Journal*, June 20, 1996; "Intermediate sanctions put on back burner," *Association Management*, June 1996; "House approves new excise tax," *Association Trends*, May 17, 1996; "Tax-Exempt Groups That Violate Tax Rules May Soon Face a New Penalty," *Wall Street Journal*, May 15, 1996; "The Treasury tries again to get tough on tax-exempt groups," *Wall Street Journal*, Aug. 8, 1995; "Nonprofit Review," *USA Today*, June 20, 1995; "IRS taking close look at nation's 'sophisticated' nonprofit groups," *Lexington* [Ky.] *Herald-Leader/Associated Press*, June 20, 1995; "Tax Exemption Accountability Act Introduced in House," *Association Management*, March 1995; and "Too Charitable to Charities?" *Financial World*, Sept. 1, 1994.

Researchers with the Council of State Governments aided me in tracking down data on state proposals to tax nonprofit property and revenues. In addition, these articles identified attempts in various states to extend the long arm of government oversight further into the nonprofit community: "NH Bill Allows 'In Lieu' Nonprofit Fees," *Association Trends*, May 3, 1996; "US High Court to Hear Maine Tax-Exempt Case," *Association Trends*, April 19, 1996; "Council Members Confirm D.C. Assns May Be Taxed," *USAE*, Feb. 14, 1995; "Pay Now or You May Pay Much More Later," *Chronicle of Higher Education*, July 17, 1994; and "In Era of Fiscal Damage Control, Cities Fight Idea of 'Tax-Exempt'," *New York Times*, Feb. 2, 1993.

## Chapter 12   Nonprofits, Police Thyselves

When it comes to nonprofits policing themselves, three national organizations have become the Good Housekeeping seals of approval for effective, efficient nonprofit management practices: the National Charities Information Bureau, the Philanthropic Advisory Service of the Council of Better Business Bureaus, and the American Institute of Philanthropy. Representatives of these three groups granted me access to their screening processes and (where applicable) public awareness programs to teach donors and volunteers how to choose nonprofits wisely.

*Leading the Association: Striking the Right Balance Between Staff and Volunteers*, written by association management consultant James Dunlop, outlined the standards functions of board members and volunteer leaders in various types of trade associations. The book was based on a study funded by the Foundation of the American Society of Association Executives (ASAE).

ASAE's government affairs department and its public relations and market research division forwarded to me the tips given to ASAE members in the wake of the United Way of America scandal, to give associations direction in screening their own operations for potential landmines and in handling media calls comparing the United Way lapses with the management practices of other nonprofit groups; "How to Turn a Negative Story Into a Media Opportunity" and "CEO Salaries Under Scrutiny? Sure-Fire Tips on How to Handle the Media" proved especially illuminating. Also, I gathered additional ideas on the subject (specifically, codes of ethics for nonprofit group members) from "Codes of Ethics, Antitrust Rules Tricky for Assns" in *Association Trends* (April 5, 1996).

David Shenk's article "Board Stiffs: How William Gates and Paul Tagliabue Helped William Aramony Bilk America" in *Washington*

*Monthly* (May 1992) documented the behind-the-scenes lax oversight exercised by United Way of America's board of directors that led, at least in part, to the criminal conviction of the United Way president.

Nancy Axelrod, president of the National Center for Nonprofit Boards, gave me extensive feedback on proposed strategies for nonprofit board members to become more active and involved in policing the activities of their groups. I learned about her organization by reading her article titled "Balancing Act: Nonprofit Boards and Chief Execs" in *Association Trends* (Sept. 8, 1995). The National Committee for Responsive Philanthropy also contributed ideas for improved nonprofit self-regulation.

David R. Bywaters, CMC, a noted management consultant with Lawrence-Leiter and Company in Kansas City, Mo., outlined steps for an effective, fair evaluation of the performance of a nonprofit's board of directors for me, using his article "What Does It Take to Evaluate an Assn's Board?" (*Association Trends*, Feb. 9, 1996) as a starting point.

Former Colorado governor Richard Lamm delivered his "additions to the Ten Commandments" for tax-exempt groups at the Colorado Association of Nonprofit Organizations Ethics Conference in Denver on June 21, 1991. I excerpted his remarks from the actual speech, as reproduced in *Vital Speeches of the Day*.

Examples of nonprofit groups that exemplify the new movement among altruistic business types toward "social entrepreneurism" were featured in various installments of the "Events & Promotions" column in *Advertising Age* in 1995 and 1996, as well as in "Going It Alone in Nonprofits" in *Fortune*, Feb. 20, 1995.

## Chapter 13    Protecting Yourself

Providing extensive assistance with recommendations for potential donors and volunteers working with nonprofit groups were the American Association of Fund-Raising Counsel, the Philanthropic Advisory Service of the Council of Better Business Bureaus, the American Institute of Philanthropy, and the National Charities Information Bureau.

Association law experts Jerald Jacobs and Bruce Hopkins also offered suggestions for the chapter, particularly the impact of proposed volunteer protection legislation in Congress in 1996.

As I began researching the latest wrinkles in nonprofit laws and proposals affecting the liability and tax deductions for donors and volunteers, I gained a stronger sense of direction after reviewing these articles: "Many Charities Fret Over How to Comply With Record-Keeping

Rules," *Wall Street Journal,* June 19, 1996; "Risk Mgmt First Line of Defense in Assn Liability," *Association Trends,* June 7, 1996; "Testifying Before the House," *Association Trends,* March 8, 1996; "Charity Begins With Homework," *Lexington* [Ky.] *Herald-Leader,* Dec. 11, 1995; "Cheers Greet Proposed New Treasury Record-Keeping Rules on Donations," *Wall Street Journal,* Sept. 13, 1995; "Some Charities Fail to Follow New Tax Rules on Substantiating Donations," *Wall Street Journal,* March 15, 1995; and "House Tackles Volunteer Protection," *Association Management,* March 1995. I also depended upon the *Annual Charity Index,* gauging charities' management practices, and the *Give But Give Wisely* list of national philanthropies that generate the most calls from consumers, both publications offered by the American Institute of Philanthropy.

Transcripts of hearings before the House Judiciary Committee in February 1996 on proposed nonprofit volunteer legislation gave the positions held by interested groups like the National Coalition for Volunteer Protection and ASAE.

# Suggested Reading

Bennett, James T., and Thomas J. DiLorenzo. *Unhealthy Charities: Hazardous to Your Health and Wealth*. New York: Basic Books, 1994.

Business Coalition for Fair Competition. *Unfair Competition in the States*. Washington, D.C.: Business Coalition for Fair Competition, 1985.

Drucker, Peter. *Managing the Non-Profit Organization: Principles and Practices*. New York: HarperCollins, 1992.

Gaul, Gilbert M., and Neill A. Borowski. *A Free Ride: The Tax-Exempt Economy*. Kansas City: Andrews & McMeel, 1993.

Gersher, Howard. *A Guide to Giving: 250 Charities and How They Use Your Money*. New York: Pantheon, 1991.

Glaser, John. *The United Way Scandal: An Insider's Account of What Went Wrong and Why*. New York: John Wiley & Sons, 1994.

Hopkins, Bruce. *Charity, Advocacy and the Law*. New York: John Wiley & Sons, 1991.

————. *The Law of Fund-Raising*. New York: John Wiley & Sons, 1991.

————. *The Law of Tax-Exempt Organizations*. New York: John Wiley & Sons, 1992.

————. *A Legal Guide to Starting and Managing a Nonprofit Organization*. New York: John Wiley & Sons, 1993.

————. *Nonprofit Law Dictionary*. New York: John Wiley & Sons, 1994.

Independent Sector. *A Portrait of the Independent Sector: The Activities and Finances of Charitable Organizations*. Washington, D.C.: Independent Sector, 1994.

Morris, Charles. *The AARP and You*. New York: Times Books, 1996.

Ostrower, Francie. *Why the Wealthy Give: The Culture of Elite Philanthropy*. Princeton, N.J.: Princeton University Press, 1996.

Peterson, Peter G. *Facing Up: How to Rescue the Economy From Crushing Debt and Restore the American Dream*. New York: Simon & Schuster, 1993.

Philanthropy Advisory Service. *Annual Charity Index*. Arlington, Va.: Philanthropy Advisory Service/Council of Better Business Bureaus, 1996.

Webster, George D. *Law of Associations*. Chicago: Matthew Bender & Co., 1996.

Weisbrod, Burton A. *The Nonprofit Economy*. New York: Columbia University Press, 1990.

Wolinsky, Howard, and Tom Brune. *The Serpent and the Staff*. New York: Jeremy P. Tarcher/Putnam, 1995.

# Index

Aamodt, Gary J.N., 75–77
*AARP and You, The* (Morris), 215, 219
Abraham Lincoln Opportunity Foundation, 135
Abramson, Alan, 17
Adams, John Hurst, 117–18
Advertising space, donated to nonprofit groups, 47
Albrecht, Kenneth, 84
Alexander, Irvin, 183
America's Battered Children, 33–34
American Association of Fund-Raising Counsel, 17–18, 61–62, 215
American Association of Retired Persons, *xiii, xiv,* 16, 73–74, 103–4, 120–21, 130–31, 133, 156, 219, 222, 223–24
American Bar Association, *xv,* 128
American Cancer Society, *xiv,* 12, 24–25, 68, 80, 81, 104–5, 184, 195
American Civil Liberties Union, 195
American College of Physicians and Surgeons, 69
American College Testing Program, 29
American Dental Association, 102
American Federation of Labor-Congress of Industrial Organizations, 126
American Financial Corp., 136
American Heart Association, 68, 102–3, 195
American Hospital Association, 59, 217
American Humane Association, 195
American Indian Heritage Foundation, 138–39, 224
American Institute of Certified Public Accountants, 82, 220
American Institute of Philanthropy, 184, 185, 186, 227
American International Group, 136
American Lung Association, 68, 195
American Medical Association, *xiv,* 123
American Parkinson's Disease Association, 91–92, 220–21
American Philosophical Society, 5
American Red Cross, 101, 135–37, 195

American Society of Association Executives, *x,* 10, 131–32, 133, 174, 213, 221, 227, 229
AmeriCares Foundation, 72
Anderson, H. George, 76
Anderson, Jack, 88, 220
Andreas, Dwayne and Inez, 135–36
Andreasen, Alan, 221
Andrew W. Mellon Foundation, 65
Annas, George, 102–3
Annenberg, Walter H., 67
*Annual Charity Index,* 185, 228
Appalachian Regional Healthcare Inc., 32
Aramony, William, *xiii–xiv,* 86–89, 173–74, 214, 220, 227–28
Archer Daniels Midland, 136
Archer, Dennis, 44
Arthritis Foundation, 101–2
Association of Church Presses, 172
Association of Fund-Raisers and Direct Sellers, 79
Association for Healthcare Philanthropy, 23, 215
*Association Law Handbook* (Jacobs), 180–81, 187–88
Association of Spermaceti Chandlers, 5
*Associations: A Family Portrait* (American Society of Association Executives), 213
Atwater Foundation, 60–61
Augsburg Fortress, Publishers, 75–77
Awtrey, Jim, 67
Axelrod, Nancy, 146, 228
Baade, Robert, 44
Babbage, Bob, 154
Baran, Jan, 126
Bauer, Herbert, 119–20
Beach, Jeff, 21
Benefit dinners, 187
Bennett, James T., 68
Bennett, John G., Jr., *xv,* 139–46, 225
Bennison, John C., 225
Bernardi, Roy, 165
Bernfeld, Jerry, 45